THE BIG GAME HUNTERS

Also by Michael Brander
Deer Stalking in Britain
A Concise Guide to Game Shooting
The Sportsman's Press

THE BIG GAME HUNTERS

MICHAEL BRANDER

· THE ·
SPORTSMAN'S
PRESS
LONDON

Published by The Sportsman's Press, 1988

© Michael Brander 1988

Brander, Michael, *1924–*
    The big game hunters.
    1. Big game. Hunting. Biographies.
    Collections
    I. Title
    799.2'6'0922

ISBN 0-948253-23-1

Photoset and printed in Great Britain by
BAS Printers Limited, Over Wallop, Hampshire

CONTENTS

In fond memory of my Uncle
Samuel Everett Johnson
Who introduced the Kheddah into Burma
and taught me at a tender age
all I ever needed to know about
building a Machan and waiting up for Tigers

ACKNOWLEDGEMENTS

Acknowledgement must be made to many individuals, particularly families and descendants of some of those who figure in the text for their assistance in numerous ways. In alphabetical order I must thank particularly the Baker family, Dr & Mrs John R. Baker and the late Colonel and Mrs E. Baker, for access to the Baker papers; Mr Alexander Dunbar of Pitgaveny for access to James Brander Dunbar and Archie Dunbar Brander's papers and collection of heads at Pitgaveny; Sir William Gordon Cumming for details on the Gordon Cumming family; Colonel Bruce Kinloch, grandson of Brigadier-General Angus Alexander Airlie Kinloch and his sister-in-law, Mrs Ann Kinloch, for their help; various members of the Millais family for help concerning John Guille Millais; Commander Jocelyn Raban Williams for details of his father's life; Mr Hamish Wallace, Hon. Secretary of The Shikar Club, for referring to their records and for help regarding his father.

I must also thank the many librarians throughout the country who have assisted me through the Inter-Library Lending System. In particular I must thank Miss Jessie Macleod, the Librarian of the East Lothian District Library, also Mrs Veronica Wallace and others of the very helpful staff. My thanks must also go to Mrs Gavan, the Librarian, and the always helpful staff of the Haddington Library. I must finally thank the Librarian and staff of the National Library of Scotland, who piled loads of books on trolleys and found me abstruse references without complaint. Without the help of all the above, mine would have been an impossible task.

Also for their very great help in reading and commenting on the typescript my thanks also to Phil Harris and to my old friend Kenneth Grose as well as always to my wife, Evelyn. Finally, my special thanks are due to Edward H. Bryant of Vandeleur Antiquarian Books, London, who provided many of the illustrations used in the book and generously allowed me to reproduce pages from C. H. Stigand's unpublished diary and Mr Geoffrey Boothroyd for allowing me to use his photographs of big game rifles. For any mistakes and omissions, however, and in a book of this nature I am aware there must be many, I am completely responsible.

INTRODUCTION

Hunting big game goes back to the earliest days of Mankind. The caveman who hunted the sabre-toothed tiger and the mammoth, often being in turn hunted by them, left cave paintings and the remains of bones and primitive weapons behind as evidence of his activities. The real proof of his success lay more perhaps in the fact that the sabre-toothed tiger and the mammoth died out, but Man survived. Rather than proving anything about his abilities as a hunter, however, it might well be argued that this merely proves that Man, even then, was more ready to adapt to a changing environment.

Soon after the dawn of civilisation around the Mediterranean basin, the early Egyptian kings hunted elephants, lions and tigers as a matter of course. Pharoah Tuthmoses III in the year 1464 BC was credited with killing 120 elephants at a water-hole. This, of course, must have been in the manner of the large mass hunt with the animals surrounded by warriors. Under the Assyrians and Persians, as almost certainly also under the Egyptians, game of all kinds was preserved in walled enclosures. Mass hunts reached new heights under the Assyrian King Ashurnasipal II in 850 BC when 30 elephants, 450 lions, 390 wild bulls and 200 ostriches were killed in the course of one mass hunt.

Gradually, as the Greeks and Romans in turn held sway over the Mediterranean and as civilisation advanced, so the animals known to the Egyptians and Assyrians vanished from their familiar surroundings, retreating into the interior of Africa, or further into Asia. The chief reason for this, however, was not so much continual hunting as the steady changes wrought by Man in the land itself. Wars had damaged the wells and water supplies used to irrigate the land. Monoculture had changed formerly fertile ground into desert. Those animals which had not been killed by over-hunting were forced to move into the interior in search of suitable habitat and feeding.

In Europe the wolf, the bear, and the wild bull were hunted for centuries in the dense forests which covered much of the area, but as successive waves of Germanic tribes pressed westward the forests steadily diminished. Mention of aurochs and bisons is still to be found in Julius Caesar's account of the Gallic Wars, but with the passing of the Romans and the rise of the Frankish Empire the first game laws were gradually introduced into Europe.

With the rise of the Carolingian Empire the hunting of beasts in the forests became the province of the aristocracy. In Britain the Norman kings adopted the Game Laws, first introduced by Canute, and used them unscrupulously as a form of direct taxation as well as a means of control over their Barons and the conquered Anglo-Saxons alike.

Amongst the last of the great bear hunters in Europe was Gaston III, Count of Foix et Bearn in the Pyrenees. Born in 1331 he was married to a daughter of the King of Navarre and kept 600 horses in his stables as well as a vast kennel of hunting dogs. He was an ardent exponent of *par force* hunting, a favourite sport also of the Norman kings. This sport was epitomised by a single huntsman following hounds on the scent of stag, boar or bear. When in full view, he unleashed greyhounds, or gaze-hounds, to bay the beast, which he then finished personally with a hunting knife, spear, or sword. This arduous form of hunting was already giving way to easier methods, such as following packs of hounds on horseback, but Gaston Phoebus, as he was known, followed the old method of hunting until he died, no doubt in the manner he would have wished, at the end of a strenuous and successful hunt after a bear on a hot August day in 1391.

Towards the end of the thirteenth century, in 1298, Marco Polo, visiting the court of the great Kubla Khan had reported his methods of hunting thus: 'He hath two Barons . . . "The Keepers of the Mastiff Dogs". Each of these brothers hath 10,000 men under his orders, each body of 10,000 being dressed alike, the one in red, the other in blue, and whenever they accompany the Lord of the Chase, they wear this livery in order to be recognised. Out of each body of 10,000 there are 2,000 who are each in charge of one or more great mastiffs, so that the whole number is very large. And when the Khan goes a-hunting one of these Barons, with his 10,000 men and something like 5,000 dogs, goes towards the right, whilst the other goes towards the left with his party in like manner. They move along all abreast with one another, so that the whole line extends over a full day's journey on horseback and no animal can escape them. Truly it is a glorious sight to see the working of the hounds and their huntsmen on such an occasion. And as the Lord rides a-fowling across the plains you will see these great hounds come tearing up, one pack after a boar, another pack after a stag, or some other beast, as it may hap, and running their game down now on this side and now on that. So that it is really a most delightful sport and spectacle . . . Meanwhile the Emperor himself is carried upon four elephants in a fine chamber made of timber, lined inside with plates of beaten gold and on the outside with lion skins . . .'

Thereafter in India the big game was hunted in recognisably similar fashion by the Rajahs and their followers until the arrival of the Europeans in the seventeenth and eighteenth centuries. Then gradually the introduction of fire-arms brought new methods of big game hunting, which developed new concepts of hunting by individuals rather than en masse. Meanwhile, in Africa the methods of the Arab Hamran hunters witnessed by Samuel White Baker and graphically described by him in the nineteenth century were no doubt continuing. Riding on horseback these fearless sword hunters hamstrung the elephants they hunted and finally killed them. Such methods, along with pitfall traps dating back to Stone Age hunting practices, were the principle forms of hunting in existence in Africa until the advent of firearms in the eighteenth and early nineteenth centuries. The Boers, with their massive 'Roers', smooth-bore heavy muzzle-loaders, were the first to hunt big game from lions to elephants using these primitive weapons and it was thus that Cornwallis Harris first described big game hunting in detail in Southern Africa.

From Pester and Williamson in India at the turn of the eighteenth century and Cornwallis Harris in the 1840s in Africa, big game hunting developed along with the rapid development of firearms in the nineteenth century until the world finally exploded into chaos in the First World War in 1914 and Man concentrated on killing his fellows. Thereafter big game hunting may have continued in a controlled form under licence, but the old big game hunters had ceased to hunt. Any subsequent decrease in big game numbers could not be laid at their door. Their day was over, as is apparent from their own chronicles. As the keenest observers on the spot, they were well aware their day was run.

The chapters that follow describe the history of their times, largely in their own individual words. The reader will see for himself that, although very diverse characters, they included the early hunter/naturalists, conservators and explorers; men who were interested not merely in slaughter but in the animals they encountered and in the new lands they discovered. Although some of them undoubtedly killed large numbers of animals this was mostly to feed the natives who accompanied them; their depredations had little more real effect on the game itself than a passing rainstorm on a lake at the edge of the jungle.

Officers of the 93rd Highlanders with rifles and game trophies, India,
c1864. Courtesy of the National Army Museum.

EARLY SPORTSMEN
IN INDIA

John Pester 1778–1856

Walter Campbell 1812–1871

Mustering forces for a tiger hunt. *Illustration from* The Old Forest
Ranger *by Walter Campbell*.

John Pester 1778–1856

Indian Journal 1802–1806

Heroic Georgian Soldier from Somerset

There is something . . . so awful . . . in their charge . . . that it is
apt to shake the hand a little . . . I cannot otherwise account for
a tiger being ever missed at a near distance . . .

One of the earliest sportsmen to leave any lengthy record of his activities, including big game hunting, was John Pester, who kept a diary of his experiences in India both as a soldier and a sportsman between 1802 and 1806. Born in 1778, the son of a Somerset squire near Yeovil, he was clearly a hard-riding horseman, accustomed to following hounds at breakneck speed over the hilly moors and valleys of his native county. At the start of these diaries he was aged twenty-three and a Lieutenant in the 1st Battalion of Bengal Native Infantry. Such was the mortality amongst the European officers, caused as much by the climate and disease as by warfare, that before two years had passed he was already acting Major. It is obvious, however, that this accelerated promotion also owed a great deal to his personal bravery and outstanding qualities of leadership.

He was very much a product of the hard-drinking hard-living Georgian Age and at one point in his diary declared his attitude: 'I am convinced that if an officer would wish to *get forward* he should pray for opportunities to distinguish himself and let none escape him that offer. To be first and foremost in danger be his object: if he falls, he falls gallantly and respected and it is a thousand to one if he is not rewarded should he succeed in doing his duty in the *style of a soldier.*'

It is difficult now to envisage the warfare of those days, when both sides were armed with flintlock or, still in some cases, primitive matchlock muskets firing a round ball; when cannon also fired solid ball or grape-shot and when to be wounded in the body meant almost certain death, or in a limb instant amputation, often followed by a painful death from gangrene. The infantry officers, of course, led their men mainly on horseback, but the baggage train and the impedimenta of a marching army was very considerable by modern standards. Officers' equipment would be carried in bullock carts, on camels, or transported by elephants. Each officer as a matter of course kept a good stock of wine. Preparing for a campaign Pester noted on one occasion: 'Packed ten dozen of Madeira and four dozen of port, with some beer in grass for the march . . .'

The climate to a large extent dictated the activities of the Europeans in India. They would normally rise before dawn and indulge in vigorous activity until shortly after sunrise. By about ten o'clock in the morning most activities would cease and the heat of the day would be passed within doors if possible until about four o'clock, after which they might indulge in further activity until the evening meal, following which steady drinking was likely to continue until early in the morning.

It seems to have been customary to drink at least one bottle of claret or similar wine each evening and frequently a great deal more. For instance, Pester recorded just prior to leaving a fort they had taken by storm: 'It was the last night we were to pass in Sarssney and I believe the first that ever fourteen *honest gentlemen* drank within its walls. Three dozen and a half of claret and proportionable quantity of Madeira – everyone sang his song, and this was as gay an evening and terminated as pleasantly as any I ever passed in my life. We concluded by breaking our candle-shades and glasses, pranks which too frequently finish drinking parties in this part of the globe . . .'

His diary starts in August 1802 with the bald account of how, at the head of his company of eighty men and accompanied by only one volunteer white ensign, he stormed a fortified village held by several hundred enemy forces. He led the final charge at the head of thirty men, which took a fortified round tower in the centre of the village. At least four of his grenadiers were killed at his heels but the victory was his – and all this after marching thirty-six miles, often through water up to their waists. The entire action took sixteen hours to complete throughout the heat of the day and it is indicative of the man that he mentions almost as an afterthought: 'Poor Marsden [the ensign who volunteered to accompany him] never recovered his fatigue and died soon afterwards.'

Some idea of the man's vitality can be gauged from the fact that by contrast he seems positively to have revelled in the events, ending: 'In the evening I dined at Plumer's when there was a large party and as soon as the cloth was removed I fell asleep in my chair and slept undisturbed until near eleven o'clock after which I took my bottle of claret and returned to my palanquin.'

His sport was equally vigorous and he was as unsparing of himself in it as he appeared to be in action against the enemy. He was especially interesting on the subject of boar hunting, or pig-sticking, mentioning on one occasion how he and a group of officers: 'At four this morning . . . met on the edge of a low cover by appointment, the distance not more than five miles from the cantonments. Hogs we found in great abundance and had most glorious sport. In the course of the morning there were many very severe falls, but fortunately no bones were broken. My grey horse Major carried me the first two runs in very high style and I had the first spear in each boar. They charged

16

most furiously, but with an expert horse they may in general be avoided and you may deliver your spear with little danger.'

On the other hand he considered: 'With a hard mouthed ungovernable horse, hog hunting is by far the most dangerous sport of any I ever engaged in and there are few instances of a large boar and a horse coming in contact without either the [horse] or his rider being much cut and frequently the horse is killed on the spot. Our ground today was very dangerous, full of holes and old wells and many of them quite covered with grass which grew over them. In these cases it is usual to follow the exact trail of the hog; he is almost invariably well acquainted with the country where you find them. An experienced hunter always sticks as close after them as possible and by doing so very often saves his bones. Hog hunting beyond a doubt requires the most desperate riding of all field sports. The danger of the ground is in my opinion much greater and more difficult to avoid than that of the fiercest boar − for with skill they are easily struck but a blind hole or well is the very devil . . . '

It is plain that when on the march the officers took every opportunity for sport that was available. Almost every day of the march seems to have an entry such as: '. . . we killed a great deal of game, viz. partridges, hares, two fine deer and a boar and returned home by ten to breakfast.' Or '. . . we killed about twenty brace of quail, three brace of hares and six brace of black partridge and were back . . . at eight o'clock.'

On one occasion he noted making camp near the Black River in a stretch of jungle teeming with game. At ten in the morning, having pitched camp, he and his friend Cumberledge, 'swallowed our breakfast and set off instantly to shoot . . . Not three hundred yards from the piquets we found a herd of hogs, but owing to the height of the grass found it in vain to ride them. We penetrated the cover and killed deer, florikin, niel ghy (blue wild cows) [sic.], partridges, hares and quail in great abundance . . . Remained out till nearly sunset and galloped furiously back, leaving our people with the guns and dogs, to find their way after us as well as they could . . .'

Taking time off during the siege of a fortress he wrote: 'Being off duty this morning, Wemyss and myself injudiciously rode a couple of miles in the rear of our camp, with the greyhounds − this frolic was attended with the imminent risk of our lives as the enemy had constantly strong parties of horse patrolling in the neighbourhood with a view to cutting off supplies. We found plenty of hares among the young wheat and were not long in killing two brace and a half, and a brace of jackals . . . our horses were completely knocked up, but we returned unmolested to camp . . .'

On another occasion along with Wemyss, Wallace and Shairpe (obviously all Scots), he tried 'the speed and bottom of our Arabs after a niel ghy (or blue deer) for three miles . . . The ground was dangerous and we were literally at speed the whole time over several wells and deep broken ground . . . none but madmen would have tried it. Wallace had first spear at him and missed him. I speared him through the loins and he staggered a few paces and fell. Wemyss's spear went to his heart. There was scarcely ever an instance before known of a niel ghy being speared . . .'

Every inch a product of the Georgian Age Pester greatly admired bravery. On the death of a Major Nairne 'an uncommonly gallant fellow' he noted: 'Nairne was a great favourite of General Lake who once saw him spear a tiger on horseback . . . General Lake shot the tiger, which was a very large one, after Nairne had put his spear in him. The tiger tore it out and instantly smashed it to shivers in its teeth. The tiger's skin and broken spear were sent home by the Commander-in-Chief to the Prince of Wales . . .'

After one of his early campaigns Pester was given two months leave and with a group of friends equipped with elephants visited Bareilly, where they had learned there were numerous tigers '. . . committing the most horrid depredations . . . destroying daily men and cattle and obliging whole villages to decamp . . . We felt rather keen to be at them and made up an additional quantity of double-headed shot for our tiger guns . . .'.

He and his friend Peyron, also from Somerset, stayed with a civilian at Bareilly named Thornhill, who showed them great hospitality. Pester noted: 'Breakfasted with Thornhill after which we went to a strong jungle in the neighbourhood and killed two tigers; they were small but exceedingly fierce and showed good sport: we were not absent more than two hours . . .'

On the next occasion they met with more opposition: '. . . we were suddenly saluted with a tremendous roar and charge of one of the largest royal tigers I ever beheld . . . he came down roaring hideously, lashing with his tail and looking savage and fierce beyond description.

'The sight was truly noble. He commenced his charge at the distance of about two hundred yards from us. Peyron, Martin, Boileau and myself fired at about fifty yards; he reeled very much and was evidently severely wounded though not mortally . . . the elephant immediately opposite him . . . ran off. Boileau's and Martin's elephants instantly followed . . . I was the next in line on an elephant that was never known to flinch . . . I gave the monster a shot from my rifle at twenty paces; it entered just above the forehead and rolled him completely over. He gave such a roar as I never heard and was striving to recover himself when Peyron and Anderdon [another friend from Somerset] both fired. He then received both barrels of my two-ounced gun and we soon despatched him . . .' Pester noted later: 'There is something to a person not in the habit of killing tigers so awful and really tremendous in their charge, the roar and their actions in attacking, that it is apt to shake the hand a little. I cannot otherwise account for a tiger ever being missed at a near distance . . .'

It was not all tiger shooting. They spent much time coursing hares and shooting small game; as when he wrote that the party 'Shot this morning in a barley field within a mile of the bungalow. Anderdon to his own share shot eighteen quail without missing a shot. We returned to breakfast with nearly thirty brace and after one of the prettiest morning's sport I ever saw in my life. The quail fly exactly like a miniature partridge and indeed are partridges in miniature, in general very fat and delicious eating . . .'

A little later he noted: 'Accounts having reached us of some tigers having committed horrid depredations at a village in the jungle about sixteen miles from Barielly, at daylight this morning our elephants, guns and servants were despatched and Peyron, Anderdon and myself left Macan's at twelve at night and about two we crossed the Rham Gungah . . . river . . . We were well assured that the intelligence of tigers being in the neighbourhood was *perfectly correct*, for about mid-way between the river's side and our tents we heard them roaring and howling hideously and that at no very great distance from us. Some of the villagers who were conducting us left us and took to the top of the trees. The men carrying the torches remained with us! We drew our pistols and at the head of a party of matchlock men we advanced and got safe to our tents which were pitched at the village end. Went immediately to bed . . . At four this morning we mounted our elephants and within the distance of half-cannon shot from our tents, the villagers pointed to a break of briars in which they assured us there was a tigress and four half grown cubs! The brake was not three hundred yards round and we instantly encircled it with our elephants. To penetrate it was impossible and we commenced shouting and firing into the jungle but all in vain . . . one of the drivers attached to my elephant dismounted and looked under the cover, which we were unable to do from our elephants. The man instantly remounted and in a terrible funk declared that he saw one of the young tigers stalking along under the briars . . . I suspected that fear had got hold of the man who dismounted to reconnoitre and was therefore induced to go down to look myself! I had no sooner reached the ground when I discovered two of the young tigers and plainly saw the immense feet and paws of the tigress. I instantly ran up the elephant's side by a rope and communicated this glorious intelligence . . . The tigress . . . made a most savage and desperate charge on us. The roar was really like a clap of thunder. Peyron and Anderdon both fired and wounded her, but she sprang on the elephant nearest her. She . . . was nearly the size of a Bengal bullock and presented a fair mark to me though closed with the elephant and I immediately fired my two-ounced double barrel at her; she instantly quitted her hold and slunk back, apparently stupefied into the jungle, all of us saluting her as she returned . . . evidently mortally wounded . . . The young tigers now came out and although not half-grown attacked the elephants with all imaginable fury . . . They afforded us excellent diversion and we despatched the whole party. The tigress was stone dead in the jungle and such a monster my eyes never beheld! . . . The inhabitants of the village, men, women and children, came to express their gratitude . . .'

Several days later they had another exciting encounter with a tigress: 'She

19

came down roaring and lashing her tail in a truly glorious style . . . the sight was enough to strike terror into the system of anyone not confident in his gun and the resolution of his elephant. On approaching at the distance of about thirty paces in our front we gave her the contents of four double barrels loaded with a couple of balls in each barrel. The tigress tumbled completely over, and in a moment recovered her legs again and closed with the elephant nearest her . . . It was impossible for us to take a shot although we were completely round them so close and entangled were they with each other.

'The tigress at length extricated itself and was advancing to renew the combat when we brought her down and twenty balls were in or through her before she could get herself again on her legs and we settled her after a fight of at least a quarter of an hour from the time we first saw her . . . Our elephants were bellowing and shewed every inclination to join in the combat; they seemed almost as furious as the parties engaged; in short, we were *all mad together* and the roaring and shouting might have been heard for many miles in the woods . . . We had *noble sport* and every luxury at command that the country afforded besides, while we were doing no small service to the poor wretches who . . . so constantly fall victims to the merciless monsters we destroyed . . .'

Soon after his return to his regiment Pester suffered a severe attack of fever, probably malaria. His Company was ordered to attack a village and he recorded that 'The Colonel wrote me a most kindly note, strongly advising me, in my present state, not to think of marching with the detachment . . . I thanked him in the most kindly terms I could, but told him that as my Company was under orders I should assuredly march with it. (Memo. Never to remain behind on those occasions!)' Despite the fever he remained in command of his men throughout the action, although admitting in his diary that he felt exceedingly ill.

On another occasion with his friends Wemyss and White, they had reports of a tiger being seen nearby and agreed to follow it up, sending off their elephants in advance. On their arrival the mahouts showed a dislike of the jungle; '. . . and we were obliged to have recourse to the butts of our guns before they would enter the forest, reminding them that the danger (of being crushed on the back of the elephants if they bolted in the forest) was greater to us than to them . . .

'After beating each side of a stream . . . I perceived his streaked side through a thick bush of briars . . . Never did I behold a more glorious sight. He lay lashing his tail and crouched waiting only for us to near him a little so that he might make his spring with effect. We were aware of our awkward situation and the elephants began to back when Wemyss and I fired together. He gave a most hideous howl and in endeavouring to make at us staggered back and fell directly into the water, the blood streaming from him as he swam towards White on the opposite side. We fired three double barrels each at him in the water, but could not prevent him reaching the opposite bank, where he landed and drew himself instantly into cover and as we speedily pursued him. About fifty yards down the stream we discovered him lying in the agonies of death, howling in such a manner as to make the forest ring again; he struggled and made every savage exertion to get at us again, but he was mortally wounded and could only rise on his forelegs. His tremendous roaring made the elephants appear very *uncomfortable*, and they showed symptoms of wishing to make off.'

The scene which followed was perhaps typical of the Georgian Age's attitude to 'the Brute Creation'. He continued: 'We did not wish to despatch the tiger immediately as the sight of a tiger in such a situation was really a most glorious one . . . [it] lay under a small tree, the roots of which it tore up and appeared perfectly frantic with rage and pain . . . After we had enjoyed the sight a full hour, I dismounted and walked up near him and with my rifle shot him stone dead. The villagers began to cheer and made us a thousand salaams for having destroyed the monster which would otherwise most likely have destroyed many of them. [It had killed a man and a bullock a few hours before their arrival.]'

The following morning they saw the beast skinned: 'The first round that Wemyss and myself had fired at him, our guns were loaded with plugs [double-headed shot] two in each barrel, four double barrels; they were the only shot of that description fired at him (being good only at close quarters) and every one of them, eight in number were cut out of the tiger and a great number of round shot. He measured eleven feet . . .'

During the latter part of 1803 and much of 1804 Pester was a very sick man, but he refused to let this stop him doing his military duty to the full although it is noticeable that he did not indulge in as many sporting activities, simply because he was clearly not fit enough to do so. He was with the Brigadier at the siege of the fortress of Gwalior and from having been Brigade Quarter-Master Major under General Lake, he was appointed Prize-Major, a post depending largely on his popularity with his fellow officers.

He sailed home on well earned sick leave in 1806, then returned to India. He was married in 1811 and retired as a Lieutenant Colonel in 1826. Although always ready to lead a forlorn hope against all odds, or face a wounded boar or charging tiger, his only absences from duty seem to have been caused by sickness and it is plain from his diary that even when severely affected by fever he was still ready to lead his men into action. He certainly seems to have led a charmed life. He died in retirement near Southampton in 1856 at the ripe old age of seventy-eight.

Hunters going out in the morning *by Samual Howitt, from an original
drawing by Captain T. Williamson.* Courtesy of Hobhouse Ltd.

Notes on two contemporaries: Thomas Williamson and Daniel Johnson

Captain Thomas Williamson's book *Oriental Field Sports*, published in 1807
and superbly illustrated with sumptuously produced drawings in colour by
Samuel Howitt, and his contemporary, Dr Daniel Johnson's book *Sketches of
Indian Field Sports*, between them complement John Pester's experiences of
field sports in India. At this stage it was a free-for-all and wherever warfare
was taking place it may be assumed that everything might be shot. The pre-
serves of the native rulers were ruthlessly shot by the European officers
without any controls beyond their own consciences, which were clearly no
great check. As Dr Daniel Johnson indicated, however, the natives had their
own methods of hunting game, including waiting for tigers in machans, or
platforms in trees, armed with matchlocks loaded with double balls. This was
the Georgian Age and animals, or the Brute Creation, as the British saw it,
were there for their benefit. On the other hand it seems likely that, tigers apart,

22

even at that time more game was probably trapped and killed by the natives than was hunted or shot by the British.

Captain Thomas Williamson served with the military forces of the Honourable East India Company in Bengal from around 1787 for a full twenty years. In 1813 he wrote another book entitled *The European in India*, again very well illustrated and providing numerous illuminating sidelights on life in India at the time. He also wrote *The East India Vade Mecum, or Complete Guide to Gentlemen Intended for the Civil, Military or Naval Service of the Hon. East India Company* in two volumes. This was reprinted in a single volume edited by J. Gilchrist in 1825, so presumably Williamson by this time was dead, though how, or when, does not seem to be on record.

Not a great deal more is known about Dr Daniel Johnson, although it is recorded that he was born in 1767 and was appointed assistant surgeon in the Bengal Medical Service in 1789, being promoted to full surgeon in 1805 and retiring in 1809. He settled down in retirement as a general practitioner in Torrington in Devon and did not write his book on field sports until 1822. It was probably the considerable success of Williamson's book, published by Edward Orme, of which it is plain he was somewhat jealous, that inspired him to write his book with the aid of a local bookseller's daughter 'not more than eight and a half year's old'. He dedicated the book to the directors of The Honourable East India Company and clearly he must have found a demand for it since in 1827 he published a second edition with an extra chapter on 'Hunting the Wild Boar'. Subsequently he also published a small book entitled *Observations on Colds, Fever and Other Disorders*, which also seems to have been modestly successful. He died at Torrington in 1835, aged sixty-eight.

Walter Campbell of Skipness 1812–1871

Indian Journal 1829–1833

Sporting Military Highlander

Never attack a tiger on foot – if you can help it. There are some
cases when you must *do so. Then face him like a Briton and*
kill him if you can; for if you fail to do so he will certainly kill
you . . .

Walter Campbell was born in 1812 in the Highlands of Scotland at Skipness, a small fishing village on the Mull of Kintyre in Argyll, opposite the north-west tip of the Isle of Arran. He wrote: 'My father died when I was only seven years of age, leaving me, two brothers and a sister, to the care of my mother – an Englishwoman by birth, but romantically attached to her adopted Highland home. In her younger days she had lived much abroad, mixed in the best society and had the courtly manner of a well-bred lady of the last century. But with all her courtly manner my mother had a dash of the Spartan in her. Her theory was that boys could not be brought up too hardy; that a man, worthy of the name of man, should not know what fear meant; and that if not courteous to the fair sex, as a knight errant of romance, he was unworthy to live. The consequence was that my brothers and I lived – out of doors – the lives of young savages; wandering among the hills . . . swimming across the river in our clothes (consisting merely of a kilt and flannel shirt) which we allowed to dry on our backs; riding unbroken Highland ponies with nothing but a halter to guide them; and going to sea in open boats in all weathers. But within doors no savagery was allowed. In the drawing room we were expected to behave like well-bred pages and tend the ladies as such . . . During the six winter months we attended the old High School in Edinburgh and spent the Summer in the Highlands studying with a private tutor, who, being a Highlander, naturally sympathised with us in our preference for rifles, salmon-spears and fishing-rods, over Latin grammars, Greek lexicons and the problems of Euclid . . .'

He went on: 'I joined the army at the age of seventeen: and soon after I obtained my Lieutenancy, the regiment in which I served received orders to embark for India. This news fell like a thunderbolt on many. India was for them a land of hopeless banishment – a living grave . . . a land from whence, if they escaped an early death, they were to return with sallow cheeks, peevish tempers and shattered constitutions. And such, alas, was the fate of many . . .'

The youthful Walter Campbell, however, was keen to go to India and on his arrival after the lengthy voyage out round the Cape he was not long in settling down. He was soon writing: 'The following is a list of the principal things required previous to taking the field in India:

A tent – single poled for a subaltern and double-poled for a captain or field officer – with two or four bullocks to carry it according to size.

A portable camp table, chair and basin-stand.

A camp cot, consisting of a light framework of wood with a rattan bottom, and a thin cotton mattress, on which is packed the table, chair and other light articles – the whole being carried by two coolies on their heads.

A good horse – or two of them if you can afford it – with his attendants, a 'gorah wallah' or horsekeeper and a grass cutter – one of each being required for each horse,

A sufficient number of bullocks to carry your baggage.

Two servants; a 'dobah' or head man and a 'maty boy'.

Two 'cowrie baskets' containing a sufficient stock of sugar, coffee, brandy and wax candles, carried by a coolie, and suspended from the ends of an elastic slip of bamboo.

A couple of hog spears – the spear heads made by 'Arnatchalem' at 'Salim' and the shafts of male bamboo brought from the 'Conkan.'

A hunting knife also made by 'Arnatchalem' if possible.

A hunting cap, strong in proportion to the respect you have for your skull – a thin plate of iron let into the crown is not a bad thing in stony country.

A good stock of cheroots and 'plenty' of ammunition – it being taken for granted that you are already provided with a gun, a rifle and a telescope.

Some men who study their comfort, rather than their purse, indulge in a palanquin, a Chinese mat, a tent carpet and many other little luxuries: but the fewer things of this kind a man hampers himself with the better.

Arab horses are almost universally used by Europeans . . .'

He recounted a tiger hunt in the following terms: 'March 1st . . . Elliot's native hunters, who have been on the trail of the tiger for a week past, brought intelligence that they had at last succeeded in marking him down . . .

'"Old Anak", a fine elephant which we have borrowed from a neighbouring rajah was instantly despatched with guns and ammunition in the howdah, and Elliot, my brother and I, followed soon after on horseback. On arriving at the ground, eight miles from the camp, we found . . . The tiger had been marked into a small open ravine . . . we mounted the elephant and the tiger was roused by a rattle of "tom-toms" . . . He was on foot in a moment and with a loud roar dashed from the ravine . . .

'The elephant and the tiger passed us at a distance of 150 yards . . . and just as he was topping the hill a long rifle shot appeared to touch him for a short angry roar was borne back upon the breeze . . . We followed at the best pace old ''Anak'' could muster and on reaching the summit of the hill saw the tiger slowly stealing down a ravine . . . for he was evidently wounded . . . One man . . . intoxicated with opium, disregarded every warning signal; the tiger was going straight towards him . . . Elliot ordered the ''mahout'' to urge the elephant forward at his utmost speed. My brother and I, both novices at tiger hunting, were almost in a rabid state; and in our anxiety to rescue the doomed wretch from his impending fate, we stamped with impatience . . . But all was in vain . . . the poor helpless drunkard . . . appeared paralysed by fear when he saw the tiger making directly towards him with terrific bounds . . The brute was upon him . . . One savage roar . . . and he was dashed to the ground . . . It was over in an instant. The tiger . . . being now excited to madness by the taste of blood, stood boldly awaiting our attack . . .

'The elephant was pushed forward with all speed, the tiger roaring furiously as we advanced, and the moment his splendid head appeared, a volley from six barrels sent him back staggering into the centre of the bush. He rallied instantly and made a brilliant charge close to the elephant's trunk, when he was again turned by a well-directed volley from the spare guns and retreated growling to his lair.

'We now retired a short distance to reload: and when we advanced again the tiger, although bleeding at every pore, rushed forth to meet us as savage as ever. He was again turned before he could spring on the elephant and again dragged forward his bleeding body to the charge roaring as if his heart would burst with impotent rage. We now let him come up quite close, so that every ball might tell, and gave him shot after shot, till he crawled back exhausted into the bushes. We followed him up and in a last expiring effort to reach the elephant he was shot dead while struggling to make good his charge. He was game to the last and Elliot who has killed many tigers says he never saw one die more gallantly . . .

Campbell went on to note: 'He was a male, about the medium size, and his dimensions . . . length from point of nose to point of tail 9 feet 5 inches . . . A tiger 9 feet 5 inches may be pronounced by some sportsmen accustomed to hear of tigers of 12 and even 14 feet in length to be a small specimen. But such was by no means the case. The animal in question was a full-sized specimen of very thick robust shape and was measured with scrupulous accuracy and without the natural wish of young sportsmen to magnify the size of their victim. There are various ways in which measurements of large game are taken. Many, I may say most men, content themselves with taking the length of the skin when pegged out to dry after the beast has been flayed. It is thus that 12 and 14 feet measurements are obtained. From examination of a great number of individuals − not less than 200 to 300 carefully measured − I am satisfied that few tigers exceed ten feet in length, and that the majority fall short of that limit. There is as great a variety of form and proportion amongst tigers as amongst men. Some individuals are the long lanky animals, while others are short and stout. Again there is a great diversity in the length of the tail, which is always taken into the notation of the length. Some tigers have long, others short tails in proportion to their bodies. It is obvious how these several circumstances modify the idea of size formed from a statement of the total length alone.'

On one occasion Campbell recorded following a black buck on his Arab horse and spearing it. 'After the first two miles I gained on him rapidly. The antelope went less collected, his gallop lost its springy bound and he began to turn short, his flanks heaving like a pair of bellows. I now felt that if I did not blow my horse I must kill him . . . I took a hard pull at my horse's head drove in the spurs and pressing the antelope to do his best for a few yards further I fairly burst him and down he went with the spear through his heart . . . He was a fine old buck in high condition with twenty-inch horns; and his having been ridden down by a single horse is one of those unaccountable things which seldom happens twice in a lifetime . . .'

With his experience of deer stalking at home Campbell found he quite often knew better than the native shikaris and especially so when it came to choosing ground where animals were likely to pass on a beat and also the best points of vantage at which to take his stance. For instance, he wrote that 'The advantage to sportsmen of an elevated position cannot be doubted . . . because it presents a wide field of view and affords earlier notice of the approach of game. Wild animals, moreover, not only smell danger – they see it, they hear it. The quickness of the senses of the beasts of the chase and the readiness with which they detect an unusual sight or sound is very remarkable. But . . . they never, unless specially attracted, look up . . . Hence the advantage of a post in a tree.'

He recorded an occasion when, tiger hunting with his brother George, he was waiting in a tree: 'The beat was long, the day hot, and I had fallen asleep on my perch. A pressure of the arm from my attendant woke me, and I saw the tiger emerging stealthily from the cover within 70 or 80 yards. The click of the rifle-lock, although so slight a sound, caught his ear . . . He instantly stopped short . . . and peered cautiously round on every side, but never looked up. So beautiful was the sight that I paused in admiration for several seconds before firing. Then with a short roar he bounded high in the air, the blood spurting from his mouth, and disappeared. George, who could see him from his post on the opposite side, shouted, "Dead!" and descending we found that the ball had gone right through his heart.'

Later he wrote: 'I have now had three days experience of driving game in the jungles with two hundred beaters and a line of twenty guns – five of them in the hands of European sportsmen – and what is the result – one bison, two sambar, and a rib-faced deer, which is not more than any one of us might have killed in a day's stalking. Beating is all very well where there is no possibility of approaching your game on account of the thickness of the cover. But

27

there is no doubt at all that in all places where the timber is large, the grass burnt down, and the underwood tolerably open, far more game may be killed by stalking than by beating . . .'

Campbell killed numerous tigers, including at least one notorious man-eater and his descriptions were racy and detailed. His views on the subject were quite decided: 'Never attack a tiger on foot – if you can help it. There are cases when you *must* do so. Then face him like a Briton and kill him if you can; for if you fail to kill him he will certainly kill you . . .'

He wrote of the tiger: 'Some idea may be formed of the havoc committed by tigers from the fact that . . . in one district alone three hundred and fifty men and twenty-four thousand head of cattle were destroyed in the course of four years . . . an average of nearly ninety men and six thousand cattle per annum!

'The general character of the tiger is that of a cowardly, treacherous and bloodthirsty animal. But he occasionally displays extraordinary courage in his attack; and when once in action the obstinacy of his defence and the silent game with which he dies, cannot be exceeded. The capricious nature of his ferocity sets at defiance all theories founded on individual instances. One sits crouched in his lair till he is shot to pieces, dying like a sullen savage without making any effort either to charge or to escape. Another avoids the combat at first, but when wounded becomes desperate and fights to the last gasp. While a third will charge the elephant before a shot has been fired . . .'

He decreed firmly: 'Next to a good elephant, the chief essential of a sports-man's establishment in a tiger-country, is an experienced ''shikari'': a fellow who ought to have the eye of an eagle, the heart of a lion, the constitution of a rhinoceros and the patience of Job. In parts of the country where good ''shikaris'' were not to be obtained, I used to find tigers by fastening a bullock near some ravine or thicket known to be frequented by them; the poor animal was generally carried off in the course of the night; nothing further was neces-sary than to follow up the trail of the tiger to some neighbouring cover, where we were sure to find him lying gorged . . .'

In emphasising the importance of the elephant, he wrote: 'A really good sporting elephant is invaluable. He beats for his game like a pointer; and carries his rider in safety over the most dangerous ground, and through the thickest covers, which he searches inch by inch, with a degree of patience and sagacity that make instinct amount almost to reason. Trees that oppose his progress are levelled by his head or torn down with his trunk; and at the word of command the sagacious brute picks up stones and hands them to his driver to throw into the thicker parts of the cover.

'On finding the tiger the elephant gives warning of his proximity by throw-ing up his trunk and trumpeting; and if well trained should remain perfectly steady, ready to obey every command of his ''mahout'' . . . Some elephants are so steady as to allow a tiger to rush up to their heads without flinching; but there are few that are not more or less alarmed by a determined charge . . .

'On a really good elephant the sportsman is exposed to little danger; less perhaps than in most Indian field sports. He is raised from ten to twelve feet off the ground, on a comfortable seat, from whence he can fire in all directions and he must be a bad shot indeed if he fails to stop a tiger in his charge. But even supposing that he does miss – which he has no business to do – and allows a savage tiger to spring upon the elephant, still the man is seldom the object of the attack, and he ought to be able to blow the brute's brains out before he does much mischief . . .

'In the absence of an elephant, tigers may be beat up, and shot from trees without any risk, for it is a curious fact, that tigers never attempt to climb, although their form appears peculiarly well adapted for so doing . . . I have frequently shot very savage tigers from trees not more than ten feet high, but never saw any attempt to climb, even when they saw plainly from whence the shot was fired. In most cases, however, the tiger, when hit from a tree, is quite unconscious of the sportsman's position; very rarely looking up to seek his foe, but springing forward as if he always looked for danger in front.

'A common method of shooting tigers is by watching them at night and shooting them from a tree when they return to feed on the carcase of a bullock which they have killed on the previous day. But this is a plan both tedious and uncertain and is more congenial to the taste of the Hindoo than that of a European sportsman.

'I have known men who were in the habit of shooting tigers on foot; but this is a sport attended with so much danger that few experienced sportsmen ever indulge in it; and I have remarked that those who did were pretty sure, sooner or later, to come to an untimely end.'

Campbell recorded that in one expedition, he, his brother George and his friend Elliot 'bagged thirteen royal tigers, besides panthers, bears, wild hog and deer!' He was then called back from leave and his brother gave him a beautiful Arab colt called Turquoise, who quickly became a favourite: 'he did thirty miles at a hand gallop in little more than three hours and came in fresh and playful as a kid . . .'

When recalled to his regiment he was perfectly capable of roughing it with the best, as might be expected, and his hunting experiences no doubt helped. He recorded gleefully: 'Turquoise (my good little Arab nag) and I arrange our domestic matters this wise: The weather being too wet for him to sleep out of doors without some covering, I have allowed him to take shelter in my tent, and in return, he lends me his rug to sleep on. The tent being very small there is not much room to spare but he being the most discreet of horses, never thinks of turning or kicking his legs about at night; and so we sleep side by side as comfortably as possible . . . He is as good as a watch dog, allowing no one to enter the tent without my leave and always wakens me in the morning by pushing me with his nose the moment he hears the bugle sound . . .'

29

When cholera in an insanitary regimental encampment at Masulipatam became very rife, after five years service in India Campbell accepted the offer of post as aide-de-camp to General Sir John Dalrymple, an old friend, and returned home. Characteristically he had refused £120 for his Arab, Turquoise, but as the horse had a strained tendon when the time came to leave India he gave him instead to a friend and was subsequently happy to learn that he had made a complete recovery.

Campbell noted that his original book *The Old Forest Ranger*, written in the form of a novel, which he published in the 1830s at his own expense since he could not find a publisher, had sold more than three editions. His much better *Indian Journal*, published thirty years later, was compiled from the original diaries he had written during his five years service. It is good to know that on his retirement as a Colonel he returned to Skipness and passed his days stalking the deer in his beloved Highlands.

Notes on two contemporaries:
Lt. Col. William Gordon Cumming and 'The Old Shekarree'

Lt. Col. William Gordon Cumming, nephew of the African sportsman Roualeyn Gordon Cumming (see pp. 44), dedicated his book *Wild Men and Wild Beasts* to 'Colonel Walter Campbell. My dear Walter, As the perusal of the writings of 'The Old Forest Ranger' in the days of my early youth first turned my thoughts to the hunting grounds of India, to him the following pages are dedicated by his affectionate Kinsman.' Published in 1871 it covered the period from before the Mutiny, during which he served, and contained much interesting material on sport. He was latterly a political officer amongst the Bheels, where he obtained plenty of opportunities for sport. Although not of quite the same calibre as Colonel Walter Campbell he was another of the many Scots who found their service in India an opportunity to indulge their sporting instincts to the full and who left very readable chronicles of their times.

The author of the small book *The Spear and the Rifle or Recollections of Sport in India*, writing under the pseudonym of 'An Old Shekarree', has been confused by many readers with H. A. Leveson (see pp. 72), who wrote under the pseudonym of 'The Old Shekarry', but this was clearly of a much earlier date. The author claimed to have been left by his father in Europe when the latter departed for Indian service. He ran away from his tutor and returned to England, then followed his father to India. From the age of thirteen onwards he appears to have led a free life in the cantonments and hunted game, mostly on horseback. Apart from being an expert horseman he was also, by his own account, a good rifle shot. Of interest chiefly as an example of early sport in India, although undated, it can be placed as roughly in the 1830–1840 period and as such has a certain interest in spite of the somewhat bombastic style of the unknown author.

2

EARLY SPORTSMEN
IN AFRICA

William Cornwallis Harris 1807–1848

Roualeyn George Gordon Cumming 1820–1866

William Cotton Oswell 1818–1893

Captain H. Butler, 59th Regiment, a contemporary of William Cornwallis Harris, hunting eland in the Cape, c1839.

William Cornwallis Harris 1807–1848

Africa 1835–1837

Georgian Military Engineer/Administrator

*Never shall I forget the tingling excitement of that moment. At last
the summit of my hunting ambition was actually attained and the
towering giraffe laid low . . . The secret of cameleopard hunting
discovered . . .*

William Cornwallis Harris, the younger son of a Kentish squire, was born at
Wittersham in 1807, and from a very early age admitted to 'shooting madness',
which to judge by his own accounts was at times no exaggeration. A product
of the late Georgian age he was clearly a bright lad, possessed of considerable
artistic ability fostered at an early age by Bewick's drawings, including his
'eccentric figure of the gnoo', which nourished the boy's early interest in
Africa. He graduated from Military College at sixteen and in December 1823
was commissioned as a Second Lieutenant in the Engineers in Bombay. By May
1824 he was commissioned full Lieutenant, and at this time his favourite possession appears to have been a muzzle loading rifle with which he claimed he
could kill a kite at one hundred and fifty yards. Very soon he was stalking
sambur deer and shooting lions and tigers from the back of his favourite hunting elephant.

Clearly he found the sport to be had in India very much to his taste, but
this does not seem to have detracted from his abilities as an engineer, for his
promotion was rapid. He was appointed assistant-superintendent engineer in
Bombay in September 1825 and executive engineer in Candleish in November
of the same year, subsequently transferring to Deesa in 1830. In 1834 he was
promoted to Captain, but by this time the combination of the climate and
various fevers he had suffered began to take their toll, as on so many Europeans
in India. It seems that the examining Medical Board gave him little chance
of surviving, so physically reduced had he become, and in 1835 he was
invalided to the Cape of Good Hope for two years, and advised to travel.

It was unfortunate for Harris, if perhaps fortunate for the wildlife of Africa,
that a ship entering Bombay harbour as he sailed out was carrying three new
rifles he had ordered from England two years previously. On the ship with
him, however, was William Richardson of the Bombay Civil Service and the
two soon found a lot in common, being both keen naturalists as well as sports-

men. They resolved to make an expedition to the interior of Africa and when they arrived at the Cape they were not long in sailing on to Algoa Bay. However, their choice of guide and interpreter, a one-eyed Hottentot named Andries, proved unfortunate for he turned out to be a treacherous liar and coward, who on several occasions in different ways was nearly responsible for their deaths. Several other Hottentots, all ex-convicts, were also enrolled in their expedition and these too, without exception, proved cowardly and troublesome.

In the end their expedition consisted of only eleven members in all. This was not for want of trying to collect more followers but, as Harris noted, it was all too plainly felt that 'two poor Indian gentlemen' stood no chance of making such a 'long and perilous journey'. Their final starting point was the 'picturesque little Dutch village of Graaff Reinet' where they put themselves in the hands of a Mr John Burnet Biddulph who obtained for them 'a capital waggon with thirty draught oxen; and we had in the meantime completed our stud of horses to twelve, of all sorts and sizes, conceiving these would suffice, though in this . . . we were greatly mistaken.'

Harris recorded: 'Our waggon fitted up with water-casks, tar-buckets, side-chests, beds, pockets and other appurtenances for the long journey before us, during which it was to be our only abode, might now not inaptly be compared to a ship proceeding to sea. Besides ourselves and our personal conveniences, it contained, with the addition of a barrel of gunpowder . . . six sacks of flour, two bags of rice, and two of sugar, with chests of tea and bales of coffee. The baggage-waggon carried tent, camp-stools, table and cooking utensils; hams, tongues and cheeses in profusion; salt and dried fish, biscuits, wax candles, soap . . . sauces and pickles . . . a few dozens of brandy, and a small barrel of inferior spirits for the use of the followers. Crevices and empty spaces were filled up with spades, pickaxes, hatchets, sickles and joiner's tools, together with nails, screws, spare bolts and linchpins; and . . . no less than eighteen thousand leaden bullets, duly prepared . . . [with] a large additional supply . . . in pigs, to be converted . . . as . . . required . . .'

They intended to leave Graaff Reinet on 1st September, only to find that their Hottentots had pawned their muskets for gin and were in a drunken stupor. Finally, by 25th September they had reached Kuruman, a missionary centre 200 miles into the interior run by a Scot, the Rev. Mr Moffat. From him they learned that the Matabele chieftain, Moselekatse, whose territory they intended to cross in order to reach the Vaal river, had sent a force of warriors to attack the emigrant Boers recently established there and it was thus a highly unsuitable time to visit him. Moselekatse was a very despotic chieftain who had built up his own savage empire on the same lines as the Zulu chieftain, Chaka, against whom he had revolted. He had established a reign of terror over a large region and had destroyed every tribe which had opposed him. Against all the advice Harris and Richardson received, however, they decided to continue as planned.

Harris wrote in disgust as one point: 'It was unfortunately requisite, during the greater part of our journey to furnish the Hottentots with ammunition for their protection whilst tending the cattle; and their incessant firing, which no remonstrance could control, soon disturbing the whole of the game in our neighbourhood, we found it useless to remain more than one day in one place. Compared with the quantity of powder expended by these scoundrels the number of animals they killed was exceedingly limited – the supply of meat for the camp generally depending upon my success; but the beasts of the forest having been unmolested all their lives and unaccustomed to the report of the gun, fled before their attacks in consternation . . .'

As they approached the Chooi Desert, Harris noted that, 'we passed a long line of pitfalls . . . Upwards of sixty of these were dug close together in a treble line; a high thorn fence extending in the form of a crescent a mile on either side, in such a manner that gnoos, quaggas and other animals might easily be driven into them. They are carefully concealed with grass and . . . render escape almost impossible. . .'

On 9th October, having crossed the desert, they found themselves in a land of sandy flats, thorn bushes and long grass with deserted villages from which the inhabitants had been driven by the chieftain Moselekatse. It was here that Harris recorded: '. . . I turned off the road in pursuit of a troop of brindled gnoos, and presently came on another, which was joined by a third still larger – then by a vast herd of zebras and again by more gnoos, with sassaybes and hartebeests pouring down from every quarter until the landscape literally presented a moving mass of game. Their incredible numbers so impeded their progress that I had no difficulty in closing with them, dismounting as opportunity offered, firing both barrels of my rifle into the retreating phalanx, and leaving the ground strewed with the slain. Still unsatisfied I could not resist the temptation of mixing with the fugitives, loading and firing until my jaded horse suddenly exhibited symptoms of distress and shortly afterwards was unable to move. At this moment I discovered that I had dropped my pocket compass and being unwilling to lose so valuable an ally, I turned loose my steed to graze and retraced my steps several miles without success; the prints of my horse's hoofs being at length lost in those of the countless herds which had crossed the plain. Completely absorbed in the chase, I had retained but an imperfect idea of my locality . . .'

He was now completely lost and was forced to spend a night in the wilds. Fortunately for him he found the nearly dried-up river which was intended to be their next stopping place and at least was able to quench his thirst before knee-haltering his horse and retreating inside a thorn bush to the sound of lions all around. In the morning his horse was missing, as he thought eaten, but he eventually found him grazing in a hollow by the river and once mounted again was not long in finding the waggons camped on the plain, they having had to stop when darkness overtook them.

In writing of another hunting expedition Harris demonstrated to the full that remarkable ambivalence of feeling towards 'the Brute Creation' which seems to have been typical of many hunters of the Georgian age. 'The reports of four savages of the Batapli tribe who joined us yesterday determined us to halt a day for the purposes of hunting. Richardson and myself left the waggons at daybreak . . . We soon perceived large herds of quaggas and brindled gnoos which continued to join each other until the whole plain seemed alive. The clatter of their hooves was . . . [like] a tremendous charge of cavalry . . . I could not estimate [them] at less than fifteen thousand . . . clouds of dust hovered over them . . . the long necks of troops of ostriches were also to be seen . . . Groups of purple sassaybes, and brilliant red and yellow hartebeests . . . beggars all attempts at description. The savages kept in our wake, dexterously despatching the wounded gnoos by a touch in the spine with the point of an assegai and instantly covering up the carcasses with bushes, to secure them from the voracity of the vultures, which . . . descended with the velocity of lightning . . . Two . . . elands . . . [were seen] and pressing our horses . . . we found ourselves for the first time on the heels of the largest and most beautiful species of . . . antelope . . . Notwithstanding the unwieldy shape of these animals, they at first greatly exceeded the speed of our jaded horses, but being pushed they soon separated: their sleek coats turned first blue and then white with froth: the foam fell from their mouths and nostrils, and the perspiration from their sides. Their pace gradually slackened, and with their full brilliant eyes turned imploringly towards us, at the end of a mile, each was laid low by a single ball. They were young bulls measuring upwards of seventeen hands at the shoulder.

'I was engaged in making a sketch of the one I had shot, when the savages came up and in spite of all my remonstrances, proceeded with cold-blooded ferocity to stab the unfortunate animal, stirring up the blood and shouting with barbarous exultation, as it issued with each newly inflicted wound, regardless of the eloquent and piteous appeal, expressed in the beautiful clear black eye of the mild and inoffensive eland.'

On nearing Chief Moselekatse's kraal they found the road more difficult. 'Game-traps and pit-falls were to be seen through every avenue, many of the thorn fences extending across the path and impeding the waggons until cut away with the hatchet . . .'

Of their meeting with the Chief, Harris wrote: 'The expression of the despot's features, though singularly cunning, wily and suspicious, is not altogether disagreeable. His figure is rather tall, well turned and active, but through neglect of exercise, leaning to corpulency . . . He appeared about forty years of age . . .'

They presented him with a many caped coat, lined with crimson cloth and fastened by an ornate clasp, also a two-foot square mirror, fifty pounds of blood-red beads and a fifty-pound coil of brass wire. In addition there was a tartan suit from Mr Moffat, the missionary. Harris wrote: 'Hitherto the king had considered it beneath his dignity to evince the slightest symptom of astonishment . . . but the sight of so many fine things at once threw his decorum off the balance . . . Putting his thumb between his teeth and opening his eyes to their utmost limits, he grinned like a schoolboy at the sight of ginger-bread . . .'

After this first formal meeting Harris recorded: 'We were shortly afterwards visited by the king without either pageant or ceremony. This he considered a confidential interview and said he had come 'to see what we had got for him'. The weather being cold, he was attired in a handsome black leathern mantle; its ample folds reaching to his heels, well became his tall and manly person; and he looked the *beau ideal* of an African chief. He had completely thrown aside that reserve and gravity which in a public assembly he had conceived most becoming and now appeared in high good humour, joking, laughing and familiarly pulling our beards, of which the luxuriant growth elicited his admiration and surprise. We thought this an auspicious moment in which to revert to the subject of our desired exit by the Vaal River, but took especial care to exclude Andries from the conference. Besides being a bad interpreter, we had seen he was personally opposed to the measure . . .'

Inevitably they were held up for several days while the chief attempted to squeeze more and more 'presents' from them, but despite losing a few articles they had not intended to give him they managed to achieve their object, largely they suspected, because the chief was worried about their presence when his warriors returned from raiding the Boers. Thus, after presenting further gifts of beads, at last they were given permission to go on to the Vaal River and on 28th October they started on their way, whereupon Harris could not resist recording his feelings of justifiable self-congratulation.

'Visiting this capricious savage as we had done, at an inauspicious juncture, when he was embroiled with white men and might not unreasonably have regarded us as spies – a suspicion which the pusillanimous conduct of our Hottentots and Andries in particular, was calculated to inspire and confirm – we had had throughout a difficult and somewhat hazardous part to perform. The probabilities were in favour of our being detained . . . but by closing our eyes upon passing events, and preserving through our intercourse with the despot a firm, conciliatory and confiding demeanour – not only had we succeeded in convincing him of the honesty of our intentions – but now pursued our journey with every reason to believe in the good faith of his professions towards ourselves. As we were now considered to be on terms of close intimacy with his Majesty we had no danger to apprehend from any of the native tribes through whose territory we might have occasion to pass.'

The next day he shot a hartebeest for the natives, accompanying them and noting that they almost invariably ate their meat raw. 'They usually seize a piece of flesh by the teeth, cutting a large mouthful off it with the assegai close to the lips, before masticating it which they do with a loud splutter and noise. The meal being finished they never failed to wipe their hands on their bodies, and then being generally gorged, they lay themselves down to repose . . . doubtless it will be ever found that uncultivated man is a compound of treachery, cunning, debauchery, gluttony and idleness . . .'

Later on that day Harris saw his first giraffe in the distance and the chase that followed was somewhat abortive: 'Putting spurs to my horse and directing the Hottentots to follow I presently found myself, half choked with excitement, rattling at the heels of the tallest of all the Mammiferes . . . Sailing before me with incredible velocity . . . he . . . seemed to leave whole leagues behind him at each stride . . . For the first five minutes I rather lost than gained ground . . . I dismounted and had the satisfaction of hearing two balls tell roundly upon his plank-like stern. But I might as well have fired at a wall: he neither swerved . . . nor slackened his pace . . . Closing again . . . I repeated the dose on the other quarter, and . . . down I came headlong – my horse having fallen into a pit . . . close to an ostrich's nest . . . There were no bones broken, but the violence of the shock had caused the lashings of my rifle to give way, and had doubled the stock in half – the barrels only now hanging to it by the trigger guard. Nothing dismayed by this heavy calamity, I remounted my jaded beast and one more effort brought me a-head of my wearied victim, which stood still and allowed me to approach . . .'

At this stage he found his rifle 'so bent' the hammer would not come down on the nipple. He had lent his knife to one of the Hottentots to deal with the hartebeest, so he was unable to hamstring the giraffe and there were no stones handy with which to hit the cap. The Hottentots did not appear and 'in a few minutes the giraffe having recovered his wind, and being only slightly wounded in the hindquarters . . . walked a few steps then broke into a gallop, and . . . disappeared . . . Disappointed and annoyed, I returned towards the waggons . . . and . . . overtook the Hottentots . . . who . . . having come to the conclusion that "Sir, would not catch the kameel" . . . did not think it worth while to follow as I had directed.'

He continued: 'My defeat did not cause me to lose sight of the flesh-pots. Any change from the monotony of an unvaried bread-and-meat diet being highly agreeable, I went back to the nest of the ostrich . . . Twenty-three gigantic eggs were laid on the bare ground . . . Having broken one, to ascertain they were worth carrying home, a Hottentot took off his trowsers in which (the legs having first been tied at the lower end) the eggs were securely packed . . . we found them a highly palatable omelette . . . I employed the rest of the day in repairing my . . . weapon with the iron clamp of a box, binding it with a strip of green hide from the carcase of an eland.'

After crossing the Mariqua River Harris saw 'an unwieldy white rhinoceros . . . standing stupidly under the shade of a spreading acacia' and the natives

William Cornwallis Harris hunting giraffe.

urged him to shoot it. He went on: 'I crept within thirty yards before firing, but it was not until he had received six two-ounce bullets behind the shoulder that he yielded up the ghost – charging repeatedly with his snout almost touching the ground in so clumsy a manner, that it was only necessary to step on one side to be perfectly safe . . . It is the larger, but less ferocious of the two species of African rhinoceros, neither of which is clad in a panoply of plate armour like their Asiatic brethren . . . These animals may be readily approached within a few yards, against the wind, and being heavy and inert, their attacks are easily avoided.'

A few days later they came on a valley where 'the whole face of the landscape was actually covered with wild elephants. There could not have been fewer than three hundred . . .' They were able to find a convenient place to lie in wait and sent Andries the Hottentot round to drive them past and they were soon passing within fifteen yards. 'Thus situated we might have killed any number we pleased, their heads being frequently turned towards us in such a position and so close that a single ball to the brain would have sufficed for each. But whilst we were yet hesitating a bullet suddenly whizzed past Richardson's ear and put the whole herd to immediate flight . . . I rested my rifle against a tree and firing behind the shoulder of the leader she dropped instantly . . . Andries now came up in high good humour . . . being pleased altogether to

39

overlook the fact . . . that his own ball, whether designedly or not, had all but expended my worthy and esteemed fellow-traveller.'

The next day not an elephant was to be seen, but near the corpse of the cow 'a calf of about three and a half feet high . . . saluted us with mournful piping notes . . . Entwining it little proboscis about our legs . . . it accompanied the party to the body of its dam . . . It ran round its mother's corpse with touching demonstrations of grief . . . I confess that I had felt compunctions in committing the murder the day before and now half resolved never to assist in another; for in addition to the moving behaviour of the young elephant, I had been unable to divest myself of the idea that I was firing at my old favourite, *Mowla Buksh*, from whose gallant back I had vanquished so many of my feline foes in Guzerut – an impression which, however ridiculous it must appear, detracted considerably from the satisfaction I experienced . . .'

This did not stop him going out the next day after elephants, when he 'entered a strip of forest . . . On the outside of this stood a mighty bull elephant . . . I crept silently behind a block of stone and levelled my rifle at his ample forehead. The earth trembled under the weight of the enormous brute as he dropped heavily uttering one deep groan and expiring without a struggle. His height at the shoulder was eleven feet and a half and his tusks measured more than seven feet in length . . .'

The following day it rained so heavily that 'we were unable to open the canvas curtains on the waggon. Peeping out, however . . . we perceived three lions squatted within a hundred yards, in the open plain, attentively watching the oxen. Our rifles were hastily seized, but the dampness of the atmosphere prevented their exploding. One after another, too, the Hottentots . . . snapped their guns at the unwelcome intruders . . . Fresh caps and priming were applied and a broadside was followed by the instant demise of the largest, whose cranium was perforated by two bullets . . .'

Nevertheless he recorded: 'The country now literally represented the appearance of a menagerie; the host of rhinoceroses in particular that daily exhibited themselves almost exceeding belief . . . On our way from the waggons to a hill not half a mile distant we counted no less than twenty-two of the white species . . . and were compelled in self defence to slaughter four . . .'

Near the Limpopo River he noted: 'Another rare species – the roan antelope is an inhabitant of the elevated downs and ridges about the source of this river and, being utterly destitute of speed, may be ridden to a standstill without difficulty. This most imposing animal, which charges viciously when unable to continue its flight, is the size of a large horse . . . Here too I first met and slew the koodoo. Majestic in its carriage and brilliant in its colour.'

Harris's enthusiasm however was raised to fresh heights when he finally killed his first cameleopard, or giraffe: 'The blood coursed through my veins like quicksilver . . . as . . . from the back of Breslar, my most trusty steed with a firm wooded plain before me I counted thirty-two of these animals . . . in

a mimosa grove . . . They were within a hundred yards, but . . . I reserved
my fire . . . [and] away bounded the giraffes . . . soon leaving me far in the
rear . . . In the course of five minutes . . . I arrived at a small river . . . and
after floundering to the opposite side . . . I perceived that their race was run.
Patting the steaming neck of my good steed, I urged him again to his utmost
and instantly found myself by the side of the herd. The stately bull being
readily distinguishable . . . by his superior stature, I applied the muzzle of
my rifle behind his dappled shoulder with the right hand and drew both trig-
gers; but he still continued to shuffle along and being afraid of losing him
. . . I sat in the saddle, loading and firing behind the elbow, and then placing
myself across his path until, the tears trickling from his full brilliant eye, his
lofty frame began to totter and at the seventeenth discharge from the deadly
grooved bore, like a falling minaret bowing his graceful head from the skies,
his proud form was prostrate in the dust. Never shall I forget the tingling
excitement of that moment. At last then the summit of my hunting ambition
was actually attained and the towering giraffe laid low . . . Two hours were
passed in completing a drawing . . . I cut off the tail, which exceeded five
feet in length and was measurelessly the most estimable trophy I had gained
. . . The spell was broken and the secret of cameleopard hunting discovered.
The next day Richardson and myself killed three . . . From this time we could
reckon confidently upon two out of each troop we were fortunate enough to
find . . .'

He recorded later: 'Few other sporting incidents occurred of an extraordinary character except the death of a very large black rhinoceros, which being
pent up in an old stone enclosure, forming a *cul de sac*, the entrance to which
I closed up, received no less than twenty-seven shot before it fell, dyed with
crimson gore and embossed with the white foam that rage had churned around
its chaps. A troop of brindled gnoo . . . dashed into a narrow defile . . . at
the outlet of which . . . I disposed of two with each barrel . . .'

It was scarcely surprising by this time after endless slaughter he noted that
'both our vehicles were now so crammed with *spolia* that being unable to find
room for any more ivory, we were reluctantly compelled to leave the ground
strewed with that valuable commodity . . . The list of large animals killed during the campaign now exceeded four hundred head of various sorts and sizes.
Of these the minimum height at the shoulder had been three feet and not a
few had measured ten or twelve . . .'

Having broken his double-barrelled rifle again Harris was using a flintlock
he had bought from the missionary, Moffat, when he saw 'a herd of unusually
dark looking antelopes . . . I at once exclaimed that they were perfectly new
to science . . . In vain was it that I pulled the trigger of my rifle . . . I fairly
rode my horse to a standstill in the attempt to overtake them. Cursing my
bad fortune as I dashed the hateful weapon to the ground, I hastened to the
camp to repair my broken rifle . . .' Three days later, however, they found

41

A buffalo hunt drawn by Captain H. Butler, 1839.

the same species and shot a buck. Referring for once to his companion, Harris then triumphantly quoted Richardson as saying 'the sable antelope would doubtless become the admiration of the world.' Having drawn it, the specimen was carefully skinned and eventually was stuffed in Capetown and finally sent to the British Museum.

By this time they were approaching the Vaal River. Harris observed 'vast troops' of bles-boks on the plain ahead of the waggons. He recorded blithely: 'Never having killed any of these antelopes and our stock of provisions requiring to be recruited, I mounted Breslar, my favourite Rosinante, and never heeding whither I sped, dashed into the thick of them. The pine-apple hill bore east about five miles and I fancied was a never failing landmark . . . Dealing death around I continued to scour the plain, the herd before me increasing from hundreds to thousands . . . when crying "Hold enough!" I stayed my hand from slaughter. Having divested some of the slain of their brilliant parti-coloured robes and packed the *spoila* on my horse I set out to rejoin the waggons, but ah! how vainly did I seek them in the area of mirage that environed me . . . The monotony of the landscape baffled all my attempts at recognition and my search was utterly fruitless . . .'

He was forced to bivouac in the open and, seeing a fire, approached it only to find a group of hostile Bushmen who fortunately did not see him. He cooked himself a bird he had shot for his Christmas dinner and spent another fruitless day searching for the waggons. On the third day, luckily for him, he found their trail and encountered some natives who led him safely back.

He had been given up for dead by the others and later wrote: 'On comparing notes with my fellow traveller I was concerned to find that in some respects he had scarcely fared better than myself; the knuckle bone of a tainted ham having supplied the place of a smoking sirloin and richly-dotted plum-pudding – and with a cup of dirty water constituted alas! his Christmas dinner.'

Their native escort then left them and they had an unfortunate encounter with Bushmen who stole and killed their oxen, but by this time they were close enough to the Boers to get help and from this time onwards they returned with all speed through comparative civilisation to their starting point. 'Sixty-nine casualties had already occurred amongst our oxen: and on the 24th another victim being left . . . [and] we had barely a sufficient number remaining to drag our waggons into the village of Graaff Reinet.' The cost of the entire expedition he estimated at 'around £800'.

He concluded: 'In addition to the sable antelope . . . my collection consisted of two perfect crania of every species of game quadruped to be found in Southern Africa, together with the skins of lion, quagga, zebra, ostrich &c, tails of the cameleopard and tusks of elephant and hippopotami besides elaborate drawings of every animal that interests the sportsman from the tall giraffe to the minutest antelope.'

In all, Harris and his companion were away from India from March 1835 to December 1837, when he returned triumphantly, apparently totally recovered. In January 1838 he was appointed executive engineer at Belgaum and, in December of the same year, field engineer to the forces in Scinde. He clearly had made a name for himself for in 1840 he was appointed Superintendent Engineer for the Southern Provinces and in 1841 he was selected for a Mission to conclude a commercial treaty with Ethiopia.

In 1844 he was knighted for his services on this expedition and returned to India, where, however, his old illness overtook him once more. In 1848, still aged only forty-one, he died in Poona of 'lingering fever', but in the pages of his book *Wild Sports in South Africa* he continues to gallop across the veldt in pursuit of the cameleopard. As the first sportsman to write an account of the animals in South Africa and draw them faithfully he deserves recognition. While his actions and attitudes may perhaps be regarded as fairly typical of his time many of them would be seen as totally inexcusable by subsequent generations.

Roualeyn George Gordon Cumming 1820–1866

Africa 1844–1849

Highland Adventurer and Showman

I may remark that lion hunting . . . is a decidedly dangerous pursuit.
It may, nevertheless, be followed . . . with comparative safety by
those who have naturally a turn for that sort of thing . . .

Born on 15th March 1820 Roualeyn George Gordon Cumming was the younger son of Sir William George Gordon Cumming, Bart., of Altyre and Gordonstoun in Morayshire. After being sent to Eton at the age of nine, like many another younger son of that period and station in life, he ended up with a commission in the Honourable East India Company's Service as a Cornet in the Madras Cavalry. The climate, however, proved too much for him and after only eighteen months his health was so seriously affected that in 1840 he resigned his commission and returned home. He then took a commission as an Ensign in the 'Royal Veteran Newfoundland Company', but finding this not to his taste exchanged in 1843 into the Cape Mounted Rifles.

Once established in Africa, and despite the warnings of many of his sporting friends at the Cape he decided to trek into the interior, collecting together a couple of waggons and teams of oxen. He recorded: 'My ordnance was as follows: 3 double barrelled rifles by Purdey, William Moore and Dickson of Edinburgh – the latter a two-grooved, the most perfect and useful rifle I ever had the pleasure of using: one heavy single barrelled German rifle carrying 12 to the lb. This last was an old companion . . . having been with me in several campaigns on the plains and in the jungles of Hindoostan. I also had 3 stout double-barrelled guns for rough work when hard riding and quick loading is required: several lead ladles of various sizes, a whole host of bullet-moulds, loading-rods, shot-belts, powder-flasks, and shooting-belts; 3 cwt of lead, 50 lbs of pewter for hardening the balls to be used in destroying larger game; 10,000 prepared leaden bullets, bags of shot of all sizes; 100 lbs of fine sporting gunpowder, 300 lbs of coarse gunpowder; about 50,000 percussion caps; 2,000 gun flints, greased patches and cloth to be converted into the same . . . With the above and £200 in cash which I carried with me, I considered myself prepared to undertake a journey of at least twelve months amongst the Boers or Bechuanas, independent of either.'

He found in practice that he got on very well with the Boers who, he noted, 'are rather partial to Scotchmen although they detest the sight of an Englishman . . .'

Early on in his journeyings he saw and described a migration of springboks thus: 'This was, I think the most extraordinary and striking scene, as connected with beasts of the chase, that I have ever beheld. For about two hours before the day dawned, I had been lying awake in my waggon, listening to the grunting of the bucks within two hundred yards of me, imagining that some large herd of springbok was feeding beside my camp; but on my rising when it was clear, and looking about me, I beheld the ground to the northward of my camp, actually covered by a dense living mass of springboks, marching slowly and steadily along and extending from an opening in a long range of hills on the west, through which they continued pouring like the flood of some great river to a ridge about a mile to the north-east over which they disappeared. The breadth of ground they covered might have been somewhere about half a mile. I stood upon the fore chest of my waggon for about two hours, lost in wonder at the novel and wonderful scene which was passing before me, and had some difficulty in convincing myself that it was reality which I beheld and not the wild and exaggerated picture of a hunter's dream. During this time vast legions continued streaming through the neck of the hills in one unbroken compact phalanx. At length I saddled up and rode into the midst of them, with my rifle and after-riders, and fired into the ranks until fourteen had fallen, when I cried "Enough." We then retraced our steps to secure the venison which lay strewed along my gory track . . .

'A person anxious to kill many springboks might have bagged thirty or forty that morning. I never in all my subsequent career, fell in with so dense a herd of these antelopes, nor found them allow me to ride so near them . . . Vast and surprising as was the herd of springboks which I had that morning witnessed . . . on our clearing the low range of hills through which the springboks had been pouring, I beheld the boundless plains, and even the hillsides which stretched away on every side of me, thickly covered and not with "herds," but with "one vast herd" of springboks; far as the eye could strain the landscape was alive with them, until they softened down into a dim red mass of living creatures . . .'

Gordon Cumming's descriptions of how he shot various animals is quite enough to turn the stomach of today's sportsmen, although not differing so very greatly from Harris. His description of shooting his first giraffe is similar in many ways to Harris's account.

'The giraffes stood looking at the waggons till I was within sixty yards of them . . . ten colossal giraffes . . . from seventeen to eighteen feet high. On beholding me they at once made off . . . My senses were so absorbed by the wondrous and beautiful sight before me that I rode along like one entranced . . . The ground was firm and favourable for riding . . . after a short burst at a swinging gallop, I was in the middle of them and turned the finest cow out of the herd . . . In a few minutes I was riding within five yards of her stern, and firing at the gallop, I sent a bullet into her back. Increasing my pace, I next rode alongside and placing the muzzle of my rifle within a few feet of her I fired my second shot behind the shoulder; the ball, however, seemed to have little effect. I then placed myself directly in front, when she came to a walk. Dismounting I hastily loaded both barrels, putting in double charges of powder. Before this was accomplished she was off at a canter. In a short time I brought her to a stand in the dry bed of a water-course where I fired at fifteen yards, aiming where I thought the heart lay, upon which she again made off. Having loaded, I followed, and had very nearly lost her; she had turned abruptly to the left and was far out of sight among the trees. Once more I brought her to a stand and dismounted from my horse. There we stood together, alone in the wild wood. I gazed in wonder at her extreme beauty while her soft dark eye, with its silky fringe, looked down imploringly at me, and I really felt a pang of sorrow in this moment of triumph for the blood I was shedding. Pointing my rifle to the skies I sent a bullet through her neck. On receiving it she reared high on her hindlegs and fell backwards with a heavy crash, making the earth shake around her. A thick stream of dark blood spouted out from the wound, her colossal limbs quivered for a moment and she expired.

'I had little time to contemplate the prize I had won. Night was setting in and it was very questionable if I should succeed in regaining my waggons . . . I took "one last fond look" and rode hard for the spoor of the waggons, which I succeeded in reaching just as it was dark.

'No pen nor words can convey to a sportsman what it is to ride in the midst of a troop of gigantic giraffes; it must be experienced to be understood. They emitted a powerful perfume, which in the chase came hot in my face, reminding me of the smell of a hive of heather honey in September.'

Gordon Cumming was, at times, the most consummate boaster and humbug. His description of the qualities required by a lion hunter, which by inference he possessed to the full, he made clear when he wrote that '. . . lion hunting, under any circumstances is a decidedly dangerous pursuit. It may, nevertheless, be followed, to a certain extent, with comparative safety by those who have naturally a turn for that sort of thing. A recklessness of death, perfect coolness and self-possession, an acquaintance with the disposition and manners of lions, and a tolerable knowledge of the use of the rifle, are indispensable to him who would shine in the overpoweringly exciting pastime of hunting this justly celebrated king of beasts . . .'

Particularly nauseating is his account of how he killed a large bull elephant: '. . . an excited native . . . led me through the forest a few hundred yards, when . . . I came full in view of the tallest and largest bull elephant I had ever seen. He stood broadside on to me at upwards of a hundred yards, and his attention at the moment was occupied with the dogs . . . Halting my horse,

Roualeyn George Gordon Cumming dressed in the kilt, his customary
hunting dress in South Africa, with a rhinoceros in hot pursuit.

I fired at his shoulder and secured him with a single shot. The ball caught
him high upon the shoulder-blade, rendering him instantly dead lame; and
. . . I plainly saw the elephant was mine. The dogs now came up and barked
around him, but . . . limping slowly to a neighbouring tree, he remained station-
ary, eyeing his pursuers with a resigned and philosophic air.

'I resolved to devote a short time to the contemplation of the noble elephant
before I should lay him low; accordingly, having off-saddled the horses . . .
I quickly kindled a fire . . . and in a very few minutes my coffee was prepared.
There I sat in my forest home, coolly sipping my coffee with one of the finest
elephants in Africa awaiting my pleasure beside a neighbouring tree. It was
indeed a striking scene . . .

'Having admired the elephant for a considerable time I resolved to make
experiments for vulnerable points, and, approaching very near, I fired several
bullets at different parts of his enormous skull. These did not seem to affect
him in the slightest; he only acknowledged the shots by a 'salaam-like' movement of his trunk, with the point of which he gently touched the wound with
a striking and peculiar action. Surprised and shocked to find that I was only
tormenting and prolonging the suffering of the noble beast, which bore his
trials with such dignified composure, I resolved to finish the proceeding with
all possible dispatch; accordingly I opened fire upon him from the left side,

aiming behind the shoulder; but even there it was long before my bullets seemed to take effect. I first fired six shots with the two-grooved, which must have eventually proved mortal, but as yet he evinced no distress; after which I fired three shots with the Dutch six-pounder. Large tears now trickled from his eyes, which he slowly shut and opened; his colossal frame quivered convulsively, and, falling on his side, he expired . . .'

As well as apparently lacking any feeling, Gordon Cumming was also totally unscrupulous. He traded muskets which had cost him less than £1 each for £30 of ivory, assuring the gullible natives they were the equal of his first class double-barrelled rifles. He also deceived them in other ways calculated to cause trouble for the next traders dealing with them. For instance he accepted the present of a leopard skin and and elephant's tusk in return for 'cutting' a native chieftain to make him shoot straight. He made incisions in the chief's arm and anointed them with gunpowder and turpentine, then he placed his finger on pictures of various wild animals, telling the chief that his gun would have power over them 'provided he held it straight.' Dr Livingstone was naturally much shocked when he heard of these proceedings, since they totally undermined his own teachings and probably coloured adversely his views on 'hunters'.

In 1850 Gordon Cumming published his book entitled *Five Years of a Hunter's Life in the Far Interior of South Africa*. In 1851 he exhibited the trophies of his hunting exploits at the Great Exhibition. Thereafter, for some years he successfully toured the country lecturing on African sport, dressed in the kilt with his red beard flowing down his chest. His lectures appeared to have been so outrageous at times that he came to be regarded as a mountebank. Then in 1858 he set up a museum at Fort Augustus, calculated to attract the travellers on the Caledonian Canal. In 1866 he died, shortly after his forty-sixth birthday, having ordered his coffin two days' prior to his death.

Undoubtedly a showman, and something of a humbug, Roualeyn Gordon Cumming was, like Harris, a product of the late Georgian period. Armed with inadequate weapons he survived five years in the interior of Africa – and if he made rather more of his adventures than perhaps they may have merited, at least he survived, which in itself was no mean achievement in those days.

William Cotton Oswell 1818–1893

India 1832–1844; Africa 1844–1855

Old Rugbeian Heroic Victorian

*I saw the burly brute from chest to tail as he passed directly over
me lengthways, one foot between my knees and one fourteen inches
beyond my head and not a graze! Five tons at least!*

The grandson of the Rev. Thomas Oswell of Oswestry on his father's side and
of Joseph Cotton, Master of Trinity House, on his mother's, William Cotton
Oswell was born at Leytonstone in 1818. He was sent to school at Rugby where
Dr Arnold, the supreme headmaster of the Victorian public school, and epitomised in the pages of *Tom Brown's Schooldays*, had also just arrived. Oswell
is said to have been the original of the portrait of 'Young Brooke', the hero
of the school. He was certainly the right build for athletics and the life of
a hunter in the wilds. At eighteen he was six-foot tall, broad shouldered and
very strong, being nicknamed 'the Muscleman'.

His contemporaries described him as 'a rare mixture of kindliness and gentle-
ness, with marvellous strength, activity and fearlessness.' In short, he was the
beau ideal of the Victorian public schoolboy and surprisingly he seems to have
continued to be a modest hero in adult life. After Rugby, Oswell went on to
Haileybury, then the training college for the Honourable East India Company.
Here he did exceptionally well, achieving good grades in Sanscrit and Persian
and passing out second of his year with first-class honours.

Once in India he proved himself an able linguist, soon dispensing with an
interpreter and teaching himself a sound basic medical knowledge in order
to deal with the numerous diseases he encountered amongst the natives up-
country. His post as Collector and Judge kept him very busy, but he found
plenty of time for pig-sticking and shooting, from deer to tigers. So much so
that in a casual aside in a letter home to his mother he asked, 'By the by,
are bear, tiger or cheetah skins any use to you? They are to be had for the
taking here . . .'

He was ten years in India before disease, in his case diagnosed as malaria,
overcame even his magnificent constitution. From Madras he wrote to his
brother in August 1844 '. . . I sail for the Cape of Good Hope on the 2nd . . .
Since my last letter I have done nothing but improve and am almost ashamed

of going after all . . . Have you read Harris's book on Africa? If not, do so, and envy me . . .'

Shortly after writing this he had a relapse and later he wrote: 'Reduced from 12 st. 2 lbs. to 7 st. 12 lbs. by many attacks of Indian fever caught during a shooting excursion in the valley of the Bhavany River, I was sent to the Cape as a last resource by the Madras doctors; indeed whilst lying in a semi-comatose state, I heard one of them declare that I ought to have been dead a year ago.

'I gained strength by the voyage and shortly after reaching Capetown, hearing that a Mr Murray of Lintrose, near Coupar Angus, had come from Scotland for the purpose of making a shooting expedition to the interior, I determined to join him. The resolve was carried out early in the Spring of 1844 (the beginning of the Cape winter); we started out from Grahamstown to Colesberg, buying on the way horses, dogs, waggons and stores, crossed the Orange River and set our faces northwards. We were all bitten in those days by Captain, afterwards Sir Cornwallis Harris, whose book published about 1837 was the first to give any notion of the capabilities of South Africa for big game shooting and, Harris excepted, ''were the first that ever burst into that 'sunny sea''' as sportsmen. Murray was an excellent, kind-hearted, gentleman, rather too old, perhaps, for an expedition of this kind, as he felt the alterations of climate very much; and no wonder for I have known the thermometer to register 92° in the shade at 2 p.m. and 30° at 8 p.m. I was younger and though still weak from the effects of the fever, the dry air of the uplands daily gave me vigour, and the absolute freedom of the life was delightful to me.'

Inevitably with the inferior muzzle-loading firearms of those days he had some very narrow escapes. He wrote: 'One morning while the waggons were moving slowly through the low bush three bulls (buffalo) crossed the line of march. I was on my horse Superior and with a shout to Murray that I meant to make sure of a bag, galloped after them, and singling out one, got alongside of him within five feet and fired. He pitched upon his head and lay perfectly motionless. Making sure he was dead I would not give him the second barrel and turned the horse to ride after the two others which were still in view; but before I could get my animal into his stride the wounded beast sprang up and struck him heavily. I felt the thud, but the horse did not fall and cantered on for twenty yards, when the whisk of his tail dabbled my trousers with blood and getting off I found a hole thirty inches deep and nearly wide enough to get into in the flank, for the horn had been driven up to its base. The bull was too weak to follow up the attack and died where he stood; the horse crawled a few yards, and then, seeing it was a hopeless case, I put a ball through his head.'

Reminiscing afterwards he recalled: 'I once found myself in an immense herd. The bush was full of them. I was surrounded and had nothing to do but stand still. They dashed about me like rooks after the wireworm in a newly ploughed field and I had the sensation of drawing myself in very tight about the waistband. Till they thinned out into a tail I could not begin to shoot, but there were such numbers that even then I knocked over six at exceedingly close quarters. The danger was being run over or butted down in the headlong stampede. The same thing has happened to me, and I daresay to many all round shots with elephants. How they avoided or missed you – for they didn't seem to try to avoid – you can't tell; you come out of it without a scratch and therefore as a rule think no more of it . . .'

Towards the end of their expedition he and Murray were approached by the chief of a tribe called the Ba-Kaa, who were suffering from starvation. He took six hundred of them with him on a seven-week hunting expedition during which he and Murray shot enormous quantities of meat for them, including on one occasion fourteen hippopotami. These were the first they had shot and were somewhat unexpected. Oswell heard shot after shot being fired some distance from him and hurried to the sound, to find Murray firing into a large pool formed by a backwater of the river Limpopo alongside which they had been travelling. One hundred and fifty yards long by fifty yards wide, with high banks, the pool was full of maddened hippopotami at which Murray was firing, with his after-rider loading his guns. Oswell joined in and for a quarter of an hour they pumped bullets into the beasts, but not one seemed to die.

One big bull made straight for the bank on which Oswell was standing and he fired within three feet of its head, blowing it back into the water.

'I'll swear I hit that fellow,' he shouted to Murray on the other bank.

'I'll swear I've hit all I've fired at!' was the reply.

As evening was approaching they ceased firing, to find the body of only one beast floating on the surface. They went back feeling somewhat depressed by the results of their shooting, not realising that hippopotami will sink when shot and only surface some time later when the gases in the body have distended their stomachs. In the morning they were relieved to find fourteen hippopotami floating on the pool, a considerable contribution towards curing their starving camp followers.

Oswell generously gave Murray full credit for killing the first rhinoceroses of their expedition and he also noted that Murray killed their first giraffe. His generous spirit was very unlike the attitude of Harris, who barely mentioned his companion at all and, like Gordon Cumming, was unduly boastful of killing animals which Oswell regarded as very easily shot.

On the plains with Murray on this first expedition he wrote: 'the springboks were met with in vast herds; for an hour's march with the waggons – say two and a quarter miles – I once saw them to the left of the track along a slightly rising ground, thicker than I ever saw sheep . . . They were to be counted only by tens of thousands . . .'

It was during this expedition that Oswell first made the acquaintance of the missionary-explorer, Dr Livingstone, and his wife and family, with whom he was to become close friends. In December of that year he returned to the Cape with Murray, who then returned to Scotland, leaving Oswell to begin re-fitting for another expedition the following year.

His companion on the next year's expedition was Major Frank Vardon of the 25th Madras Native Infantry. In Oswell's opinion he was 'the finest fellow and best comrade a man ever had . . . [the] brightest, bravest-hearted of men and the most unselfish of dispositions, totally ignorant of jealousy, the most trustworthy of mates; a better sportsman and better shot than myself at all kinds of game save elephants and only a little behindhand at that because he was a heavyweight and poorly armed with a single barrelled gun; yet he was always rejoicing at my success and making light of his own disappointments . . .'

Despite his comments on Vardon it is clear the latter was lucky to have Oswell with him, for on one occasion 'Though they [the Mahoho, or white rhinoceros] were a very meditative inoffensive lot there was a point at which they drew the line. I once saw Vardon pull a Mahoho's tail; this however was taking too great a liberty and if I had not been near he might have suffered, but as the heavy brute swung round to give chase, a ball at very close quarters stopped him . . .'

Writing fifty years after his expeditions he noted (prematurely at the time): '. . . one species of rhinoceros, the Mahoho, is extinct! I am very sorry. He was never I believe found north of the Zambesi, but between that river and the Molopo . . . he was formerly in great force. Poor old stupid fellow, too quiet as a rule, though when thoroughly upset (like a good natured man in a passion) reckless, he was just the very thing for young gunners to try their 'prentice hand on and directly the kafirs got muskets he was bound to go; though considering the numbers there used to be, I hoped he would have lasted longer . . .'

He went on sadly: 'I am sorry now for all the fine old beasts I have killed but I was young then and there was excitement in the work and I had large numbers of men to feed . . . every animal save three elephants was eaten by man and so put to good use . . . But I am writing of close upon fifty years ago. Africa is nearly used up. She belongs no more to the Africans and the beasts: Boers, gold-seekers, diamond-miners and experimental farmers – (all of them from my point of view mistakes) – have changed the face of her. A man must be a first-rate sportsman now to keep himself and his family; houses stand where we once shot elephants and the railway will soon be whistling and screaming through all the hunting fields of the Zambesi . . .

'I was in the saddle from ten to twelve hours a day for close upon five seasons and general immunity perhaps produced carelessness. I may say now, I suppose, that I was a good rider and got generally to terms with my game. I was, however, never a crack shot and not very well armed according to present notions, though I still have the highest opinion of a Purdey 10 bore which

William Cotton Oswell.

burnt five or six drachms of fine powder and at short distances drove its ball home. This gun did nearly all my work. I had besides a 12 bore Westley Richards, a light rifle and heavy single barrelled one carrying two-ounce belted balls. This last was a beast of a tool and once – I never gave it a second chance – nearly cost me my life by stinging without seriously wounding a bull elephant. The infuriated brute charged me nine or ten times wickedly and the number would have been doubled had I not at last got hold of the Purdey, when he fell to the first shot. We had no breech loaders in those days save the disconnecting one and that would have been useless for we had to load as we galloped through the thick bush and stock and barrel would soon have been wrenched asunder or so strained as to prevent their coming accurately into contact again . . '

The actual loading was described thus: '. . . the smooth ten bore ten lbs Purdey specially made . . . the balls wrapped in waxed kid or linen patch, rolled between the hands and the folds cut off. A paper cartridge, the end bitten off and thrust into the barrel together with the paper covering. The ball would be placed above it and the whole could be rammed down by a single movement with a powerful loading rod if great expedition should be necessary. Although the actual loading could thus be accomplished easily the great trouble was the adjustment of the cap upon the nipple which with an unsteady horse was a work of difficulty . . .'

Oswell lent this gun to Samuel White Baker during his exploration of the Nile and referred to Baker as 'the best shot, sportsman and writer that ever made Africa his field . . .' Baker in return wrote of Oswell: 'Unlike Gordon Cumming who was accustomed to fire at 70–80 yards Oswell invariably strove to obtain close quarters with elephants and all other game . . .'

Oswell himself advised: 'Get as good a start as possible, press your game as much as you can for 300 to 400 yards – for press them you must or you may ride after their tails all day – and you are alongside: a shot in the gallop with the gun across the pommel brings the poor thing to the ground and you are ashamed of yourself if it has been done wantonly. Eland hunting from horseback may be called with giraffe as very tame after the novelty is over . . .'

Referring to his friend the famous missionary and explorer, Dr Livingstone, he noted: 'I am afraid he despised the role of sportsmen. Perhaps he was right . . . He could talk to the kafirs ears and hearts, we only to their stomachs; . . . I would fain believe that his grand work was occasionally made a little smoother by the guns . . .'

Of the kafirs he wrote: 'Buffalo were abundant, the bravest and most determined of all game when wounded and at bay . . . The kafirs will hunt a blood spoor of elephant, lion and rhinoceros or any other animal right ahead of you like hounds, but when they are on wounded buffalo trails they will *follow* you at a respectful distance as they know the ways of him and his character . . .'

It is abundantly clear now that one of the reasons Oswell never wrote about his exploits at the time they took place was that he would have found it difficult to avoid criticising Harris and Gordon Cumming, at least by inference, and so ruin their somewhat over-inflated reputations. He obviously abhorred the cruelty involved in constantly peppering game from a distance and reckoned always to kill his game, from elephants downwards, with one shot or at the most two, simply by approaching them so closely that he was sure of doing so. He detested the Boer methods of killing elephant, recording: 'The Boers have an effective though cruel way of killing them. Their legs are solid, not hollow with marrow . . . The Jaegers . . . are not fond of getting too near . . . so they take their first shots at the forelegs of two or three. The ball splinters and weakens the bone and he instantly stands immovable . . . The hunters follow the rest of the herd . . . then return to the cripples who fall an easy prey to the Boers at close range. I witnessed this butchery but once and willingly would never again . . .'

Oswell was undoubtedly a magnificent rider and was known on occasions to ride alongside a hyena at full gallop and, unfastening his stirrup leather, brain the beast with a blow from his heavy stirrup iron. In describing him, Baker said, 'I have always regarded Oswell as the perfection of a Nimrod. Six feet in height, sinewy and muscular, but nevertheless light in weight, he was not only powerful but enduring. A handsome face with an eagle glance, but full of kindness and fearlessness bespoke the natural manliness of character which attracted him to the wild adventures of his early life.'

Oswell was always patient and considerate towards the natives with whom he dealt, while expecting and receiving respect in return. He noted proudly, 'I never had occasion to raise a hand against a native and my foot only once, when I found a long lazy fellow poking his paw into my sugar-tin . . . One chief and one only wanted to hector a little, but he soon gave it up. And with the rest of the potentates and people generally I was certainly persona grata for I filled their stomachs . . .'

He was the first to bring the attention of the outside world to the Tsetse fly and noted: 'On the low Siloquana hills . . . we made our acquaintance with the Tsetse fly which we were the first to bring to notice, Vardon taking or sending to England some he caught on his favourite horse . . .' At the end of their expedition he wrote; ' Vardon went home to England and I returned to India to finish my time before taking furlough in 1847. Early in 1849, hearing Livingstone intended to make an attempt to reach Lake 'Ngami, Murray and I again left England to join him.' He did not regard this as a hunting expedition, but the fact remains that his and Murray's efforts kept the expedition fed and it is very doubtful if Livingstone by himself could have completed his exploration successfully.

Unlike most hunters of the period Oswell never hunted with dogs, but he made special mention of them: 'I have said little of our dogs, but they deserve mention. I never shot with them; but besides guarding the camp from surprise they were invaluable . . . in helping us to pick up wounded lion or in telling us the whereabouts of a hard-hit ambushed buffalo – I have known them to hold a lion at bay for nearly an hour, the larger one heading him continually and the little Skye-looking fellow running in at intervals, nipping him in the rear and scuttling off at full speed.'

In describing native pit-fall traps, one of the hazards of Africa in those days, he wrote: 'From end to end the banks of the Zouga are lined with pit-falls. Eleven of our horses fell in – one only died . . . but two of the oxen buried themselves – fortunately we had a few spare ones. We ourselves were all caught . . . while searching for and opening the holes to prevent mishaps amongst the cattle.' He went on, 'They are most artfully concealed; loose sand is sometimes thrown over the covering reeds and grass and the impressions of animal's feet together with their dung placed on top. They make the game very wild. One animal falls in and alarms the whole herd. They retreat far off and only return to drink and flee. From the elephant to the steinbuck nothing escapes.'

He himself had many hairsbreadth escapes from being killed. On two different occasions he was tossed by a rhinoceros. On the first occasion, one of his favourite horses was killed but he was unharmed. In the second incident

Oswell hurled into the air. Both Oswell and his horse survived this adventure in the Cape.

he himself was gored and his thigh gashed for eight inches down to the bone and the femoral artery. On yet another occasion a lion chased him and leaped on his horse's hindquarters so that he was thrown, together with the lion, in the horse's maddened buckings to escape. Perhaps his closest shave with death, however, was when elephant hunting. With great difficulty he had been following a wounded elephant on horseback through dense bush.

'After a time the thorns thinned out and I caught sight of the wounded elephant . . . and when he entered the tropical forest beyond I was in his wake and very soon compelled to follow where he broke a way. Lying flat on my pony's neck and guiding him as best I might by occasional glimpses of the tail of my now slowly-retreating pioneer, I laboured on in the hope that more open ground might enable me to get up alongside him. A most unpleasant ride it was . . . I was at one time nearly pulled from the saddle by heavy boughs and at another nearly torn to pieces by the wicked thorns of the wait-a-bit . . . I have killed elephants on very bad ground, but this was the worse piece of bush I ever rode into in my life . . . peering at the broad stern of the chase, I saw him suddenly put his head where his tail ought to have been; the trunk was tightly coiled . . . [and] forward flapped the huge ears, up went the tail,

56

and down he came like a gigantic bat ten feet across. Pinned above and on either side, by dismounting I could neither hope to escape, nor kill my opponent. I therefore lugged my unfortunate animal round and urged him along. But I had not taken into account with what great difficulties and how slowly I had followed the bull. He was now in full charge and the small trees and bush gave way before him like reeds . . . I was well mounted and my spurs were sharp. Battered and torn by branch and thorn, I yet managed a kind of gallop, but it was impossible to keep it up . . . in fifty yards we were fast in a thick bush and he was within fifteen of us. As a last chance I tried to get off, but in rolling round in my saddle my spur galled the pony's flank and the elephant screaming over him at the same moment he made a convulsive effort and freed himself, depositing me in a sitting position immediately in front of the uplifted forefoot of the charging bull. So near was it that I mechanically opened my knees to allow him to put it down and throwing myself back, crossed my hands upon my chest, obstinately puffing myself out with the idea of trying to resist the gigantic tread, or at all events of being as troublesome to crush as possible. I saw the burly brute from chest to tail as he passed directly over me lengthways, one foot between my knees and one fourteen inches beyond my head and not a graze! Five tons at least! As he turned from chasing my pony which without my weight and left to its own instinct escaped easily . . . he swept by me on his way to rejoin his companions and I got another snapshot at his shoulder. As soon as I could I followed his spoor, but must have changed it in the thick bush, for in five minutes I had run into and killed a fresh elephant in a small open space. The Bushmen found the first, next morning, dead. Of all my narrow escapes this was the only one that remained with me in recollection for any length of time . . . One hears of night-mares – well for a month or more, I daresay, I had night-elephants!'

Oswell's life was thus spent from 1832 to 1844 in India, and from 1844 to 1855 in Africa. Along with Cornwallis Harris he was one of the earliest to experience the different forms of hunting available in the two continents. On returning to England he married a Miss de Rivaz and settled down in Tonbridge Wells for the rest of his long life, only finally being persuaded to write of his big game hunting exploits by his friend and admirer, Sir Samuel White Baker, with whom he had much in common.

He died peacefully at Tonbridge Wells in 1893, aged seventy-five, after contracting a chill which brought on a recurrence of his old fever.

Notes on a contemporary: William Charles Baldwin

William Charles Baldwin, another of the early African hunters and writers, was in fact inspired to go out to Africa in the first place by the publication of Gordon Cumming's book. A much more modest and clearly infinitely more likeable character than Gording Cummings, he spent eight years in Africa from

William Charles Baldwin.

1852 to 1860. His subsequent book, *African Hunting from Natal to the Zambesi*, was the first plain and unvarnished account published to tell of the discomforts and drawbacks involved. He described the deaths of his companions from disease and privation with as honest an eye as he had for the wildlife around him. He was the first writer to write without purple passages and glowing enthusiasm about all he saw.

He was also engagingly frank about his early life. Brought up in the country he spent, according to his own account, two days a week with the local harriers from the age of six onwards until he was finally packed off to school. After an undistinguished career at school he was 'placed in a large merchant's office with a view to being fitted for going abroad.' Predictably with his roving spirit, apart from his beagles and bull terriers, this did not work out successfully. As he put it rather engagingly, 'upon comparing notes with the junior partner we arrived at the same conclusion, viz. that quill-driving was not my particular vocation.' He then was sent, by a no doubt increasingly anxious parent, to Forfarshire to learn to farm. Not finding himself compatible with the farmer he went on to the West Highlands, where he enjoyed himself enormously, but learned precisely nothing. It was while here that he read Gordon Cumming's account of Africa and decided to try it for himself.

He wrote subsequently: 'I landed at Natal, December 1851, after a ninety-two days' passage. I was most anxious to be introduced to "Elephant White," as he was called, a great hunter; but whether he earned that title from his own elephantine proportions, six feet four inches, or from his prowess with the animal from which he derived his name, I have yet to learn. I believe he had been very successful formerly when elephants were more plentiful, but

58

he had grown idle and left the work to younger hands.' In the event, within three weeks of his landing Baldwin had joined White's party, making up nine white men in all. Their object apparently was to shoot sea cows in the neighbourhood of St Lucia Bay, a notoriously bad area for white men. It is indicative of the climate and the conditions that after many months of hardship and sickness he and one other were the only survivors of the entire party.

It also says much for Baldwin's tenacity and toughness that on his return to civilisation he almost immediately set about equipping another expedition into the interior, this time into Zulu country. It is apparent that apart from being a good shot and a first-class rider, the result of his childhood training, he was also able to get on well with the natives. It is clear that he was soon able to speak to them in their own language and he noted that most of the differences between natives and white men were simply caused by a mutual misunderstanding.

His yearly expeditions were filled with the sorts of anecdotes which are to be found in most hunter's accounts. Like Gordon Cumming, he met Dr Livingstone. He suffered fever and sickness, and had narrow escapes from

Baldwin has a narrow escape.

59

death both at the hands of hostile tribes and from wild beasts. Problems such as these, or the difficulties of dealing with unpredictable native chieftains and the treachery likely to be encountered, were points which he brought out fully and fairly, the first of many travellers in Africa to do so. His descriptions of African life in the interior at this time were unaffected and straightforward. They were also indicative of the trials and tribulations which had to be faced by anyone aspiring to be a professional hunter.

It is apparent that he was successful in making enough from his hunting expeditions to return home after eight years and retire. Like so many others of the early big game hunters, little seems to have been recorded of his life after the hunting days were over. We are left with the record of his eight years as a hunter in his youth and it is as a heavily-bearded, sturdily built young man, determined to make his way that he remains in the pages of his book.

3

EARLY SPORTSMEN IN INDIA, AFRICA AND NORTH AMERICA

Samuel White Baker 1821–1893

Henry Astbury Leveson 1828–1875

Samuel White Baker and his companions riding for their lives. An impression by the Victorian illustrator, Stanley Berkeley.

Samuel White Baker 1821–1893

India/Ceylon 1846–1855, Africa 1861–1866, 1869–1875

The Perfect Victorian Hero

*One second more and at this headlong pace he was within three feet
of me; down slashed his trunk with the rapidity of a whip thong
and with a shrill scream of fury he was upon me . . .*

Samuel White Baker was born in London in 1821, the son of a wealthy merchant who had made a fortune in the West Indies. His grandfather had commanded an eighteen-gun privateer during the war with France and defeated a thirty-two gun French frigate in a fierce battle in the English Channel. Young Samuel was brought up in Enfield and when the family moved to Gloucestershire he attended Gloucester College, the local grammar school. Here his superior size and strength were outstanding and at the age of only seventeen he laid out a notorious local bully with one well-placed punch. G. A. Henty, the Victorian novelist, used this and many other episodes in Baker's life as inspiration for his novels. When full-grown, Baker stood five feet ten inches, but with very broad shoulders and a deep chest he weighed some fifteen stone. Nevertheless, he was always very quick and agile on his feet and at seventeen must have been a formidable opponent.

His early interest in using both rifle and shotgun were fostered on the family estate in Gloucester, but he learned little at school. It was only when he attended a private tutor, the Rev. P. H. Dunster, that he first started to apply himself, and his tutor noted that he had 'plenty of natural ability and had been well grounded in earlier years. He read fluently, spelt correctly, wrote a good hand and could express himself well and easily.' After two years tuition young Samuel was sent to Frankfurt to learn German.

Meanwhile his interest in guns had reached the stage where he persuaded George Gibbs, the Bristol gunsmith, to make a rifle to his own design. Despite the gunsmith's protests that the design was 'preposterous in the professional opinions of the trade' he was later to use this rifle and others like it with great effect on big game such as elephants and buffalo. It had a barrel thirty-six inches long and carried a belted ball with three ounces, or a conical bullet of four ounces with a charge of no less than sixteen drachms of powder. It had two grooves of rifling and since breechloaders were not introduced until the 1850s it was, of necessity, a muzzle loader. Only someone with his great strength could hope to fire such a weapon with accuracy after carrying it for any length of time. He wrote, with justifiable pride: 'The twist was one full turn in the length of the barrel. The rifling was an exceedingly deep and broad groove (two grooves) which reduced the difficulty of loading to a minimum, as the projecting belt enabled the bullet to catch the channel instantly and to descend easily when wrapped in a greased silk patch without the necessity of hammering. The charge of powder was inserted by inverting the rifle and passing up the loading rod with an ounce measure screwed to the end; this method prevented the powder from adhering to the sides of the barrel and thus fouling the grooves.

'An extraordinary success attended this rifle, which became my colossal companion for many years in wild sports with dangerous game. It will be observed that the powder charge was one-third the weight of the projectile and not only a tremendous crushing power, but an extraordinary penetration was obtained never equalled by any rifle that I have since possessed.

'This weapon was in advance of the age as it foreshadowed the modern Express and the principle was thoroughly established to my own satisfaction, that a sporting rifle to be effective at a long range must burn a heavy charge of powder, but the weight of the weapon must be in due proportion to the strain of the explosion.'

After eighteen months in Germany Samuel White Baker returned to London, fluent in written and spoken German, but it soon became apparent that he was not suited to life in his father's London office. Then both he and his brother John, always closest to him, married in a joint ceremony their childhood sweethearts, the sisters of their local Vicar. Sam married Henrietta, the eldest, and John her younger sister, Elizabeth. The marriage took place in 1843 when Sam was just twenty-two, prior to the brothers being sent out to manage the family plantation in Mauritius.

Once established there, although the brothers and their wives were happy together, they found they did not like the island, chiefly from Sam's viewpoint because the fauna was remarkable chiefly by its absence. An article on elephant hunting in Ceylon, which he read in *Blackwood's Magazine*, made him decide to investigate further. His approach was sensible and methodical.

He was to write later: 'When I arrived in Ceylon one of my first visits was to the museum of Colombo. Here I carefully observed the transverse section of an elephant's skull until perfectly acquainted with its details. From the museum I went straight to the elephant stables and examined the head of the living animal; comparing it in my own mind with the skull until I was thoroughly certain of the position of the brain and the possibility of reaching it from any position . . .'

Fortunately for Sam, in Ceylon he met an old friend from Gloucester who was serving in the army. In his experienced company he made his first sporting expedition into the interior, shooting elephants, buffalo and deer. He then sent word enthusiastically to his brother John to come and join him with their combined families.

On John's arrival they set off together and, as Sam noted, '. . . tried the rough system of travelling, and started off with nothing but my guns, clothes, a box of biscuits and a few bottles of brandy — no bed, no pillow, no tent, nor chairs, or table . . . I literally depended on my guns for food and my cooking utensils consisted of one saucepan and a gridiron . . . with a large leaf as substitute for a plate, cocoa-nut shell for a glass, my hunting knife comprising all my cutlery . . .'

The brothers enjoyed themselves immensely. Some idea of the hazards involved in shooting with muzzle-loaders is, however, clear from Sam's account of following an elephant so closely through the jungle, 'that I could have slapped her'. He continued: 'At length, losing all patience, I fired my barrel under her tail, giving it an upward direction in the hope of disabling her spine. A cloud of smoke hung over me for a second and throwing my empty gun on one side I put my hand behind me for a spare rifle. I felt the welcome barrel pushed into my hand at the same moment that I saw the infuriated head of the elephant with ears cocked charging through the smoke! . . . I had just time to cock the two-ounce rifle and take a steady aim. The next moment we were in a cloud of smoke, but as I fired I felt certain of her. The smoke cleared from the thick bushes and she lay dead at *six feet* from the spot where I stood. The ball was in the centre of the forehead . . . Had she been missed I would have fired my last shot. This had been a glorious hunt . . .'

But Sam was no fool and he later wrote very sensibly: 'One great cause of danger in shooting in thick jungles is the obscurity occasioned by the smoke of the first barrel: this . . . effectually prevents a certain aim with the remaining barrel . . . I dislike shooting in thick jungles and I very seldom do so. It is extremely dangerous and is like shooting in the dark . . .'

At this stage both Sam and his brother were still utter novices and it was not long before he realised that they were guilty of the same fault. They were contemptuous of the game they sought to bring down and did not appreciate the very real dangers they faced. When they had learned to respect and admire the game they hunted they began to mature and develop into experienced hunters.

After a prolonged and successful hunting expedition the brothers decided that they wished to move permanently from Mauritius to Ceylon. The coffee market had just collapsed and many estates were available in choice parts of Ceylon at a fraction of the price they had previously commanded. They sailed for Britain, determined to convince their father that it was a sound place for investment.

The two young men soon managed to persuade their father that this was the case and an estate was bought at Newera Eliya, in the interior. After the inevitable initial setbacks, the brothers' enthusiasm and keenness finally triumphed and the estate became soundly established and prosperous. Sam learned the language and acquired the more simple skills in doctoring wounds and treating the commoner complaints, experiences which were to serve him well throughout his subsequent travels.

Sam and his brother hunted with hounds and unwittingly rediscovered the old method of *par force* hunting beloved of the Normans. They would set out with deep-scenting hounds at dawn and, after finding a scent, would follow it up until the quarry was in view. Then their greyhounds or 'gazehounds' would be released and, hunting by sight, they would follow up until the stag, boar, or leopard was brought to bay by the hounds. Sam, or the brothers jointly, would then arrive and with the aid of a hunting knife put an end to the hunt. Against boars weighing three or four hundredweight, capable of slitting a man from knee to chin, the Normans considered this to be the finest form of hunting imaginable.

Sam and John enjoyed a great many hunts of this nature. They also hunted elephants and buffalo in the jungle with their rifles, for the Government at this time were paying a reward for all elephants killed, owing to the damage they caused to the plantations. Hunting them with his heavy double-barrelled rifle Sam once bagged thirty-one in five days and on one occasion bagged fourteen in a single day. He was also often lucky to escape with his life. He recorded with his usual vivid pen one occasion when his party had killed nine elephants.

'I had one barrel still loaded . . . when I suddenly heard Wallace shriek out. "Look out, sir! Look out – an elephant's coming!"'

'I turned round . . . and close past Wallace . . . came . . . a "rogue" elephant in full charge. His trunk was thrown high in the air, his ears were cocked, his tail stood erect . . . as a poker, and, screaming exactly like the whistle of a railway engine, he rushed upon me through the high grass . . . His eyes flashed . . . and he had singled me out as his victim.

'I have often been in dangerous positions, but I never felt so totally devoid of hope as I did in this instance. The tangled grass rendered retreat impossible. I had only one barrel loaded and that was useless as the upraised trunk protected his forehead. I felt myself doomed . . . and I resolved to wait for him until he was close upon me before I fired, hoping that he might lower his trunk and expose his forehead.

'He rushed along at the pace of a horse in full speed; in a few moments as the grass flew to right and left before him, he was close upon me but still his trunk was raised and I would not fire. Once second more and at this head-long pace he was within three feet of me; down slashed his trunk with the rapidity of a whip thong and with a shrill scream of fury he was upon me.

'I fired at that instant; but in the twinkling of an eye I was flying through the air like a ball from a bat. At the moment of firing I had jumped to the left but he struck me with his tusk in full charge upon the right thigh and hurled me eight or ten paces from him. That very moment he stopped . . . and turning round commenced a strict search for me. I heard him advancing close to the spot where I lay still as death . . . Although I had not felt the sensation of fear while I stood opposed to him, I felt like what I never wish to feel again while he was deliberately hunting me up . . . Fortunately . . . the powder and smoke had nearly blinded him and had spoiled his acute sense of scent. To my joy I heard the rustling of the grass grow fainter . . . at length it was gone!

'Not expecting to be able to move . . . I with difficulty reached a stream of water near the spot, where I bathed my leg, but in a few minutes it swelled to the size of a man's waist.'

Regardless of this handicap he was back hunting inside a couple of days.

After eight years sojourn in Ceylon, during which he established his plantation at Newera Eliya, Sam noted with misgivings: 'Every year increases the number of guns in the possession of the natives and accordingly diminishes the number of animals. From the change which has come over many parts of the country within my experience of the last eight years I am of the opinion that the next ten years will see the deer shooting in Ceylon completely spoiled and the elephants very much reduced. There are now very few herds of elephants in Ceylon that have not been shot at by either Europeans or natives and it is a common occurrence to kill elephants with numerous marks of old bullet wounds . . . at the report of a gun every herd within hearing starts off for the densest jungle.

'A native can now obtain a gun for thirty shillings and with two shillings' worth of ammunition, he starts up a hunting trip. Five elephants at a reward of seven shillings per tail more than pay the prime cost of his gun; to say nothing of the deer and the other game he has bagged in the interim . . . there is no rest for the animals; in the daytime they are tracked up, and on moonlit nights the drinking places are watched and an unremitting warfare is carried on. This is sweeping both deer and buffalo from the country and must eventually annihilate them . . .'

Within a decade, as Sam had foreseen, Game Laws had to be introduced into Ceylon. It might be argued that Sam himself was in some measure responsible, since he certainly killed a considerable head of game. In 1851 for instance, in a three-week hunting trip with his brother Valentine on leave from the army, and two other friends, his party accounted for fifty elephants, five deer and two buffalo, of which Sam shot twenty-two elephants and three deer, by far the largest share. On the other hand this was deliberate culling of elephants, while they were still a threat to the plantations. As Sam clearly indicated, the threat to the wildlife was from constant irresponsible shooting by natives intent on recouping the cost of their guns and ammunition, regardless of whether they were shooting females heavy with young, or young and immature beasts.

Sam was also honest enough to give an account of the drawbacks of Ceylon from the hunter's viewpoint: 'Ceylon is at all times a frightful place for vermin; in the dry weather we have ticks; these little wretches which are not larger than a grain of gunpowder find their way to every part of the body and the irritation of their bites is indescribable. Scratching is only adding fuel to fire; there is no certain prevention or relief from their attacks; (the best thing I know is cocoa-nut oil rubbed daily over the whole body, but the remedy is almost as unpleasant as the bite.); in the wet weather mosquitoes and, what are still more disgusting, ''leeches'', which swarm in the grass and upon the leaves of the jungle. These creatures insinuate themselves through all the openings in a person's dress – up the trousers, under the waistcoat, down the neck, up the wrists and in fact everywhere, drawing blood with insatiable voracity and leaving an unpleasant irritation for some days after.

'All these annoyances form great drawbacks to the enjoyment of the low country sports . . . When the day is over and the man, fatigued by intense heat and a hard day's work, feels himself refreshed by a bath and a change of clothes, the incurable itching of a thousand tick bites destroys all his pleasure; he finds himself streaming with blood from leech-bites, and for the time feels disgusted with the country. First-rate sport can alone compensate for these annoyances.'

In 1855 Sam and his family left Ceylon for a holiday in England, as Sam was in very poor health after a severe attack of fever and Henrietta was pregnant. Unfortunately, Henrietta died soon after the birth and Sam was for a long time inconsolable. For the next couple of years he could not settle to anything, trying at first to join his brothers Valentine and James serving in the army in the Crimea, but arriving there only as peace was declared. He even for a short period contemplated entering the Church.

Then he spent some time stalking in Scotland, including a famous occasion when he proved to a sceptical audience on the Duke of Athol's ground that he could run down a stag with the aid of a couple of deer hounds, in the manner he had described in his recently published book *With Rifle and Hound in Ceylon*. Sam also tried to persuade Dr Livingstone to let him join his party exploring the Zambesi, but was rebuffed. He then approached the Royal Geographical Society with a view to letting him mount an expedition at his own expense, but again was turned down.

In 1860, on a short visit to London, he obtained the blessing of the Royal Geographical Society for an exploration of the tributaries of the Nile in Eastern Abyssinia. He also met his friend William Cotton Oswell who loaned him his favourite rifle, the ten-bore Purdey, which he had found so useful in Africa. At this stage in his life he married a young Hungarian girl, Florence Von Sass, a girl not much older than his eldest daughter.

Sam then took a brief hunting trip to the town of Sabanja in Turkey where he and Florence roughed it in rooms in the Armenian quarter above a cow byre. It seems likely that Sam intended this as a test to see whether Florence

Sir Samuel White Baker and his wife, Florence.

was fit to accompany him to Abyssinia; if this was the case she passed with flying colours. In 1861 they set off up the Nile from Cairo with the avowed intention, revealed only to his brother, to explore the sources and possibly meet Speke and Grant coming up from Zanzibar.

The guns he took with him he listed as follows:

My little Fletcher double rifle No. 24
One double rifle No. 10 by Tatham
Two double rifles No. 10 by Reilly
One double rifle No. 10 by Beattie (one of my old Ceylon tools)
One double gun No. 10 by Beattie
One double gun No. 10 by Purdey, belonging to Mr Oswell of South African celebrity
One single rifle No. 8 by Manton
One single rifle No. 14 by Beattie
One single rifle that carried a half pound explosive shell by Holland of Bond Street: this was nicknamed by the Arabs 'Jenna of Mootfah' (child of a cannon) and for the sake of brevity I called it the 'Baby'.
(in addition) . . . My revolver and a brace of double-barrelled pistols.

During this journey Sam encountered the Hamran Arabs, who hunted elephants on horseback at full gallop, using a sharp sword to hamstring them. With the 'Baby', Sam also accounted for a considerable number of elephants. If he admired the Hamran Arabs' methods of hunting it is equally clear that they held him in awe. Even he was to admit that some of the risks he ran on this expedition were indefensible, such as entering on hands and knees a tunnel in thick thorny undergrowth into which a lion had dragged the carcase of a buffalo he had shot the previous evening. He recorded: '. . . suddenly a dark object appeared to block the tunnel. In another minute I distinguished the head and dark mane of a noble lion on the other side of a mass which proved to be the remains of the bull buffalo; another head of a lioness arose up on the right and at the same instant with a tremendous roar the scene changed before I had time to fire . . . We were actually in possession having driven the lions from their prey . . . [But] the Hamran Arabs persuaded me to discontinue this kind of exploration and my Tokrooris having taken the same view of the performance I gave up the practice.'

Finally they reached the Abyssinian border, having explored all the tributaries of the Nile they had found. At this stage their interpreter, Mahomet, who had always been tiresome, deserted. Fortunately he was no longer required, since by this time both Florence and Sam spoke excellent Arabic.

They then marched towards Khartoum and here for the first time Sam encountered the evils of the slave trade as well as obstructive officialdom at its worst, with treacherous and rebellious native followers bent on assassinating him. Overcoming every difficulty, however, Sam succeeded in pressing on to Gondokoro, the principal centre of the slave trade in the interior. There Sam met Speke and Grant, who had discovered some of the sources of the Nile, but by no means all. Sam decided to try and fill in the gaps on the map and he and Florence continued their journey. Eventually, after considerable hardships, they reached Lake N'Yanza, which they re-named the Albert N'Yanza, after Prince Albert.

Their return journey, when they were greatly debilitated by fevers and starvation, was even more of a nightmare than their outward trip. Treacherous and warring native chieftains, as well as the difficult terrain, made the journey seem interminable. It was not until February 1865 that they again set out for Gondokoro and it was May before they returned to Khartoum, where plague was raging. Eventually they reached Cairo and from there took ship to England, arriving in November of 1865 after four years of exploration.

Sam and his wife were greeted with acclaim by the Royal Geographical Society and the pair took London by storm. The ultimate recognition came when a knighthood was bestowed on Sam by Queen Victoria in 1866.

In 1869, after the publication of several successful books on his travels, at the Prince of Wales' suggestion Sam was invited by Ismael Pasha of Egypt to undertake the suppression of the slave trade. He was given a contract as

Governor General of the Equatorial Nile Basin for four years. For those four years he fought the climate, disease, the countryside and the native tribes and Turkish and Arab officials' indifference and active opposition, as well as the slave traders themselves. He also, at intervals, enjoyed some interesting sport, shooting hippopotamus, buffalo, and antelope, as well as lions and numerous other large game.

At the end of his term in office, with his task still incomplete, he was succeeded by Colonel Charles Gordon, a visionary and mystic, unable to speak Arabic. He was a very different choice from Sam Baker, the man of direct action and Arabic speaker worshipped by the natives. Florence, however, had had enough of Africa and made Sam swear never to return without her agreement, which she was clearly resolved never to give.

In 1878, by way of a rest, Sam and Florence explored Cyprus, then an unknown island in the Mediterranean and the result was another book, though perhaps one of his least successful. There followed a three-year grand tour of the world, starting with India, going on to Japan and then to North America. Wherever they went Sam enjoyed the best hunting available, ending this leisurely world tour in 1882.

Thereafter Sam settled with Florence in Devon and spent part of each year either in India or Cairo, hunting whenever he had the chance. In 1889 he was in India hunting tigers yet again at Jabalpur. Finally, in 1893 he died of a heart attack at Sandford Orleigh, his Devon home, aged seventy-two. Remembered widely as a great explorer and suppressor of the slave trade in the Sudan, he was also perhaps the greatest hunter of all time, for he had hunted big game not only in India and Africa but also in North America and around the world. He has been described as a 'kind of fulcrum' in the exploration of Africa and it was also as a fulcrum that he acted as a big game hunter, covering the change-over period from muzzle-loaders to modern weapons and combining age-old methods of hunting with the most modern. He was furthermore an observant naturalist who contributed a great deal to the knowledge of the day. It is much to his credit that he remained on good terms with almost all the men he met, both explorers and hunters, even though as a man of direct action he has had few equals. Although in reality a Georgian eccentric he truly merited the title of 'The Perfect Victorian Hero.'

Henry Astbury Leveson 1828–1875

India 1845–1853; Africa 1863–1864

Soldier, Shot and Self-Publicist

*I stepped on one side and gave him my second barrel behind the ear,
when dark blood rushed from his nostrils . . . and all was still. The
man-eater was dead and his victims avenged . . .*

Henry Astbury Leveson was born on 18th June 1828, almost certainly the illegitimate son of one of the wealthy Yorkshire mill-owning Leveson family, whose name he took. It is, however, noticeable that he dedicated his first book, *The Hunting Ground of the Old World*, to his mother, although it was probably through his father's influence that in 1845 he obtained a commission in the Honourable East India Company's military service in Madras at the age of seventeen. Once out there his natural horsemanship and good eye, aided by a sound nerve, soon had him rated as a first-class pig-sticker and shot.

He turned author after leaving India in 1853, but his purple passages, based on Walter Campbell's successful *Old Forest Ranger*, made for tedious reading. The doubtful truth of some of his passages in which he was invariably the hero also caused him to be somewhat discredited, but even allowing for occasional exaggeration, he was obviously a good shot and notable horseman and soldier.

He wrote all his books under the pseudonym of 'The Old Shekarry' (not to be confused with 'An Old Shekarree' (see pp. 30) who wrote on Indian sport under this pseudonym some years earlier.) His account of slaying a feared man-eater in his first book, *The Hunting Grounds of the Old World*, gives a good taste of his somewhat florid style.

He had called a council of the local native shikaris to discuss how this man-eating tiger might be shot, for it had accounted for numerous women and girls as well as native postmen who ran between villages. Leveson wrote that one of the leading shikaris 'said he had been thinking of a plan which though dangerous in the execution might be attended with success. It was for me to go with a man dressed as a runner down the main road at sunset, being the time the tiger generally carried off his victims and run the chance of getting a shot.

'At this proposition sundry interjectional expressions such as ''Abah!'', ''Arrez!'', ''Toba!'' escaped from the lips of the bystanders and from sundry shaking of heads and other unmistakable signs, I could see that it had not

72

found much favour in their eyes. Chineah the dhoby and one or two of the gang, however, approved the plan and Kistimah offered to accompany me as the post-runner.

'This, however, I objected to for I thought I should have a better chance of meeting the tiger if I went alone than in company; besides I preferred having only myself to look after. The plan of action once settled, I returned to the village and obtained from the patel the bamboo on which the tappel-runners sling the mail bags over their shoulders. To the end of this is an iron ring with a number of small pieces of metal attached, making a jingling noise as the man runs, which gives warning of the coming of the post to any crowd that might be obstructing the path, allowing them time to get out of his way. Having broken off the ring I fastened it to my belt so as to allow it to jingle as I walked; and arming myself with a short double rifle by Westley Richards, a brace of pistols, and a huge shekar knife, I made Kistimah lead the way down the path towards where the man-eater was said to lurk . . .

'The sun had almost set as I proceeded slowly down the road, and although I was perfectly cool and as steady as possible, I felt cold drops of perspiration start from my forehead as I approached the spot where so many victims had been sacrificed. I passed the rock keeping well on the look-out, listening carefully for the slightest sound, and I remember feeling considerably annoyed by the chirping made by a couple of little bulbuls (Indian nightingales) that were fighting in a bush by the roadside. Partridges were calling loudly all around and as I passed the watercourse I saw a jackal skulking along its bed. I stopped, shook my jangling affair and listened several times as I went along, but to no purpose.

'Whilst ascending the opposite side of the ravine, I heard a slight noise like the crackling of a dry leaf: I paused and turning to the left fronted the spot from whence I thought the noise proceeded. I distinctly saw a movement or waving in the high grass, as if something was making its way towards me; then I heard a loud purring sound, and saw something twitching backwards and forwards behind a clump of low bush and long grass about eight or ten paces from me, and a little in the rear. It was a ticklish moment, but I felt prepared. I stepped back a couple of paces in order to get a better view, which action probably saved my life, for immediately the brute sprang into the middle of the road, alighting about six feet from the place where I was standing. I fired a hurried shot ere he could gather himself for another spring, and when the smoke cleared away, I saw him rolling over and over in the dusty road, writhing in his death agony, for my shot had entered the neck and gone down into his chest. I stepped on one side and gave him my second barrel behind the ear, when dark blood rushed from his nostrils, a slight tremor passed over his limbs, and all was still. The man-eater was dead and his victims avenged.'

This sort of early Victorian melodramatic over-writing was unfortunately typical of Leveson's early style and makes for very tedious reading today. It

73

is also only too plain that while he must indeed have been both an experienced and able hunter he could seldom resist gilding each story with somewhat improbable additions.

The results of his service in India and the Crimea were recorded in a rather confused style in his book *The Forest and The Field*. From the fall of Sebastopol in 1855 Henry Leveson spent the next four years shooting in Europe, Asia Minor and Tibet. Some of his experiences in these years were included in his book *Hunting Grounds of the Old World*.

His last and best book, *Sport in Many Lands*, was a wide-ranging work with less of the bombast which marred his earlier writing. For instance he dismissed shooting gorillas in Nigeria with contempt, stating that 'a well armed man has but little danger to fear from the animal itself if he only exercises common precautions. I consider it a very tame sport . . .'

This extract from the same book, describing tiger shooting in India, compares favourably with his earlier writing even though still somewhat prolix: '. . . the line was reformed and shortly afterwards a magnificent tiger sprang out of some high reeds in the dry bed of a watercourse and I had a fair right and left shot; but unaccustomed to shoot from a jolting howdah I missed clean and a perfect shower of bullets rattled round about him as he dashed across the open. Although he was manifestly hit, from the short sharp yelps he gave,

The tables turned on 'The Old Shekarry'.

he continued to bound along through the bushes until . . . a second discharge rolled him over dead as we thought; but on hurrying up to the spot he was nowhere to be seen, having vanished as it were into the ground. Closing up our line we tracked him by his pugs to some dwarf date trees . . . when Madegan espied him stealing away . . . and let drive at him . . . Madegan ordered his mahout to press forward but he had no heart for the game, which did not add to the steadiness of the beast he was driving, who . . . turned tail and bolted. Blake and I now hurried up and this time I should have got a fair shot had not my elephant accidentally hurt his foot against a sharp stone and proved so fidgetty that I could hardly keep my feet by laying hold of the sides of the howdah, much less take a fair aim: so I reserved my fire and Blake's elephant charging boldly up to the crouching tiger gave him the chance and he hurriedly fired a right and left which wounded the infuriated beast but did not disable him: for before the smoke had cleared away, with a hoarse angry roar, the monster bounded on a low bank . . . and then . . . sprang on clean to the elephant's forehead and, with claw and fangs fastening on his head and ears dragged him to his knees . . . when my elephant . . . pluckily rushed up and, although I felt somewhat afraid of hitting my friend's elephant or mahout instead of the tiger, the case was critical and as I brushed by I planted a right and left just behind the top of the shoulder blade: and Blake, who never for a moment lost his presence of mind, leaned over the front of the howdah and almost simultaneously lodged the contents of his second gun in the nape of his neck, when the brute relaxed his hold and fell to the ground writhing in his last agony. Hardly was Blake's elephant freed from the worrying grip of the tiger, than, excited by rage mingled with revenge he curled up his trunk and uttering a terrific trumpeting noise . . . and literally lifting the prostrate carcase on his tusks chucked it on one side and commenced dancing a war dance on it to the utter discomfiture of the sportsman in the howdah and his attendant, who had to hold on like grim death . . . The mahout was dislodged from his seat . . . guns, rifle and all loose gear were pitched on the ground before the frantic animal could be quieted . . . The sight was ludicrous enough for the spectators, but Blake did not see any fun in it, and to add to his discomfiture, the stock of a valuable gun was broken in the fall, a loss not easily made good in an up country station . . .'

He also gave an account in this book of shooting grizzly bears in the Rocky Mountains as well as bison on the prairie. Since it covered sport in Asia, India, South Africa and Abyssinia, Leveson certainly had grounds for being compared with Samuel White Baker as one of the most travelled and experienced sportsmen of his times. Sam Baker, however, was always restrained in giving purely factual accounts of his sport, thrilling though these often were.

Henry Leveson, writing always as 'The Old Shekarry', simply could not restrain his pen, nor had he any pretensions to modesty. Nor, for that matter, was he as gifted or fluent a writer as Samuel White Baker. On the other hand it is perhaps easy to be too critical of his bombast, exaggeration and invention and forget that he must also have been a courageous and experienced soldier and hunter. Although he recovered to some extent from his wounds received in the Crimea and other campaigns, there is little doubt they contributed to his death in 1875 at the comparatively early age of forty-seven.

A grizzly brought to bay by 'The Old Shekarry'.

4

LATE VICTORIAN SPORTSMEN
IN INDIA

James Forsyth 1838–1871

William Rice 1832–1886

Alexander Airlie Angus Kinloch 1838–1919

Shikaris, India, c1865. Courtesy of Elizabeth Clifford Photographs.

James Forsyth 1838–1871

India 1857–1871

Sporting Conservator of Forests and Expert Rifle Shot

*. . . generally they dart off at full speed at once and then comes into
play the most difficult of all the arts of the rifleman – snap shooting
at running game off an elephant . . .*

James Forsyth was born in Scotland in 1838. After schooling in Scotland, he
gained a MA at Cambridge and went out to India in the late 1850s. He served
with distinction under Sir Richard Temple, Chief Commissioner of the Central
Provinces, as Conservator of Forests. It was in this post that he surveyed the
entire area, making numerous marches of over a thousand miles lasting months
at a time through totally unexplored country. A fluent linguist and keen sportsman, as well as an energetic stalker, he was in the perfect position to take
full advantage of all the sport available.

His first book, published in 1862, was entitled *The Sporting Rifle and its
Projectiles*. Although published at a time of great change in all forms of firearms
there was clearly a considerable demand for it as in 1867 he published a much
revised, though even then soon outdated, second edition. In the preface he
wrote: 'The progress of gunnery since the publication of the first edition has
necessitated many additions to the present work. Most of it has been re-written
and the plates are almost entirely new.

'I trust the work will now be found to be a complete guide to the young
sportsman in all matters concerned with the SPORTING RIFLE.'

He wrote at one point: 'Baker says, if I remember right, that a good shot
should be able to bag, *without fail*, everything fired at standing at seventy
yards or running at fifty. I have never met a man yet who could bag *without
fail* all animals at any distance. I think myself that if one fires at fair standing
shots within 150 yards and running within 100 yards he should kill two out
of three in the former case and one half of the latter.'

He recommended: 'As a rule the place to hit all mammals is through the
shoulders, the lungs or heart are thus penetrated and besides the bones of
the shoulder may be broken and escape prevented . . .'

In the work for which he is better known, *The Highlands of Central India:
Notes on their Forests and Wild Tribes, Natural History and Sports*, the results
of many explorations he had made, which was published in 1871, he wrote

feelingly: 'The labour of exploring such forests . . . during the hot season, when alone they are sufficiently open and free from malaria, is immense – day after day toiling over those interminable basaltic ridges, where many marches are often to be made without meeting an inhabitant, without often a single green tree for shelter, and dependant for water on a few stagnant pools puddled up by the feet of wild animals. This was often what fell to the lot of the forest officers . . . and there is not one whose health did not after a few years give way under the combined assaults of malaria and a fiery sun . . .'

On the subject of shooting the sambar deer, he pointed out that: '. . . if information can be got from the people who frequent the jungles for wood cutting, etc., of whereabouts the sambar are feeding and resting . . . capital sport can be got with them in the day time with the aid of a riding elephant. This enables you to see over the grass, and generally starts any sambar that may be lying down within about a hundred yards. The elephant must be thoroughly trained to stop dead short on deer getting up, and should not be furnished with a howdah, the simple pad or charjama being preferable for this sort of shooting; and the smaller and more active the elephant is the better . . . A standing shot may sometimes be had during a few seconds after the sambar first rise, but more generally they dart off at full speed at once and then comes into play the most difficult of all the arts of the rifleman – snap shooting at running game off an elephant. The elephant is never *perfectly* still for more than a moment and its short swing must be allowed for as well as the pace of the deer. The sambar is, of course, from its great size and distinct colour, much more easy to hit than the spotted deer, or barking, or hog, deer; but still it is amazing what a preponderance of clear misses the best shots will make at even running sambar off the elephant, until long and constant practice has given the peculiar knack which is so difficult to attain. It is, however, by far the most deadly as well as one of the most enjoyable ways of hunting the sambar.

'Driving a large extent of country with a long line of beaters is the commonest method . . . It is frequently successful and often secures a good stag; but for my own part I have very rarely resorted to it . . . The whole country is disturbed; the shooting of a creature driven up to you, without the exercise either of skill or any other manly quality on your own part is not sport . . . it has never been my fortune (not that I have much regretted it) to be out with a large hunting party in India . . .

'By far the finest sport afforded by the sambar is when he is regularly stalked in his native wilderness, without either elephant or beaters. I will not waste a word on so vile a practice as that of shooting him at night, when he comes to the crops or drinking places. None but a native shikari, or a European with equally poaching proclivities would ever think of such a thing.'

Forsyth was never afraid to speak of his misses and disasters, a sure sign of a thoroughgoing sportsman, who knows that such things must often occur to everyone. On one occasion he wrote: 'Just as we arrived some dogs . . . passed . . . in full cry after a doe sambar they had roused. Of course we flew to our rifles, but were just in time to miss her handsomely as she dashed into the thick jungle . . .' On another occasion after walking several miles along 'the backbone of the ridge beyond Bingara . . . I caught the glint of the sun on something moving, and made out a noble sambar stag . . . He was not more than a mile off in a direct line; but to get to the spot it would be necessary to go several miles round the head of a small ravine . . . we carefully marked the spot, and . . . started off at a brisk walk to circumvent him. The sun was well up by now, and it is very hot in March even at that early hour . . . At last . . . we sighted the red topped tree under which we had marked our stag . . . We were not to succeed however . . . the Bheel [his native attendant] accidentally stepped on a leaf and the game was up. Though I dashed ahead at once . . . all I saw was a dark form running low, but at a great pace . . . too far off for a shot.'

Forsyth wrote: 'No one can hunt in these scantily covered hills without wondering at the extreme difficulty of making out such large animals as sambar, bison and bears on the open hill side. The bison and bear precisely resemble the large black trap boulders that thickly strew every hill; and thus the glaring contrast of their black hides with the bright yellow grass frequently attracts no attention whatever . . .'

He recorded on another occasion when hunting: '. . . something caught my eye . . . It looked exactly like one of the bunches of twigs that grow out of old teak stumps on those hills with one or two dried leaves attached to them; and yet I fancied I had seen it move. I looked at it intently for at least a minute, trying to make out if it was a bunch of teak twigs or a sambar's head and horns. It never moved in the whole of this time; and as the Bheels who were with me said it was only a stump, I turned to pass on. The glint of my rifle barrel must have caught in the sun, for a noble stag started from his lair . . . wheeled round and clattered away. My hasty shot missed him clean . . . and I turned for home swearing to expend a bullet in future on every teak stump that bore the most distant resemblance to a stag's head. Both T. [his companion] and I were often mistaken in these hills in the same manner and have frequently gone up to within a few yards of a stump to make sure. The resemblance is so very close . . . Even the motion of the huge ears of the sambar, which they restrain only in the presence of danger, answers exactly to the stirring of a dried teak leaf in a slight breeze . . .'

With a friend, Forsyth described a gruelling hot day's hunt after a herd of bison, when eventually: '. . . I ran up to T. in time to see ten or twelve bison scrambling up the opposite side of the ravine. A bull brought up the rear . . . so we opened fire . . . and the third shot broke his leg. He had the other shots too, and, after limping on a bit, staggered, and fell down the hill. Being much fatigued by the heat of a very sultry April day, we waited there till the people came with our leathern water-sack to have a drink and then went over to the bull, who was still alive, but unable to rise . . .'

The following day they shot a sambar and another bison. Forsyth made the point that 'It is so easy to throw in half a dozen bull bison in a day's sport by the stroke of the pen . . . I have however stuck to the exact facts of a by no means heavy bag, on purpose to give a more accurate idea of what such shooting really means – namely very hard work and much exposure for an average of certainly no more than one head of game a day, and often much less . . .' adding that 'By taking every chance at cow bison and doe sambar of course the bag could be largely increased; and I heard of two men who one year murdered in this way twenty-eight bison in a week. This is not sport, nor are the performers sportsmen. The bison is already it would seem, diminishing in numbers . . . He is one of the most harmless animals in the whole world to the industry of man, and, fairly hunted, affords perhaps the best sport in India; it would be a pity, then, if his numbers should be unduly diminished by unsportsmanlike conduct.'

He noted subsequently: 'While wandering about in 1862, during the months of April and May in the teak forests of the Betul district, I devoted a day now and then to the sport of tiger-shooting; and it was the laudable custom of the forest officers to spare if possible every year, a few weeks during the height of the hot season for the purpose of making an impression on the numerous tigers which at that time rendered working in the forests and carrying timber so dreaded by the natives and consequently costly to Government.

'Although there is much in the sport of tiger-hunting that renders it inferior as a mere exercise, or as an effort of skill, to some other pursuits of these regions (for many a man has killed his forty or fifty tigers who has never succeeded in bagging, by fair stalking, a single bull bison or stag sambar), yet there is a stirring of the blood in attacking an animal before whom every other beast of the forest quails, and unarmed man is helpless as the mouse under the paw of a cat . . . which draws men to its continued pursuit after that of every other animal has ceased to afford sufficient excitement to undergo the toil of hunting in a tropical country.

'. . . the hot season, the height of which is in April and May, is the most favourable time for hunting the tiger. Then the water supply . . . is at its lowest . . . and the tiger . . . seeks the lowest valleys, where . . . much of the game he preys on has congregated . . .'

Forsyth commented that two types of tiger were generally recognised by the native shikaris. One, which lived on game alone chiefly in the hills was very innocuous, even beneficial in keeping down the herds of deer which otherwise might have attacked the crops. The other was an older, heavier animal which preyed on cattle. Forsyth argued that in reality the game-killing tiger merely graduated as it grew older onto killing cattle, growing heavier and lazier as a result. He noted, however, that 'It is useless to devote much time to hunting the hill tigers which prey on game alone. They are so scattered over extensive tracts of jungle and are so active and wary that it is only by accident that they are ever brought to the bag.' He continued: 'Favourably situated covers are almost certain to hold one or more cattle-eating tigers during the hot weather; and however many are killed, others will shortly occupy their place . . .'

He also pointed out: 'The tiger very seldom kills his prey by the "sledge-hammer stroke" of his fore paw so often talked about, the usual way being to seize with the teeth by the nape of the neck, and at the same time use the paws to hold the victim, and give a purchase for the wrench that dislocates the neck . . .

'Tigers that prey on cattle are generally perfectly well known to the cowherds . . . The damage they do on the whole is very great, sixty or seventy head of cattle . . . being destroyed in . . . a year. Generally there is . . . one native . . . whose profession is that of shikari, or hunter . . . When he hears of a bullock having been killed . . . erecting a platform . . . in the nearest tree . . . [he] watches by night for the return of the tiger . . . His weapon is a long matchlock, which he loads with six "fingers" of powder and two bullets. These fly a little apart and if they hit are usually the death of the tiger. His method of shooting is sometimes imitated by lazy European sportsmen.'

Following Walter Campbell's lead he argued: 'The best way of hunting the tiger is undoubtedly . . . to bring in the aid of the trained elephant and to follow and shoot him in his mid-day retreat . . . No sort of hunting requires more careful arrangements, greater knowledge of the animal, perseverance and good shooting, than the pursuit of the tiger by the single sportsman with a single elephant . . . Some people affect to despise . . . using elephants . . . and talk a great deal about shooting them on foot. As regards danger to the sports-man nine tenths of the tigers *said* to be shot on foot are really killed from trees, or rocks, where the sportsman is quite secure. The only danger then is to the unfortunate beaters, if used . . . In this method of hunting many more tigers are wounded than secured, the only danger lying in following up a wounded animal, which is usually avoided; and thus an innocent animal is often converted into a scourge of the countryside. A very few sportsmen do for a short period of their lives, make a practice of hunting and shooting tigers really on foot; but they are seldom very successful and sooner or later get killed, or have such narrow escapes as to cure them of such silly folly for the rest of their days. A man on foot has no chance whatever in thick jungle with a tiger that is bent on killing him. He cannot see a yard before him and is himself conspicuous to every sense of the brute . . . who can move at will through the thickest cover without the slightest sound or stir . . . The sports-man who as a rule uses an elephant in thick cover will find quite enough oppor-tunities . . . of testing his nerve on foot, particularly if he . . . tracks his own game instead of employing shikaris to do so . . . Much of the excitement of the sport depends on the . . . method of attacking the tiger . . . As a rule when an elephant is in fair ground the object should be to get the tiger to charge instead of letting him sneak away . . .'

With an acute understanding of the native mind Forsyth wrote: 'A great many reasons . . . combine to make the natives . . . very unwilling to give information about tigers. Firstly it is liable to bring down a large encampment of "Sahibs" on their village, which they, very justly in most cases, dislike. The military officer who scorns to learn the rural language and his train of overbearing, swindling servants . . . stinks in the nostrils of the poor inhabitants of the tracts where tigers are found. The tiger himself is in fact far more endurable [and] they fear that they will be made to beat for the tiger . . . with a considerable chance of getting killed and very little of being paid . . . On the other hand a properly organised expedition, where the sportsman provides his own supplies and his means of hunting is certain to meet with every co-operation from the people. They will even crowd in to help in driving the jungles, when they know they are to work for a good sportsman and shot who will not unnecessarily risk their lives.'

Forsyth was responsible for organising a tiger hunt for the Governor General of India in January 1861 when a royal tiger was secured. In recording the event he wrote that he '. . . mounted sentry over that beast for nearly a week, girding him in a little hill with a belt of fires and feeding him with nightly kine, till half a hundred elephants carrying the cream of the vice-regal camp swept him out into the plain, where he fell riddled by a storm of bullets from several hundred virgin rifles. He had the honour of being painted by a Landseer, by the blaze of torchlight, under the shadow of the British standard; and my howdah bore witness for many a day, in a bullet hole through both sides of it, to the accuracy of aim of some gallant member of the staff.'

Forsyth was clear about tiger hunting: '. . . having discovered a tract where tigers are reported a good central place should be selected for a camp . . . near a village . . . The sportsman will probably find . . . the village headman . . . waiting to receive him with a simple offering – a pot of milk, or bunch of pantains . . . If he is welcome tales will not be wanting of the neighbouring tigers . . . The usual haunts of the tiger will be described . . . The shikari of the neighbourhood will be present, or can be sent for . . . Rupees, or the prospect of them, will be wanted to loosen his tongue . . . If you are known to be a good paymaster he will willingly serve you . . . In my earlier sporting days I always went out to make the preliminary exploration for tigers myself; and this is the only way to learn the business thoroughly, so as to be able afterwards to devolve the labour on your shikaris. A sportsman who is not thoroughly master of this business will never have a reliable shikari . . . The morning is the best time for this work. It is then cool and every footprint of the previous night is sharp and clear . . . The movements of the tiger even may often be traced up to eight or nine o'clock by the voices of monkeys and peafowl, the chatter of crows and small birds and the bark of sambar and spotted deer. The whole nocturnal life of the beasts of the forest is then displayed in the clearest manner to the hunter whose eye has been trained to read this book of nature ... Everywhere the cruel tyranny of the tiger has imprinted itself on the faithful page. His track to the water is straight and leisurely, while that of the nilgai or spotted deer is halting and suspicious, and apt to end in a wild scurry to right or left when it crosses the tiger's. Here and there bleaching skulls and bones show that the whole herd have not always made good their escape ... not seldom the trampled soil and patches of blood and hair show where a stubborn boar has successfully resisted the attack of a tiger. Bruin alone is tolerably safe from the assault of the tiger; but he too gets out of his way like the rest and drinks at a different pool ...'

On another occasion Forsyth '... followed a tiger in the early morning for several miles up the bed of a stream, entirely by the demonstrations of the large Hanuman monkey, of which there were numbers feeding on the wild fruits ... Each group continued to swear at him till he passed out of sight ... The river took a broad sweep ... and by cutting across the neck I managed to arrive ... in front of the tiger ... He was travelling under the opposite bank [and] passed within twenty yards of me, making for a small ravine ... I let him get to the mouth of this before I fired; and on receiving the shot he bounded forward into its cover ... I knew he was hit to death ... but we then went round a good way to where a high bank overlooked the ravine into which he had disappeared. Here we cautiously peeped over ... and found the tiger lying stone dead shot near the heart.'

In 1865 he shot a cattle-eating tiger which was reputed to have killed over a thousand head and forced the natives to abandon one of the best grazing areas available. Forsyth wrote: 'He was a very large tiger, measuring ten feet one inch in length as he lay and was a perfect mountain of fat – the fat of a thousand kine as the cowherds lugubriously remarked ... ten feet one inch is the length of an unusually large tiger. The average length from nose to tip of the tail is only nine feet six inchs for a full grown male and for a tigress about eight feet four inches. The experience of all sportsmen I have met with, whose accuracy I can rely on, is the same ... The skin of a ten-feet tiger will easily stretch to thirteen or fourteen feet if required ... A well known sportsman and writer, whose recorded measurements have done more to extend the size of the tiger than anything else informed me that all his measurements were taken from flat skins ... [This was almost certainly a reference to William Rice: see pp. 92] the British public demands twelve feet tigers, just as it refuscs to accept an Indian landscape without palm trees ...'

Forsyth continued: 'A strange affection springs up between the hunter and his well-tried ally in the chase of the tiger ... No one who has not witnessed it would believe the astonishing caution with which a well-trained elephant approaches a tiger – removing with noiseless adroitness every obstacle of fallen timber, etc., and passing his huge bulk over rustling leaves, or rolling stones, or quaking bog with an absolute and marvellous silence; handing up stones, when ordered, for his master to fling into the cover; smelling out a cold scent as a spaniel roads a pheasant; and at last, perhaps, pointing dead with sensitive trunk at the hidden monster, or showing with short nervous raps of that organ on the ground that he is somewhere near, though not actually discovered to the senses of the elephant . . . The elephant's business is to stand like a rock in every event, even when the tiger is fastened on his head – as many a good one has done and will do . . .'

Discussing what was desirable in a good hunting elephant he wrote: 'We look for a small well-bred-looking head and trunk, a clear confident eye devoid of piggish expression, fast easy paces, straight back and croup, wide loins, and generally well-developed bone and muscle . . . A very tall elephant is seldom a good working one . . . A smaller elephant than eight feet two inches will be undersized . . . A female makes the best hunting-elephant, when she is really staunch with game, as her paces and temper are generally better . . . All elephants intended to be used in hunting must be very carefully trained and entered to their game. A good mahout, or driver, is very difficult to obtain. The elephant should first be accustomed to the firing of guns from his back . . . but their ultimate qualities will depend much on natural temperament. The more naturally courageous an elephant is the better chance of his remaining staunch after having been actually mauled by a tiger – an accident, of course to be avoided as long as possible . . . It will occur sometimes . . . and then a naturally timid animal . . . will probably be spoilt for life, while a really plucky elephant is often rendered bolder . . .'

Forsyth recorded: 'In . . . April and May of 1862 I bagged six tigers and one panther in the Betul jungles, wounding two more tigers which escaped . . . Another party was also shooting in the same district; and although they arrived after me in the field, contrary to the well-understood rule in such circumstances, proceeded ahead and disturbed the whole country by indiscriminate firing at deer and peafowl. It is scarcely necessary to say that when after tiger nothing else should be fired at. The Lalla [his favourite shikari] . . . securing . . . a monopoly of information, in which he was well served by the conduct of our rivals in harassing the people in the matter of provisions and thrashing them all round if a tiger was not found for them . . . On one occasion I reached their ground just as their last camel was moving off to a new camp. They had stayed here a week trying in vain to extort help in finding a couple of tigers whose tracks they had seen. The tigers were all the time within half a mile of their tents; and before ten o'clock that day I had them both padded. During a whole month I believe they only succeeded in getting one tiger and that by potting it from a tree at night. Some years afterwards when I shot the same country under much more favourable circumstances, the numbers of tigers had greatly diminished, owing to the high rewards and the steady attentions of the forest officers and my bag was then just the same as in 1862. Five or six tigers may in fact be considered a very fair bag for one gun in a month's shooting, even in the best parts of the Central Provinces; but two or three guns, with a proportionate force of elephants, should of course do much better.'

Forsyth went on: 'Between five and six hundred human beings and an uncalculated number of cattle are killed by wild beasts in the Central Provinces alone every year . . . For some years heavy rewards were given for every tiger and other dangerous animal killed, special rewards being placed on the heads of man-eaters and I am convinced that many more were killed during that time than previously . . . The number destroyed increased every year . . . Rewards for the killing of 2,414 tigers, panthers, bears and wolves were claimed in 1867 (the last year for which statistics are available) against 1,863 in 1865. Tigers are certainly not so numerous by a great deal in many parts with which I am personally acquainted as they were even six or eight years ago . . .'

Mentioning obvious changes which had taken place Forsyth stated that 'Jubbulpur is now rather an important place being the point of junction of the two lines of railway which between them connect . . . Calcutta and Bombay . . . At the time of which I write it was a small civil and military station . . . The steam horse has torn his way through the parks and levelled the bamboo clumps that were the glory of the place . . .'

In *The Field* of 17th May 1862 Forsyth distinguished between panthers and leopards, pointing out 'the larger size of the panther, which reaches in fine specimens to seven feet eleven inches from nose to tip of the tail, the leopard not exceeding five feet six inches; the lighter colour, and taller more slender figure of the panther and the rounder more bull-dog like head of the leopard . . .'

In writing about the panther he expressed unqualified admiration. 'In my early sporting days I fell into the mistake of most sportsmen in supposing that the panther might be hunted on foot with less caution than the tiger. On two or three occasions I nearly paid dearly for the error; and I now believe that the panther is really by far a more dangerous animal to attack than the tiger. He is, in the first place, far more courageous . . . if once brought to close quarters he will rarely fail to charge with the utmost ferocity, fighting to the very last. He is also much more active than the tiger, making immense springs clear off the ground, which the tiger seldom does. He can conceal himself in the most wonderful way . . . into an inconceivably small space. Further . . . he is far more difficult to hit in a vital place. He can climb trees, which the tiger cannot do . . . And lastly his powers of offence are scarcely inferior to those of the tiger himself; and are amply sufficient to be the death of any man he gets hold of. When stationed . . . near Jubbulpur . . . I shot seven panthers and leopards in less than a month . . . chiefly by driving them out with beaters . . . One of the smaller species, really not more than five feet long I believe, charged me three several times up a bank to the very muzzle of my rifle (of which I luckily had a couple) falling back each time to the shot, but not dreaming of trying to escape and dying at last at my feet . . . When a panther takes to man-eating, he is a far more terrible scourge than a tiger. In 1858 a man-killing panther devastated the northern part of the Seoni district killing (incredible as it may seem) nearly a hundred persons before he was shot . . . My own experience is that the majority of panthers one finds are come across more by luck than good management.'

Biased in favour of his Indian hunting as he undoubtedly was Forsyth admitted: 'Few men would probably come to India merely to shoot over this central wilderness. But as a field for general travel and even as a sporting ground, India is rapidly coming into favour among the wandering section of Englishmen . . . I will here speak only of the glorious field that the country offers to the sportsman – incomparably the finest in the whole world. Africa may be thought to be better, but it is not so if India be looked at as a whole. Perhaps more animals in number or in size may be slaughtered in Central Africa; but that does not surely imply superior *sport*. In reading accounts of African shooting I have often wondered how men could continue to wade through the sickening details of daily massacre of half-tame animals offering themselves to the rifle on its vast open plains. In India fewer animals will perhaps be bagged; all will have to be worked for, and some perhaps fought for. The sport will be far superior; and the sportsman will return from India with a collection of trophies which Africa cannot match. Africa and India both have their elephants. We cannot offer a hippopotamus; but we have a rhinoceros superior in sporting point of view to his African relative. We have a wild buffalo as savage and with far superior horns to the Cape species; and we have *four* other species of wild bovines besides, to which there is nothing comparable in Africa. In felines, besides a lion, panther and a hunting-leopard, almost identical with those of Africa, we have the tiger, and one, if not two other species of leopard. Our black antelope are unsurpassed by any of the many antelopes of Africa; and besides him we have fourteen species of antelopes and wild goats and sheep in our hills and plains, affording the finest stalking in the world, to compare with the other antelopes of Africa. Africa has no deer, properly speaking, at all . . . India on the other hand has nine species of antlered deer. We have three bears, Africa has none at all. There is no country in the world that can show such a list of large game as we can in India. And for minor sport what can compare with our endless array of pheasants, partridges and wildfowl?

'All this too is now so easy of access. Twenty-one days by overland passage lands the traveller in Bombay . . . If he joins a regular camp in the "plains" he will find the most perfect system of open air life that has anywhere been devised . . . [with] pretty nearly everything that civilised man can want, ready to move about with him at the rate of from twelve to twenty miles a day. By the help of the railways he may see almost the whole country south of

Head of an Indian elephant. Nineteenth century drawing.

Head of an African elephant. Nineteenth century drawing.

the Himalayas and shoot specimens of all its game during the pleasant cold months from October to March . . . [or] combine with some small game shooting and pig-sticking if he likes in November and December . . . By the time that April ushers in the hot blasts of summer, he may find himself, if he pleases, stalking the ibex among the snows of Kashmir . . .

'For mere sport England need not be left earlier than December . . . The help of the local civil authorities is of course of the greatest value; and I may say that it is always freely rendered to gentlemen projecting a tour through their charges. Some previous acquaintance with the language, and the general requirements of such a trip on the part of at least one of the party is almost essential to ensure success . . . The cost of such an expedition need not be very great. Most of the outfit required would be re-sold at the conclusion at no very great loss. One hill tent, ten feet square . . . would be sufficient for two sportsmen and would cost . . . about £30. A strong rough pony is the best animal to ride . . . [and] can generally be bought in Bombay at a cost of about £20 . . . Arrangements should be made to get the loan of, or purchase, a staunch shooting-elephant and howdah . . . and a really good one will not be bought for less than £200 to £300. Decent shikaris can generally be obtained on the spot . . . The current expenses, after the outfit has been bought will come to about £30 per mensem of each sportsman . . .'

It was obvious where his own sympathies lay, as he went on to explain how 'a man accustomed to rough it could get on and obtain the best of sport at much less expense than this, which is laid down for a party wishing to enjoy all the comforts of the Indian style of travelling in camp. Such an adventurous sportsman need only get for himself a small pal tent and a few necessary implements of travel and hire a camel to carry them, buy a rough pony for £5 or £10, hire a couple of servants and plunge with his rifle into the wilderness. If capable of speaking the Hindi language and conciliatory towards the wild men, he would soon have about him a knot of real jungle hunters who would take him up to every sort of game. Saddlery, hunting implements of all sorts . . . ammunition and clothes should be brought from England . . .'

By 1870 Forsyth was writing that, following the 'universal introduction of breech loading' he recommended a ·450 or ·500 Express rifle with short conical bullet 'for *all ordinary* purposes'. 'For dangerous game such as tigers there is nothing better yet available for sportsmen than the large rifle firing the spherical ball, or explosive shell of my own invention, which I have described . . . All rifles should, by preference, be double-barrelled. To use a single barrel is to sacrifice many chances, while it possesses no advantage over a well-made double. A good price, however, will have to be paid for a really true-shooting double rifle; and when this is a consideration a breech-loading single Express rifle will be found to give a wonderful command of shots.'

He ended his outstanding book on sport in central India by recommending his gunsmith friend, Mr Henry of Edinburgh's, rifle as the best he knew.

Towards the end of 1870 he returned home with his book ready for publication. Sadly in 1871, as the sheets were passing through the press, at the age of only thirty-three he finally succumbed to the rigours of the life he had led. His book was thus published posthumously in November 1871, but remains an enduring record of the man himself and the sport he enjoyed.

William Rice 1832–1886

India 1850–1882

As Lieutenant or Major General Unable to Measure Tigers

All the measurements were taken . . . after the skins had been . . .
well stretched . . . but great pains were taken to insure . . . their
proper relative breadth as well as length . . .

As a strong advocate of shooting tigers on foot rather than from elephants and as one who claimed frequently to have shot tigers measuring close on twelve feet, Rice was undoubtedly anathema to Forsyth and was certainly the person to whom he referred as responsible for twelve-foot tigers. While still a Lieutenant, Rice wrote a book entitled *Tiger Shooting In India*, published in 1857 at the time of the Mutiny, although written on the five seasons from 1850 to 1854.

Starting as an absolute novice, unable to afford the cost of an elephant, young William Rice developed shooting on foot with a group of Indian beaters to quite a fine art. Of course the country in Rajpootana, where he developed this method of shooting, unlike the Central India teak forests where Forsyth shot, was quite suited to shooting on foot, there being plenty of rock nullahs or valleys up which the tigers could be driven, allowing the guns stationed on the banks at suitable passing places a good chance of a safe shot. In Central India, Forsyth's country, the thickness and height of the grass made shooting except from the back of an elephant virtually impossible.

Rice's records of his shooting, however, are refreshingly without conceal-ment and there can be no doubt that he genuinely believed in the measurements of the tigers he shot, even if it may be, as Forsyth caustically suggested, that the shikaris saw to it that he had twelve-feet tigers because that was what they thought he wanted. Rice himself recorded his first attempt at tigers, while he was still a complete novice (or griffin in the local terminology), with obvious honesty.

'. . . having heard there was a tiger in a village . . . thirteen miles west of camp . . . Lt. Little and myself rode out there . . . But, although in several places we saw footprints quite fresh he could nowhere be found. My friend was obliged to ride back to camp in the evening, but I determined to stop in the hope of getting a shot . . . by moonlight . . . As a bait . . . I tied up by the horns a poor lame half-starved bullock to a tree stump and afterwards climbed a small tamarind tree close by. Here I seated myself with three double guns . . . and silently awaited the tiger's coming. After . . . about three or four hours the moon went down. It now became too dark to see any mark, so I let down my three guns to the foot of the tree and prepared to descend myself. No sooner had my foot touched the ground than an appalling roar from a thick bush not a dozen paces off caused me almost to jump out of my skin. I instantly seized a gun and blazed away at random both barrels into the bush in the hope that my enemy would take the hint and disperse. To my horror he only repeated the roar still louder. In the fright consequent thereon and not being able to see the tiger or well knowing what I was about I banged off the remaining guns into the bush. Each of these shots was answered by more roars. Having no other loaded guns left I ran off at a marvellous pace towards the village. Here to my great joy I met some men hastening towards me. They, it appeared, had been waiting to hear my shot from the tree, which would announce the tiger's death, but seeing from the flashes of my guns that I was on the ground and hearing the repeated shots and loud roarings, concluded that I had chosen to fight the tiger on foot and had of course killed him. After undeceiving them they volunteered to accompany me back to the tree to retrieve my guns as well as to release the bullock.

'Just as we had picked up the unloaded guns we were saluted by another roar close by which caused us all to hastily retreat, leaving the unfortunate bullock still tied up . . . After passing the rest of the night under a large tree where my horse and man were waiting, I . . . found the poor beast killed and half eaten . . . Having well paid the owner of the dead bullock I rode back to camp . . . making a vow never to be again guilty of such slow unsportsmanlike work as watching in ambush at night for any wild beast . . .'

On a month's leave in March/April 1850 he had shot a bear and lost another and continued: 'After losing this bear I mounted my horse and rode slowly across country towards my tent, taking with me two Bheels [native tribesmen], only one single barrel rifle and my large dog "Wull" . . . between a Persian Greyhound and an English bull bitch . . .

'We had not gone far when we met two travellers, who . . . declared they had just seen a large tiger lying down near the roadside and pointed in the direction he had gone off. Hoping to get a distant shot at the brute I quickly dismounted and went after him. On going up to a large thick bush about 60 yards off to my astonishment out jumped the tiger from the opposite side and in a few bounds made across the dry bed of a river that was close by. Directly "Wull" saw the tiger, which he doubtless mistook for some new sort of deer, he set off after him giving tongue all the while and keeping within two or three yards only of the brute's heels . . . Suddenly one of the Bheels . . . called out that the tiger was coming back and instantly ran off for his life . . . I looked up and sure enough saw the tiger coming straight towards me closely followed by the dog.

'The beast had nearly recrossed the river bed in a few bounds and was within thirty yards of me when, without taking any particular aim I pitched up the rifle and fired. Then flinging down the empty gun I dived among the dense thorn bushes taking in my headlong flight the same road the Bheel had done before me, for while jumping across some wide deep rocks I passed this man and left him groaning at the bottom of the rocks down which he had fallen having missed his footing. Being convinced that the wounded tiger was after us I was uncharitable enough to feel extremely glad that I was not now the last and most likely to be caught by him. The Bheel soon, however, came limping up and rejoined the two travellers in whose charge the horse had been left. While assuring them all that I was certain the tiger was hit, for he threw up his head in the air on my firing, we heard a crashing and panting noise among the bushes; this caused us all to instantly take to our heels, but the panic was soon over on someone calling out that it was only the dog. After debating some time the two Bheels agreed to return with me to recover my rifle; and very cautiously we went, half expecting to meet the tiger at every step. At length I found and quickly reloaded the rifle: and was about to return

Captain W. Rice.

94

when the thought occurred to me to see if there was any blood about the spot where I fired at the tiger. Scarcely had we gone half a dozen paces when to my great astonishment and delight I saw the tiger lying quite dead: the bullet, without entering his skull, had grazed the extreme tip of it, leaving a long wound more like a cut from an axe than a ball. This tiger measured eleven feet six inches and was very stout ... "Wull" by his loud barking had evidently confused and turned back the tiger on us. For years afterwards until it was quite worn out I used the skin as a cover for my bed – sleeping on, instead of inside it, as so easily might have been the case but for such a wonderfully lucky shot ...'

Rice himself subsequently wrote: 'The book called *Tiger Shooting in India* referred to sport obtained in the Rajpootana districts while stationed with the 25th Bombay Native Infantry from 1850–54. Before and in those days tigers were almost invariable looked for and shot from ... elephants ...

'Not being able to afford the cost of elephants and finding the country from its hilly nature would admit in almost all cases of hunting tigers on foot, the author then made the attempt with tolerable success. Since those times, thanks to the wonderful improvements in firearms – shooting every sort of game on foot has become quite the fashion, so it is hoped these pages may help to show the young sportsman how elephants may be dispensed with in many places ...

'Starting at first alone on these hunting expeditions and afterwards being joined at intervals by one or more friends, the bag made during these trips consisted of 68 tigers killed and thirty wounded: seven panthers killed and wounded: and fifty one bears killed and wounded – grand total one hundred and fifty six head of large game killed and wounded.

'N.B All the measurements recorded of tigers &c were taken after the skins had been pegged down, being well stretched in so doing; but great pains were taken to insure these skins presenting their proper relative breadth as well as length; and it will be found that when thus fairly pegged out not much can be added to a skin; but as some doubt has been expressed as to the extraordinary length of many of the tigers mentioned in the aforesaid book it maybe as well to state that several animals seemingly far larger than any killed were seen at close distances and escaped wounded or otherwise.'

He quoted from the *Bombay Gazette* of 19th July 1873, in which a Colonel Beresford wrote, 'I have measured many tigers and though I should say that on an average ten foot six for a male and nine foot eight inches for a female is about the mark I do not agree with those who say that anything over eleven feet is a stretch of imagination ... I myself shot a tiger in 1862 whom I measured as he lay on the ground at twelve feet four inches: that skin was NEVER stretched ... it then measured twelve feet four inches and that skin in England at the moment measures eleven feet six inches. On my subsequently mentioning the subject to some famous Bheel hunters they at once remarked, "Why not? Are all men the same size?"'

With his friend Lt. Little, Rice was told of a bullock-slaying tiger and continued: 'We were taken to a ravine . . . and had taken up our position on a rocky ledge . . . We cautiously advanced and looking over the steep bank of the ravine saw the tiger stretched out at full length just three yards or less below us. He looked up and grinned horribly: we instantly gave him a bullet each, whereupon he sprang into the cover below and was out of sight even before we could get a second shot. On going down the bank we soon found drops of blood and easily carried these on for some distance down the ravine [when] suddenly a man pointed to a cave formed by a large ledge of rock. We knew his meaning . . . All the men as usual were at once ordered to a safe distance in the rear, while, placing our spare guns before us, we knelt down to polish off this tiger at an unpleasantly close distance: for we were prevented by the very steep bank behind us from going further back and a view could not be obtained from any other point. As it was, all we could make out were the tiger's *two eyes* shining very clearly in the dark cave with an indistinct outline of his face. We silently agreed to fire together on the word "one", "two", "three" being given by one of us. On the smoke clearing away we were delighted to see our foe stretched out stiff on his back, the white of his belly being uppermost and very visible.

'On going closer, we saw two small holes, one over each eyebrow, from which streams of blood trickled down, causing us to congratulate each other on our good aim. We could now see that the cave was very spacious inside although it had but a very small entrance.

'Whilst talking over our lucky shots we observed one of the tiger's arms move slightly, but as if from some muscular spasm . . . On noting this I suggested that another shot should be given to make sure, but Little slightly objected on the ground that it was unnecessarily spoiling the skin. On this I agreed to fire where our knives would be used in taking off the victim's jacket, so at once . . . without putting my gun to my shoulder I placed it opposite the tiger's chest and fired the remaining loaded barrel . . . No sooner had I fired than, with a frightful roar, up jumped the tiger as lively as ever! With one bound Little, who is remarkably strong and active, gained the top of the high ledge of rock that formed the tiger's cave. For my own part in the most dreadful state of alarm I at once rushed through the men who had now come up and were crowding round us, upsetting three or four and myself in so doing. For the moment there was a dreadful panic . . . everybody seemed to fall over and trip up everybody else . . . All this time the tiger was roaring awfully. I fully believed he was outside the cave killing each man as he caught them; instead of which, being much confused, he luckily remained in the den round and round which he kept walking, seemingly without being able to find his way out. At last, on gaining my legs, I snatched up a gun and climbed up a small thin tree just in front of the den . . . From this point I fired twelve more shots at only so many yards distance into this tiger before he was quiet . . .

Captain Shakespeare, a contemporary of Rice.

'All now being still we came down from our high posts and this time found the beast really dead, riddled with balls . . .

'This was the most extraordinary and lucky escape for all of us . . . This little adventure served as a good caution to us never to fear making holes in a beast's skin to fully ascertain whether he was dead or not. This tiger was a very large old one . . .'

Having finally attained the rank of Major General, William Rice wrote a second book entitled, all-embracingly, *Indian Game (From Quail to Tiger)*, published in 1884. In this second book he is not quite so ingenuous as in his first attempt at authorship, although he does include, almost verbatim, many of his previous accounts of tiger shooting, from which it may perhaps be deduced that he had not shot many since, on foot or otherwise. On the whole, his second book seems to bear evidence of more polished editing than his first. It covers, of course, a much wider scope and is well illustrated. He included in it chapters on Small Game and Wildfowl shooting, Blackbuck shooting and Hog hunting, also mention of Cheetal, Panther, Bear, Sambar and Bison, as well as Lions and Tigers. He noted particularly: 'A native officer . . . has shot an immense number of lions in the vast "Sheer Forest" . . . He computed there were not above three hundred lions left altogether in that country . . .' The one animal Rice apparently overlooked is rhinoceros, of which there is no mention. In at least one instance, however, it is noticeable that the length of one tiger mentioned in his first book has been increased by a further six inches in his second – from eleven feet three inches to eleven feet nine inches. Even allowing for editorial interference, this does indicate a degree of carelessness on Rice's part. Nevertheless, he deserves a place amongst the big-game hunters of his day, if only for having survived.

Alexander Airlie Angus Kinloch 1838–1919

From Lieutenant to Brigadier, Mostly on Sporting Furlough

I had hoped at one time to bag every sort of 'Large Game' to be
found in the continent of India and to make my book a complete
guide to the sportsmen . . .

Alexander Airlie Angus Kinloch was born in 1838 at Logie, the family estate of 2,000 acres near Kirriemuir in Angus, and joined the King's Royal Rifle Corps in 1858 as a Lieutenant. During the Afghan War in 1867 he was promoted to Deputy Assistant Quartermaster General and was mentioned in despatches. In 1895 he retired as a Brigadier with the honorary rank of Major General. His hobbies, throughout his life, were shooting, fishing and falconry. In pursuit of these he appears to have been particularly expert in obtaining leave of absence from his military duties in India. He wrote three books, all with virtually the same title. The first, *Large Game Shooting in Thibet and the North West*, was published in 1869 while he was still a Major. The second, with the same title, but much enlarged, was published in 1876 when he was a Colonel. The final version, an encapsulation of his lifetime's interest, was entitled *Large Game Shooting in Thibet, the Himalayas, North West and Central India*, and was published in 1892 when he was a Brigadier.

He wrote, resignedly, in the Introduction to his final comprehensive volume on shooting in India: 'I had hoped at one time to bag every sort of "Large Game" to be found on the continent of India and to make my book a complete guide to the sportsmen of all three Presidencies. As, however, I see no immediate prospect of my ambition being gratified I have restricted the scope of my work and confined myself to Northern and Central India.'

He continued, mirroring familiar views: 'The love of the chase is an instinct which centuries of civilisation have been unable to eradicate . . . That this instinct like most of the promptings of healthy Nature is a pretty safe guide to follow is generally admitted; and there are few who question the advantages to be derived from field sports: but it will be found that the professors of such doctrines have very peculiar views on other subjects and seem to make it the business of their lives to prove that the world has been going on the wrong system and that they have fortunately been born to set it right. If they had their own way men would become effeminate and women would lose much that now gives dignity and charm to their sex.

'So general is the instinct which leads to the love of the chase in its many forms that it may almost be said to be universal . . .'

He then, rather hesitantly, voiced doubts which many keen sportsmen were expressing in the late Victorian period regarding the craze for record bags: 'It is unnecessary to write in defence of field sports . . . but it must be admitted that of late years there has been some foundation for the assertion that many men shoot for the love of slaughter and not for healthy excitement.

'Without going into the question whether the battue system as usually conducted is or is not a high form of sport, nothing can possibly be said in favour of the practice of turning down pheasants and even hares and rabbits, the day before a grand shooting party. It is hard to imagine what pleasure anyone can find in butchering animals under such circumstances and the introduction of the system can only be attributed to a vulgar and childish desire to show a long list of the slain at the end of the day and obtain the cheap (in one sense only) notoriety of the heaviest bag of the season . . .'

He was able, however, to enthuse about sport in India with a clear conscience: 'In India not only is the game varied but the scenes among which it may be hunted are equally so. The sportsman may hunt the mighty Elephant or Gaor among the splendid sub-Himalayan forests: rouse the Rhinoceros and Buffalo from their muddy lairs in the dense reeds on the banks of the Brahmaputra; gallop his Arab at speed over the rocky soil of the Deccan in hot pursuit of the grey Boar: stalk the Ibex and Markhur among the precipices of the pine-clad mountains surrounding the Happy Valley; invade the solitudes of Thibet in the hopes of adding to his trophies the massive head of the shaggy Yak or the ever-watchful Nyar; or content himself by riding quietly Express rifle in hand over the cultivated plains of the North West and bringing to bag many a graceful Black Buck and Gazelle . . .

'During many years residence in India I have been fortunate enough to enjoy a large share of leave; most of it has been spent travelling and shooting . . . There is hardly an animal whose habitat I have not visited, which I have not met with: and there are very few which I have not shot. I have seldom made, or indeed tried for, large bags. Travelling generally alone, after obtaining one or two good specimens of any animal I have usually given up its pursuit and set out in search of some other species only to be found perhaps at the distance of many marches. My journal then, if given entire, would often be very tedious, days of sport occurring only now and then during weeks of dreary marching; so I have thought it better merely to make extracts from my diary which was usually written every night.

'One merit at least I may claim for my work – that is truthfulness; the descriptions are as accurate as I can make them and I have in no instance drawn on my imagination for the sake of adding to the interest of my anecdotes . . .'

He then went on to take a sideways swipe at his critics and also expound on the ease of travel in India: 'When my first volume appeared one of my critics was good enough to say that my rifle was my "better half." Since then I have made two more expeditions into Thibet and . . . I was accompanied everywhere by my wife. I mention this in order to show that the difficulties in travelling in remote districts are not so insurmountable as is generally supposed and that any lady who enjoys a little adventure may accompany her husband if she can only make up her mind to undergo a certain amount of "roughing it." I need hardly say, however, that she must be a good walker and rider and possessed of the "pluck" in which English ladies seldom fail.

'My wife crossed some of the highest passes in the Himalayas and traversed certainly the very worst paths without any serious inconvenience. In Thibet she generally rode a Yak, which although slow is more sure-footed than a pony and not so apt to go lame on stony ground. In the lower hills when she did not walk she travelled in a "dandi" which may be best described as a small hammock slung to a pole and carried by four men. A short walking dress of soft Kashmir woollen stuff with loose pantaloons of the same material tucked into brown "Elcho" boots, is the best costume for a lady, who is then equally equipped for riding, walking, or climbing. A soft grey felt "Terai" hat with a good thick "pagri" is the best head-dress: while a mask, or thick veil, is absolutely necessary to preserve the complexion from the cold dry wind and burning sun . . .'

Having completed his introduction, Kinloch wrote judicially on the subject of the tiger: '. . . the different methods of shooting Tigers viz: from the backs of Elephants, from platforms and on foot – by beating, driving, or watching, have been written about a hundred times . . . there are times when shooting off Elephants is not *merely* the *safest* but the *only* way in which a Tiger could possibly be brought to bag, so, on the other hand, there are places where Elephants cannot go, yet Tigers may be shot on foot with but little risk. Even the usually despised plan of sitting in a tree over "a kill" may be the only possible way of getting a shot; and tedious as this undoubtedly is the man who is a naturalist as well as a sportsman will find much to interest him during his solitary watch. I say *solitary* advisedly for no one who does not wish to have his labour for nothing will ever permit a native to sit with him. I have never yet seen the native who could keep quite still and absolutely silent. All that I have met with would either become excited, or fidget, or cough, or talk, or go to sleep and snore.

'In the Terai the only way of shooting Tigers is off Elephants; shooting them on foot is simply impossible: the grass is so high that the Tiger could not be seen. Those who have shot Tiger on foot in the Bombay Presidency and other parts where Tigers are driven out of nullahs may disparage the Terai shooting, but the nature of the countries is so different that it is impossible to apply the same rules to both. Some will decry all Tiger shooting on foot as foolhardiness and others will compare Tiger shooting off an Elephant to "shooting a

Alexander A. A. Kinloch.

mad dog from the top of an omnibus.'' I can speak with no authority on the subject, never having had the opportunity of shooting a Tiger on foot with the exception of one wounded one . . . I think however there is little doubt that Tiger shooting on foot may be carried out with very little risk in favourable localities if properly conducted as described by Major General Rice in his most interesting book. For my own part I should not have the slightest hesitation in firing at a Tiger if he were going away from me, or if I had the advantage of being above him or behind a tree: but I think that no one who values his life should walk up to a Tiger which is expecting him, however confident he may be in his own shooting. Everyone has heard how Tigers which have been mortally wounded have struck down men in their dying agonies: and almost every year some fatal accident occurs to add to the warnings, but they are still too often unheeded . . . though men are to be found who have made a practice of stalking Tigers on foot, still more have paid the penalty for their rashness, and those who survive will usually *be among the first to point out the danger.* The crushing power of a Tiger is irresistible . . . if he *does* charge home death is nearly inevitable. With other animals this is not the case: the

101

THE BIG GAME HUNTERS

Elephant or the Gaor may be dodged or avoided; while, however unpleasant, a "rough and tumble" with Bear, Panther, or Pig is by no means necessarily ... fatal...'

In 1865 riding by himself on an elephant he recorded: 'Going over a nearly bare and most unlikely looking plain I had sat down in the howdah when ... a Tigress suddenly sprang up ... but soon brought up in a clump of grass. I went after her and found her ready for a spring. I fired and her head dropped between her fore-paws. Seeing a wound in the nape of her neck and the blood streaming over her face I thought she was done for, so would not give her another bullet, but went in search of men to assist in padding her. Having taken off the howdah, I returned on the pad and was surprised to find that the Tigress had moved into the grass. I felt sure she was past doing mischief: so, as I was anxious not to spoil her skin, I slipped off the Elephant and walked into the grass. I found the Tigress sitting up but evidently quite stupid, so I fired a bullet into her chest from a distance of two or three yards. She dropped to this and we pulled her out by the tail. After some minutes as she still continued to breathe, I fired a bullet with a small charge of powder into her chest and thought for a moment that I had finished her: to my astonishment, however, she got on her legs and began to crawl away, creating a panic among the bystanders. This would not do! So I had to shoot her through the heart. I then found that the wound in her neck was an old sore occasioned by fighting: my first bullet had struck below the eye, merely splintering the bone and had gone out again without doing much harm: it had luckily stunned her. We now padded her and took her home...'

He was certainly not afraid to chronicle his mistakes, with a view to ensuring that others did not repeat them. He recorded another occasion when he shot a panther and made many errors of judgment: 'In 1882 ... I saw a Panther galloping across the open plain ... [It disappeared] among some tufts of grass which formed the only cover ... for a considerable distance. Riding my Elephant up to these tufts I commenced examining them closely. They were much scattered and none of them seemed large enough to hide a peafowl ... I felt confident I could make out the spotted skin of the Panther. So certain was I that I at length fired into the tuft from a distance of about twenty yards ... but there was not a movement or sign of any animal. In another moment I again found that I could see spots and a still more careful scrutiny showed me the heaving flanks of the Panther. He was evidently untouched, so I fired for his spine and this time there was no mistake. He bounded out with a roar and cantered slowly across a strip of meadow, making an angry demonstration against my pad Elephant. He was much too crippled to do harm however and he soon lay down and finally rolled over on his side, apparently nearly at his last gasp. I was unwilling to spoil his skin by giving him another shot, so I dismounted and standing close to him told my Shikari to finish him off with a blow on the head with a thick stick. On being struck the Panther gave an angry growl and struck at me with his claws, but his hindquarters being paralysed he was unable to spring at me. He was so close, however, and his attack was so sudden that I fired from my hip, smashing his shoulder to pieces and singeing his fur. This effectively settled him.

'One cannot be too careful when approaching dying animals: many lives have been lost by neglecting the most ordinary precautions . . .'

He went on to underline some of the mistakes he had observed being made by 'would-be sportsmen': 'I trust that my work may be of use to real sportsmen; and . . . I would express an earnest hope that those who may be induced by these photographs and descriptions to visit the distant lands where these noble animals are to be found will enjoy good sport as long as they follow their pursuit as true sportsmen. This I am sorry to say has *not* always been the case. Too many instances have occurred of late years of "would-be sportsmen" becoming disgusted with the hard work and (being ashamed to come back empty-handed) employing their Shikaris to shoot game for them: all thus obtained being counted in the bag.

'This is not the only harm done; rifles, guns and ammunition have been given to Shikaris – sometimes I fear in payment of wages – and they are consequently enabled and encouraged to kill game during the winter. The heads thus obtained unfortunately find a ready market, being bought in large numbers and at long prices by the numerous tourists who nowadays visit Kashmir. Happily recent legislation has put a stop to this . . . A third evil is that of shooting females and young ones to swell the *numbers* of the bag.

'All these practices I consider highly unsportsmanlike. Those who give guns and ammunition to natives may consider themselves very generous; but it is a selfish generosity at the expense of real sportsmen. No native – or not one in one hundred – shoots for sport and it would be far better to give a man who had done good service a handsome present in rupees than to furnish him with the means of destroying a quantity of game and ruining the prospects of future sportsmen . . .'

Although, unlike Rice, Kinloch mentioned shooting rhinoceros, it is significant, having regard to his comments that he noted at one point: 'The Lion, I fear, is extinct, or very nearly so . . .'

Ever ready to offer advice to the less experienced, he urged them to appreciate the difficulties before starting out: 'Patience and perseverance are absolute essentials if success is to be obtained. Some men seem to expect to find "Large Game" as easily as they would find hares and pheasants at home and become disgusted if they are not constantly firing off their rifles.

'Such men had better not attempt Himalayan shooting for they will inevitably be disappointed. There is still abundance of game in the Himalayas but it is not to be obtained without hard work.'

He echoed Forsyth's views on the attitudes of the native villagers: 'In many places the natives will deny the existence of game and will tell any number

A drawing of G. P. Sanderson, a contemporary of Kinloch, with a bison,
India, 1870.

of lies to induce the traveller to leave their village and go to some other one,
where they assure him that he will obtain excellent sport . . .

'This anxiety to get rid of sportsmen is partly caused by the unwillingness
of the people to furnish the supplies required by travellers: but I fear that
it is partly to be attributed to the conduct of Englishmen who have thrashed
or abused villagers for not showing game when they were doing their best.
It is therefore always advisable to be as independent as possible of the products
of the country and to limit one's requirements to absolute neccessities . . .

'In almost every village at least one man may be found who does a little
hunting on his own account; and if you make friends with him and administer
a little judicious ''bakshish'' when he shows you sport, he will generally do
his best for you.

'Shepherds usually make the best Shikaris and even if they are not professional hunters, their knowledge of the country makes them valuable as
guides.

'The professional Shikaris who hover about hill stations and the still more numerous *soi-disant* Shikaris to be met with in Kashmir are to be looked on with the greatest suspicion. The later especially are generally arrant imposters and rogues, who know little or nothing about "Shikar." '

He ended by giving his own eleven Commandments, prefacing them thus: 'In conclusion I venture to give a few hints which though superfluous to experienced sportsmen . . . may be useful to those who are beginners in the arts of rifle shooting and stalking . . .'

1

Never give a loaded rifle to a native if you can possibly help it. Now that breechloaders are in universal use, it can seldom be necessary to do so, except when in pursuit of dangerous animals.

2

Do not have 'safety bolts' on your rifles; they are extremely dangerous and have been the cause of fatal accidents. You can load and unload a breechloader nearly as quickly as you can adjust the catches which are moreover apt to get out of order.

3

Never walk through jungle where Tigers and other dangerous beasts are known to exist without a loaded gun or rifle in your hand.

4

Do not become careless because you do not find game at once: the best chances nearly always come when you least expect them.

5

Make *sure* of easy shots. This is the grand secret of making a bag.

6

Never fire long shots. You frighten away far more than you kill: have patience and you will get your game in time. Shots should seldom be fired at a longer range than one hundred and fifty yards.

7

Always walk slowly and often sit down and look about you.

8

Avoid showing yourself against the sky line.

9

Be as silent as possible and insist on your attendants being the same.

10

Always consider the direction of the wind when hunting either in the hills or jungles.

11

Always take plenty of ammunition and carry a large knife in your belt: you *may* never want it, but the time *might* come when your life could depend upon it.

The General, unfortunately, was so enamoured of his beloved Thibet that he was persuaded to invest heavily in a concern called The Trans-China Thibetan Transport Company and his Scottish estate near Kirriemuir was one of the casualties. His grandson, Colonel Bruce Kinloch, himself a Ghurka officer and with his inherited genes a well known African Game Warden and author, recalls his grandfather well. The last of a military species now extinct, he used the army unmercifully to achieve his ends as a big game hunter. He died aged eight-one in 1919.

5

LATE VICTORIAN SPORTSMEN
IN AFRICA

Arthur Henry Neumann 1850–1907

Frederick Courteney Selous 1851–1916

Arthur H. Neumann facing a elephant. A drawing by J. G. Millais.

Arthur Henry Neumann 1850–1907

Africa 1868–1907

Sensitive Introverted Elephant Hunter

> *. . . there is . . . always when you go for them in earnest . . . a*
> *considerable amount of risk about the business . . . I always feel*
> *when I get back to camp, 'Safely through another day' . . .*

Arthur Neumann, son of the incumbent, was born at Hockliffe Rectory in Bedfordshire on 12th June 1850. At the age of eighteen he set out to work as a coffee planter in Natal and a year later was joined by his brother Charles. They subsequently diversified into tobacco and cotton but the venture does not seem to have prospered, for later they tried gold-digging in the Transvaal. By the end of ten years, during which it seems likely his father died and he became financially independent, Arthur had established a trading post in Swaziland, where he learned to speak the language and maintained friendly relations with the Swazi King, Ubandeni.

He spent much of his time shooting in Swaziland and the Transvaal until the outbreak of the Zulu War in 1879 when he was made a Captain in one of the native contingents, but later joined the Swaziland police under Captain MacLeod of the 71st Highlanders. As the native interpreter he was invaluable for his understanding of the native mentality and approach. This was well tested when a message arrived with the news that the Zulu army had overwhelmed a British force at Isandhlwana and massacred it. They were urged to see that Ubandeni did not learn of this, but MacLeod and Neumann knew that the Swazis would soon have the news anyway and that the soundest course, even if it put their own lives at risk, was to tell him the news. In doing so, they assured him that the eventual overthrow of the Zulu army was inevitable.

King Ubandeni wisely waited for more information, and on learning that it had taken the entire Zulu army to destroy a small British force, promptly joined with the British and fought on their side both then and in the subsequent Basuto War.

In 1880 Neumann again joined forces with his brother Charles, farming near Maritzburg, but for the next ten years spent much of his time hunting in the Limpopo and Sabi river areas, as well as exploring the possibilities of the new colony being founded in British East Africa. In 1890 he joined the East African

Company at Mombasa to prospect a route for the projected railway to the Victoria Nyanza, through the hostile Masai country.

The expedition successfully found a route for the railway, though Neumann was wounded in the arm on one occasion by a Masai spear when attacked in camp. Subsequently he was offered the post of magistrate in Zululand. This regular and tedious existence did not suit his roving temperament and within a year he had sickened of it. In 1893 he organised his first elephant hunting expedition from Mombasa. He spent the next three years in the then totally unknown interior around Mount Kenya and the Lorogi Mountains. He encountered his first elephants in 1894 and from then on was fairly successful, on one occasion killing eleven elephants in one day, including three rights and lefts.

In 1894 he explored the then unknown Lake Rudolf, believing himself to be the first to discover the area. It was a considerable disappointment to him later to find that Count Teleki had just beaten him to it and had already described the Lake. In 1896 he was charged by an enraged cow elephant when his Lee-Mitford .303 missed fire. She crushed his ribs very badly with her head and his faithful native followers carried him back to camp where he lay for two months living on a diet of milk, which fortunately for him was available. It was a full three months before he was fit again.

It was after this expedition that he described these wanderings in his book *Elephant Hunting in East Equatorial Africa*, published in 1898 and dedicated to his old friend MacLeod of Macleod. His account of the incident with the cow elephant which chased and gored him is vividly portrayed in his book: '. . . she came for me at a rush . . . I . . . threw up my rifle . . . The click of the striker was the only result of pulling the trigger . . . I saw at once that my case was well-nigh hopeless. The enraged elephant was . . . within a few strides of me; the narrow path was walled in one each side by thick scrub. To turn and run down the path in an instinctive effort was all I could do . . . She was now all but on me. Dropping the gun I sprang . . . to the right and threw myself down among some brushwood . . . But . . . turning like a terrier after a rabbit, she was on top of me as soon as I was down . . . I lay . . . face upwards . . . Kneeling over me (but fortunately not touching me with her legs, which must, I suppose, have been each side of mine), she made three distinct lunges at me, sending her left tusk through the biceps of my right arm and stabbing me between the right ribs, at the same time pounding my chest with her head . . . and crushing my ribs on the same side . . . What hurt me was the grinding my chest underwent . . . she then left me and went on her way . . . Though several of my ribs were broken, no limb was fractured . . . the tusk had neither severed the artery of my arm, nor penetrated my lungs . . . I had every reason to feel thankful for having got off so easily. In following this pursuit one must reckon with the risks . . . if one only keeps on at it long enough sooner or later one is bound to be caught . . . It was the fortune of war . . . For weeks I hardly slept and it was two months before I could lie in any position except on my back . . . Still the healing process went on gradually.'

In his book which at times reads very much like extracts from his diary, he chronicled the death of his favourite little terrier, Frolic, who died from a baboon bite which poisoned her system. He wrote: 'Faithful lovable little dog! I don't think I could have felt the loss of a human companion more. I felt at least her life with me had been a happy one. I buried her with my own hands by moonlight; and as I laid her in her little grave I almost wished I could rest beside her in the quiet bush by the roaring cool river. A sad, sad day.'

He also chronicled a narrow escape from an extremely venomous puff-adder thus: '. . . something that looked like a toad caught my eye beside my boot. Thinking I had inadvertently trodden on a harmless reptile, I was about to move my foot back in compassion, when I noticed a black forked-looking tongue darting viciously close to my right foot and looking more carefully saw that what I at first took for a toad was in reality the villainous triangular head of a large puff adder on whose neck I had set my foot, its body swollen out as big as my thigh. By so providential a chance had I held it fast in this way so that it could not move its head to strike. Having my rook rifle by me I put a bullet through its brain. It measured 4 feet 8 inches long . . .'

In his book he frequently mentions killing large numbers of elephants in a hunt; on one occasion, for instance, fourteen, and on another eleven. His claims seem to have been a source of much ill-informed and unjust criticism of his book which hurt him deeply, but it is an obviously truthful account of his journeying and hunting. It is difficult to ask for more.

It was soon after his book was published that he first met John Guille Millais, who became a close friend and described Neumann as 'a man of extremely shy, hypersensitive nature and subject to alternate fits of gaiety or depression, but when happy was of such a charming, lovable temperament that his society was a continuous pleasure . . . In later years he imagined that nearly everyone disliked him, and his obsession grew upon him to such an extent that he avoided all intercourse with people who were often most anxious to be kind to him.'

In 1899 he volunteered for the mounted infantry in South Africa serving throughout the Boer War and returning to Mount Kenya country in 1902. By this time he had long discarded the untrustworthy Lee-Mitford rifle and had been using a .577 by Gibbs and a double ten-bore by Holland and Holland. He now changed over to a .450 by Rigby and smaller .256 Mannlicher; these he found absolutely perfect. He used the .256 Mannlicher for everything but elephants, his only criticism being that it 'gets so hot after two double shots in quick succession that if one were not obliged to do so in self-defence one could not hold it . . . two would be the right thing: then one's gun bearer would act as loader, and one might often score an extra elephant or two by the gain of time, and even be safer in an emergency.'

In a letter to Millais after one of his infrequent visits to England he wrote: 'I often think of our last meeting at Ward's shoot . . . the leading impressions left on my mind from that visit were: first, the failure of that old brute of a butler to bring me my early morning cup of tea in my bedroom in the morning, by reason of which I (being an old crank much addicted to my own habits) was more or less upset for the whole day: second, being dragged off for a beastly walk on the Sunday, when I would much rather have pottered round with you and Selous: third, my envying Selous going off with you in the afternoon. As I am situated I don't care for England. I feel generally like a hunted fox in a strange country there, and now I never hanker after it the least bit . . .'

Subsequently he described his attitude to elephant hunting in the following very honest and revealing terms: 'I take but damned little interest nowadays in shooting any other beast but the elephant: but him I worship . . . Nothing else thrills me, but the spell of the elephant is as potent as ever . . .'

He described a hunt thus: 'There was no particular excitement – nothing much beyond the average, I mean: though there is, I truly tell you, always when you go for them in earnest, and not merely to pick off an old straggler

Arthur H. Neumann.

112

when the opportunity offers, a considerable amount of risk about the business. I always feel when I get back to camp, "Safely through another day." The last time I got on terms with a herd, after, as I say, many hard and fruitless days and much forebearance, through a reluctance to shoot anything not of good weight, I felt desperate and said to myself: "Well, I mean to get some today anyhow; the best I can, of course, but I *must* go for them and get all I can." I went in and I had a hottish time. I killed ten – all small ivory, I regret to say – but I wish some of those superior sportsmen who call one "butcher" and "slaughterer" and other pretty names when expressing (theoretical) opinions on such work could have tried it for once. I make no pretension to being anything but a humble hunter – I rather dislike the title of "sportsman": I never quite know what is meant by it. But as to *butchery* one is just as likely to be made into sausage-meat as the poor little elephants. Several times was I nearly trampled on: and whether accidently or malice prepense would make but little difference to one's appreciation of the process of being mashed into pulp. But I am more cautious than I used to be, all the same, and try not to run into unnecessary danger. I often think now of the rash way in which I have often behaved in times gone by and wonder that I was not killed over and over again . . .'

Neumann was rated by all who knew him as an extremely brave man. He regarded the elephant as the most dangerous game, but considered the danger to be from outside sources, i.e. vicious cows in the same herd encountered suddenly. Equipped only with a .256 Mannlicher his method was to creep into the centre of a herd and, choosing the best bull, shoot it in the heart, which did not usually kill it immediately and left him open to be charged suddenly by other herd members. When he started to use a .450 Rigby double Express rifle he killed elephants much more easily and was not liable to have so many narrow escapes.

It is clear that he was a genuine hunter, with a total contempt for pretension and for the attitudes epitomised by early hunters such as Harris and Gordon Cumming. He regarded shooting a giraffe, for instance, as totally contemptible. He was, however, clearly an introvert and latterly not far short of a recluse with something approaching a morbid fear of crowds, understandable in a man who had spent most of his life roving free in the wilds.

Like his contemporary, Selous, whose friendship with Millais he envied, he was amongst the last of the transitional hunters who had gone out to an untamed Africa with muzzle loaders and changed over to the breechloader. A true big game hunter although latterly chiefly an elephant hunter, he was by nature a specialist and a one-track minded man. He would not, one feels, have objected to that description.

He continued hunting in 1903 and 1904, but in 1905 new restrictions were enforced in East Africa and in July 1906 he completed his last trip at Mombasa. He was then still apparently planning to return to Kenya and build himself a house there on the slopes of his favourite Mount Kenya. In October, however, he returned to England and contracted severe influenza, which brought on a fit of deep depression. It is sad that he should have died in London at the age of fifty-seven rather than in his own wild Africa.

Millais wrote: 'He was a charming and deep character, but . . . I never knew a more lonely man, or one more suspicious of friendship . . . He was subject to dreadful fits of depression, especially in England, in crowds which seemed to obsess him and to affect him more than they did Fred Selous. Most unfortunately no-one was with him in one of these depressing periods and he shot himself.'

Notes on a contemporary: William Finaughty

Born in 1843, William Finaughty described himself as a harum scarum youth who left Grahamstown at the age of twenty-one in 1864, making his way through the Free State to Matabeland, then ruled by the Zulu king, Chaka's brother, Mzilikatse. The country was then still thick with game, but because of his lack of experience Finaughty only killed three elephants. On another trip in the following year, 1865, he killed more and in 1866 while on what was meant to be a purely trading journey he killed eighteen.

In 1867 on his fourth journey he killed nineteen, but in 1868 he had a wonderful two months when he shot ninety-five elephants with ivory weighing 5,000 pounds. In those days he said the elephants still did not know the meaning of gunfire and in one day he bagged six bulls in a river bed simply because they did not run away at the sound of the shots.

In 1869 he went into elephant country beyond the Tuli, living there for three years and sending his ivory back in the waggons that brought him fresh provisions. In five months he killed fifty-three elephants, providing 3,000 pounds of ivory. In one day he succeeded in killing five bulls and five cows, his best day ever. At this time he had probably shot more elephants than any other man alive, with the possible exception of a few Boer hunters.

It should be borne in mind that he was probably still shooting at that time with a muzzle-loader, even if he went on to a breechloader later on in life. It is interesting to note that he considered buffalo far more dangerous than elephants and from them he recorded many more close escapes. He seems, however, to have given up elephant-hunting latterly and spent the rest of his life as a trader. He was still alive in 1914 on his farm near Bulawayo.

Frederick Courteney Selous 1851–1916

Africa 1871–1894

Amongst the Greatest in and outside Africa

I was pressed down on the ground . . . but luckily behind her forelegs. Dragging myself from under her, I . . . beat a hasty retreat having had rather more than enough of elephants for the time being . . .

Selous was born in London on 31st December 1851. He was sent to a preparatory school at the age of nine, where he appeared to be the bane of the headmaster's life, constantly bird-nesting and trespassing on a neighbour's land. In 1865 he went on to Rugby, by which time he had read Baldwin's book *African Hunting from the Natal to the Zambezi* and was already fired with the ambition to become a big game hunter in Africa. In 1868 he was sent to Switzerland, then to Wiesbaden, to learn French and German and study to become a surgeon, but it was soon obvious this was not the life for him.

On 4th September 1871, aged twenty, he landed at Algoa Bay with £400. From there he went on to the diamond fields at Kimberley, where he unfortunately had a valuable double-barrelled breech-loading rifle stolen, then a serious loss. From there he took a partner on a trading trip up the Vaal and Orange rivers and wrote that '. . . there was no game whatever, not even springbucks, the Kafirs having hunted everything into the far interior, so that now there is more game within five miles of Cape Town than here where we are more than 600 miles up country.'

Selous next set out, with two partners, on the first of his expeditions into the interior. They were indifferently equipped, especially as regards guns, and he bought two 'Roers', the large-bore elephant guns used by the Boers. Cheap but effective, they used trade gunpowder and kicked like mules. Although between 1872 and 1874 he shot seventy-eight elephants with them he wrote that '. . . the punishment I received from these guns has materially affected my nerves to such an extent as to have materially influenced my shooting ever since and I am heartily sorry I ever had anything to do with them . . .'

During this expedition Selous was lost in the bush for a considerable time before finally meeting some friendly Kafirs who fed him milk and water. Of this experience he wrote: 'The next morning as soon as it was light, accompanied by the Kafir who carried my rifle, I made a start and though very tired and worn out from privation, managed to reach the wagons late in the afternoon after an absence of five days and four nights. How I enjoyed the meal that was hastily prepared for me and how delightful it was to keep out the bitter cold with a couple of good blankets . . .'

Although over twenty, when he asked his permission to shoot elephants, Lobengula, the king of the Matebele, was very disparaging about his youthful appearance. When Selous asked where he might go, he answered, 'You may go wherever you like. You are only a boy.'

He had set out with Jan Viljoen, a famous Boer elephant hunter, who in 1867 was reputed to have killed 210 elephants in one expedition with his party, but by chance Selous became separated from him and hunted instead with a Hottentot known as Cigar, also an experienced hunter. This was rough living as Selous indicated: '. . . we had nothing in the provision line but Kafir corn and meat of the animals we shot, washed down by cold water . . . I had but one youngster with me, who carried my blanket and spare ammunition, whilst I shouldered my own old four-bore muzzle-loader and carried besides a bag filled with powder, and a pouch containing twenty four-ounce round bullets. Though this was hardly doing the thing *en grand seigneur* I was young and enthusiastic in those days and trudged along under the now intense heat with a light heart . . .'

By this time, since most of the elephants had to be hunted on foot instead of horseback because of the depredations of the 'tsetse fly', most of the old Boer and English elephant hunters had given up. The distances, dangers and poor results had combined to deter all but the hardiest. Nevertheless, Selous succeeded in obtaining 450 lbs of ivory, which he had shot, and another 1,200 lbs which he traded with the natives, making a profit of £300 on his expedition with the Hottentot, Cigar, of whom he said, 'I do not think I could have had more skilful preceptor . . . he continually allowed me to have the first shot, whilst the elephants were still standing – a great advantage to give me – and never tried in any way to overreach me, or claim animals I had shot as is often done by Boer hunters . . .'

The following year he found a partner named George Wood. Within four months, apart from rhinoceros and buffalo, they had killed 92 elephants; Selous 42 and Wood 50. His adventures were numerous, but a sample will have to suffice. Here he recounts firing at and chasing after a wounded bull elephant which was being escorted away by four attendant cows: '. . . giving my gun back to Nuta to reload, I was running after him . . . when suddenly the trunk of another elephant was whirled round, almost literally above my head, and a short, sharp scream of rage thrilled through me, making the blood tingle down to the very tips of my fingers. It was one of the . . . cows, that had thus lain in wait for me behind a dense patch of bush.

'. . . the only thing I could do was to run . . . I bounded over and through thorn-bushes which in cold blood I would have judged impenetrable, but I

Frederick Courteney Selous, DSO.

was urged on by the short piercing screams which . . . seemed to make the whole air vibrate . . . After a few seconds (for I don't think she pursued me a hundred yards, though it seemed an age) the screaming ceased . . . and it was only when the trumpeting suddenly stopped that I knew I was out of her reach. I was barelegged – as I always am when hunting on foot – and my only garment when the beast charged was a flannel shirt . . . but . . . now . . . my hat, the leather belt that I wore round my waist and about three parts of my shirt had been torn off by the bushes, and I doubt if there was a square inch of skin left uninjured on the front half of my body.'

His adventures on this day were by no means over, for a gun had been accidently double-loaded by a Kafir. He described how a bull elephant charged him, whereupon: 'Taking a good sight for the middle of his shoulder I pulled the trigger . . . the gun went off – it was a four-bore elephant gun, loaded twice over and the powder thrown in each time by a Kafir with his hands – and I went off too! I was lifted clean from the ground . . . whilst the gun was carried yards away over my shoulder . . . I was almost stunned . . . and . . . found I could not lift my right arm . . . I was covered with blood, which spurted from a deep wound under the right cheek-bone . . . The stock . . . was shattered to pieces, and the only wonder was that the barrel did not burst . . . [His gun bearer then came up with the spare rifle] . . . the elephant . . . stood still [and] I went cautiously up within forty yards or so of him . . . Though I could not hold my arm out I could raise the forearm so as get a hold of the trigger: but the shock had so told on me that I found I could not keep the sight within a yard of the right place . . . After a short time . . . my nerves having got a little steadier, I . . . took a quiet pot shot . . .'

Despite the protests of his gunbearer, who was seized with panic, Selous continued: '. . . after bestowing a few Anglo-Saxon idioms upon Nuta, I again ran on . . . About a mile . . . I had now been a long time bare-headed, exposed to the heat of the fierce tropical sun, and the kick I had received from the gun had so much shaken me that I felt dead-beat and could scarcely drag one leg after another . . .'

He then sent his bearer Nuta, a good runner, ahead to turn the elephant by shouting, remaining behind with another native, Balamoya. The elephant was successfully turned and came towards them, but scented them and when the native lost his nerve and ran, it started to charge. Selous wrote: '. . . on came the elephant . . . Though very shaky just before, the imminence of danger braced up my nerves and I think I never held a gun steadier than upon this occasion . . . He came on at an astonishing pace . . . He was perhaps twenty yards off when I pulled the trigger. I aimed a little above the root of the trunk and just between the eyes and directly I fired I ran out sideways as fast as I could, though I had not much running left in me . . . I saw . . . the blood was pouring down his trunk from a wound exactly where I had aimed and . . . I cannot understand why it did not penetrate his brain . . . After standing for a short time he again turned . . . Nuta, seeing what had happened, instead of trying to turn him again . . . came back to me. Perhaps it was as well . . .'

Selous then gave up the chase without having succeeded in bagging a single elephant and it was ten days before he could use his arm again, but these were the sort of hazards he expected. Even so, he found the hunting very indifferent, for towards the end of 1877 he wrote to his father: 'On this side of the river elephant hunting is at an end. I am now going . . . to go down the Zambesi to Tete – a Portuguese settlement . . .'

His journey was dogged by illness and both he and his companions were fever-stricken, so that at one stage he even contemplated trying his luck in North America or Australia. However, things improved and in 1878 with his friends Clarkson and Wood he encountered a large herd of elephants. They killed twenty-two, hunting them until their cartridges and horses were all exhausted, but Selous still had thirteen cartridges left and wrote: 'Having picked out a good cow for my fifth victim I gave her a shot behind the shoulder, on which she turned . . . and walked away . . . As I cantered up behind her she wheeled round . . . My horse was now so tired that he stood well, so . . . I gave her a shot from his back between the neck and the shoulder, which I believe just stopped her from charging . . . she backed a few paces . . . and then stood facing me again. I had just taken out the empty cartridge and was about to put a fresh one in, when, seeing that she looked very vicious, and as I was not thirty yards from her, I caught the bridle and turned the horse's head away . . . in case of a charge. I was still holding my rifle with the breech open when I saw that she was coming . . . Digging the spurs into my horse's ribs I did my best to get him away, but he was so thoroughly done that .. he only started at a walk and was just breaking into a canter when the elephant was upon us. I heard two short sharp screams above my head . . . when, horse and all, I was dashed to the ground . . . I was half-stunned . . . and the first thing I became aware of was a very strong smell of elephant . . . I was . . . pressed down on the ground in such a way that I could not extricate my head . . . with a violent effort I wrenched myself loose . . . and saw the two hindlegs of the elephant standing like two pillars before me . . . She was on her knees, with her head and tusks on the ground and I had been pressed down under her chest, but luckily behind her forelegs. Dragging myself from under her, I regained my feet and beat a hasty retreat, having had rather more than enough of elephants for the time being . . . Almost immediately I had made my escape she got up and started looking for me . . . but never quite wheeling round . . . At length I gained the shelter of a small bush and breathed freely once more . . .'

He recovered his rifle and hunted what he thought was his attacker, killing her with two shots, but it proved to be another beast. Apart from a nasty black eye and the skin removed from much of his chest he escaped more or less unhurt and his horse, although injured, recovered within two months.

The following year, however, two of Selous's close friends were killed within months of each other. Clarkson was killed by lightning and French died of thirst and exhaustion when lost in the bush, hunting an elephant he had wounded. Selous himself ended the year with a very severe attack of fever and at the end of 1879 was close to death himself.

By early 1880, once again completely recovered, he began preparing a big expedition across the Zambesi, but this was prevented owing to lack of official permission to carry sufficient ammunition. He then wrote home indicating that he intended returning to write a book: '. . . for which I may get a little money. I know that people have got good sums for writing bad books on Africa, full of lies, though I do not know if a true book will sell well. My book at any rate will command a large sale out here as I am so well known and have a reputation for speaking nothing but the truth . . .'

Unlike Neumann, Selous had no independent income to rely on and he was often in considerable financial straits, being forced to rely on organising shooting parties for rich clients, the forerunners of later game-hunting safaris. In 1887 for instance, he was employed as a guide and hunter by three rich English

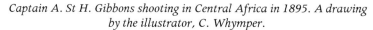

Captain A. St H. Gibbons shooting in Central Africa in 1895. A drawing by the illustrator, C. Whymper.

landowners on a big game hunting expedition. This appears, however, to have been a comparatively rare event.

In 1888 he was on an expedition of his own, deep into the hitherto largely unexplored interior, when they were attacked by treacherous hostile tribesmen. He had a party of some twenty-five native followers and was fairly well equipped, but this did not prevent the tribesmen catching them by surprise in the night. He escaped by himself armed with a rifle, but with only four cartridges, having lost touch with his men, some three hundred miles from friendly territory. He shot a wildebeest for meat the first day, but when he approached a native village his rifle was stolen and an attempt was made to shoot him, although he succeeded in escaping under the cover of darkness. He then threw himself on the mercy of a chief he knew and although his life seems to have been in considerable danger eventually he was re-united with the remnant of his following. He found twelve had been killed and six wounded, while the rest had had narrow escapes. Subsequently he learned that the reason for the attack had been a local chieftain's orders to obtain gunpowder from him, even at the cost of killing him. Despite this very close call Selous was soon planning another journey into unknown regions.

In 1889 and 1890 he was deeply involved with Cecil Rhodes and the British South Africa Company who were trying to occupy Mashunaland, later Rhodesia. The Matebele under Lobengula were opposed to this and Rhodes's original plan was to attack them with a small force, but Selous pointed out the folly and dangers of this, suggesting instead that a road be made passing south-east of the Matebele territory and going due north to the Portuguese frontier.

During 1890 Selous led an expedition which cut a road through the country from Salisbury on through good gold-mining country. Trouble with the Matebele and with the Portuguese was avoided with some difficulty, although some of the Portuguese had to be arrested. Finally Mashunaland was opened up to the British South Africa Company under Cecil Rhodes, but the conception and execution had been entirely the work of Selous. As one Boer officer said before starting, '. . . the expedition without Mr Selous would be like a swarm of bees that has lost its Queen and does not know where to go.' In fact, Rhodes exploited Selous's knowledge of the Mashuna chieftains and his ability to deal with them and promised him a great deal which never materialised. Rhodes himself introduced Selous as 'the man above all others to whom we owe Rhodesia to the British Crown', but compliments come cheap. Rhodes appears to have done precisely nothing for the one man, above all others, who had helped him to acquire the territory which was eventually to bear his name.

In 1893 the Matebele, who had a history of attacking and massacring neighbouring tribes, predictably attacked the white men they saw as invading their territory. Some Matebele, opposed to Lobengula, joined with a force of nearly seven hundred irregular white troops. Selous, acting as the Chief of

121

Scouts, was wounded in the fighting, but Lobengula's rising was soon suppressed.

In 1894 Selous returned to England and married Miss Marie Maddy, daughter of a Gloucester vicar, and after a honeymoon in Europe and Constantinople the newly-married couple set up home in Worplesdon in Surrey. Here Selous had all his vast collection of specimen heads gathered together in a large private museum. Later, in 1894, he went hunting in Asia Minor near Smyrna, where he killed a long-faced red deer. The following year he went after goats and succeeded in securing a good specimen. He was fortunate in his friendship with his publisher, Rowland Ward, for from this stage onwards his work as an author was to provide him with a living which, if not luxurious, at least gave him sufficient for many short trips abroad each year. It was at this stage in his life that his dormant passion for egg collecting, which had been a feature of his youthful school escapades, surfaced again. Each year in April he went to the best places for egg collecting in England, Scotland, Asia Minor, and as far afield as Iceland.

In pursuit of specimens Selous travelled worldwide. In 1897 he bagged his first Wapiti and mule deer in the Big Horn Mountains of North America; in 1900 he hunted moose in Canada and caribou in Newfoundland, where he shot a record forty-pointer stag. Two years later he made a successful hunting trip into British East Africa, his first visit to the area, and in the winter of 1907 he wrote his book *African Nature Notes and Reminiscences,* principally at the instigation of his friend President Theodore Roosevelt, with whom he had long conducted a correspondence. It was published the following year by Macmillan.

In March 1908 'Teddy' Roosevelt told Selous he intended to take a long holiday in Africa as soon as his final term as President was over, and asked him to make all the arrangements for him. From then until the following March Selous was busy preparing and planning for this safari, which the ex-President undertook with his son Kermit as companion. The Presidential safari was an immense success, Selous advising the employment of a notable white hunter named Judd as guide.

Selous himself continued to go on occasional hunting expeditions, or to add to his considerable egg collections, visiting Iceland for this purpose in 1913. Abel Chapman, his companion on this trip, recorded later how he asked him after a ride of eight hours in pouring rain: 'How would you like to dine with me at the Ritz tonight? A little clear soup, a grilled sole, lamb cutlets and green peas, mushrooms on toast and a bottle of Champagne '94?'

'Thanks very much,' Selous replied, 'but if I had my choice of what I should like best, it would be good fat moose and tea.'

Selous's favourite drink, which he far preferred to champagne, was tea. In his early camping days in Africa he always threw a handful of tea leaves into the pot and left it to simmer all day before freshening it with another handful

An incident during C. V. A. Peel's expedition in Somaliland, 1899.

in the evening. It was emphasised that 'the tea-leaves were *never* emptied.'

On the outbreak of the First World War, at the age of sixty-three, he volunteered and was accepted to go to Africa with the rank of Lieutenant. In August 1914 he wrote: 'I believe this war will be a terrific business . . . Freddy (his son) will not be old enough to volunteer until April next, when he will be seventeen and I fully expect that he will be wanted. *If I should be eliminated it will not matter a bit as I have had my day*, but it would be a pity if so promising a boy got scuppered at the outset of his life.'

On 4th February 1915 he was allowed to go to East Africa as Intelligence Officer, despite his age. Subsequently, in a series of actions during which he acquitted himself extremely well, he earned the DSO, but inevitably the end came. Aged sixty-five he was killed in action in 1916 leading his company against the German forces. In 1917 the tragedy he had feared earlier took place when his son Freddy was killed in action as a Captain in the RFC. At least Selous was spared knowledge of the event he had so obviously dreaded. He himself lies buried in the continent for which he had done so much and where he had spent the greater part of his life, leaving a name behind him which is still widely remembered and respected.

6

EDWARDIANS IN AFRICA AND AROUND THE WORLD

John Guille Millais 1865–1931

Theodore Roosevelt 1858–1919

John Guille Millais.

John Guille Millais 1865–1931

Africa 1893–1898 and 1923

Soldier, Sailor, Artist, Zoologist, Author, Wanderer

*I left the army and went off to South Africa . . . I have never
regretted that step I took in . . . 1893 and thirty years of wandering
. . . are my ideal of freedom*

John Guille Millais was born in 1865, the son of the famous artist Sir John
Millais. He was sent to Marlborough at the age of eleven and it was then that
his deeply felt interest in nature first surfaced fully. Like his close friend,
Frederick Selous, he soon became an expert shot with a catapult and began
his collection of British birds and their eggs, one of the many natural history
collections which were to be an enduring feature of his life. At Marlborough
he was constantly in trouble for using his catapult, both as a weapon to kill
birds and in defence against gangs of local boys. For such offences he was
birched no less than four times (then considered a heinous punishment) and
was close to being expelled.

During one of his holidays he went with his parents to stay at the home
of a wealthy eccentric, Mr Reginald Cholmondely at Condover Hall, 'a superb
Elizabethan mansion' in Shropshire. Mr Cholmondely was interested in collecting birds and insects and also kept a private zoo. Taking a liking to the young
Millais and recognising a keen fellow collector who shared his interest in birds,
he invited him to visit Condover Hall whenever he wished during the holidays,
and he appears subsequently to have been a regular guest.

By the time Millais was thirteen he was already an experienced shot with
the fully choked twenty-bore he had been given by his father. It was in those
early days that be began his holiday coastline wanderings, from Dunbar to
the south through to Loch Eriboll in Sutherland, and it was here that he completed most of his bird collection. In 1880 he bought a retriever-collie mongrel
bitch named Jet, which was to be his constant companion for fifteen years,
capable of entering the roughest seas and retrieving any bird he had shot for
his collection. With her as his only companion he wandered the coastline of
Scotland, often spending nights in the open amongst the sand dunes. A great
deal about Millais' upbringing may be inferred from a casual entry in his book
Wanderings and Memories, published in 1919, when he noted: 'My father and
mother were always opposed to these constant absences on my part, but being

good-natured and broad-minded people, and having regard to the fact that I always returned at some time or another, they had got accustomed to my perpetual wanderings and ceased to wonder.

'My usual plan was to go by train to some point on the coast and send my bag forward some thirty miles . . . and then work towards it. Many a day I never reached my dry clothes and extra cartridges, because I had seen some rare visitor at which a shot could not be obtained. Then it meant a night and sometimes two out in the open, until the specimen was bagged or lost. It was rough work for one so young, but I loved the life as only a young naturalist can do . . .'

In 1882 young Millais had finished his first term at Cambridge and was somewhat pleased with himself for having won eighty pounds (then a considerable sum) at live pigeon shooting, still then a very popular pursuit on which large sums were gambled at every meeting. His father was not amused, and it is an interesting sidelight on the changing attitudes of the period that Millais quoted him as saying firmly, 'I will give you anything you like in reason for the sake of sport or your Natural History, but I draw the line at pigeon shooting. It is not a clean game and I won't have you mixed up with that crowd. So give me your promise you will not shoot pigeons again.' Millais added, 'It did not take me long to find out the wisdom of the old man's advice and I have never fired at a tame pigeon since.' Within a little more than two decades by force of public opinion the so-called sport had been banned in Britain.

In 1886 John Millais received his first commission for drawings published in the *Graphic*. He then was sent to a well-known crammer and finally passed into the army, being commissioned into the Scots Guards, thanks to 'the interest of Sir Garnet Wolseley'. He remained in the Scots Guards for only four days, however, and then transferred into the 2nd Battalion of the Seaforth Highlanders. For the next five years he served in this regiment, during which time he published *Game Birds and Shooting Sketches*, the first of the modern books on natural history. In 1892, aged twenty-seven and just short of attaining his captaincy, he left the army against his father's advice and went off to South Africa, where he spent a year hunting in the interior.

From then on Millais led a wandering life, making a number of expeditions around the world, but particularly in Africa, where he shot big game and portrayed the life, both in pictures and in words. He was as talented at written description as he was at depicting the same subject on canvas. He was also, throughout his life, a shot of considerable accuracy, with both rifle and shotgun.

In the latter part of the nineteenth century and in the early years of the twentieth he was friendly with many big game hunters and notables throughout the world. Frederick Selous, with whom he shared many interests, from big game hunting to bird and egg collecting, was a close friend and after he was killed in the First World War Millais wrote an admirable biography of him. Like Selous, he had a son who was killed in the war, although Selous himself was killed in action before the death of his son. Millais also wrote a brief and understanding biography of Arthur Neumann, who was another close big game shooting friend.

Amongst his other such acquaintances Millais included Oswell, whom he clearly regarded as a very fine character, as did all who knew him. More interesting perhaps was his attitude towards C. H. Stigand, whom he also knew quite well. He seems to have held a certain objection to what he clearly felt were Stigand's arrogant attitudes in his books, especially his views on the ease of shooting on the plains, as opposed to shooting in the bush. It is possible that Millais failed to appreciate that Stigand was not a natural writer of easy flowing prose as he was himself, but it seems more likely that the two were simply not compatible.

More interesting, perhaps, were Millais' comments on President Theodore Roosevelt, when he betrayed an artist's loathing of indifferent photography, combined with a sportsman's dislike of pretension. He wrote: 'The only thing I have against Roosevelt, who is a delightful man and a personal friend, is that he has an abominable habit of being photographed with every Zebra and Kongoni he shoots for the pot as if it was some great feat. Personally I loathe these wretched amateur photographs of the successful hunter posing in front of mangled corpses. It is of no earthly use or scientifically instructive and gives no correct representation of the animal . . . I think it is deplorable.'

Just before the war Millais spent a period in East Africa on safari with William Judd, one of the leading 'white' hunters of the day who, with Selous, had made all the arrangements for President Theodore Roosevelt's tour of Africa in 1909. Millais noted: 'It is one of the charms of East African hunting that when you have arrived in camp and possess so excellent a camp manager as Judd you have nothing to do but just to hunt and enjoy yourself . . . when the arrangements of the safari are in the hands of such a thoroughly experienced man, the hunter is relieved of all camp worries and arrangements and can come and go at will. Personally I prefer to hunt alone, with one black follower, so after a hasty meal, as there were yet two or three hours of daylight, I wandered into the bush, accompanied by my gun-bearer, Mabruki, a silent and keen-eyed Wakamba savage, who in his youth had been a cannibal . . . We immediately encountered a great herd of Thomson's gazelle, numbering at least two hundred . . . I made for a high anthill close by . . . Here was Africa untouched and still as prolific as it was a hundred years ago. Man the destroyer has not yet made his mark . . . It was just Africa as we who love the wilds and its game wished to see it . . . Wherever we looked there was game . . . in herds, battalions and individuals, stretching away in thousands over to the billowing uplands. One herd of five hundred Zebra were at the moment emerging from the open forest on our left, and the whole country seemed to be moving with animals attracted by the succulent pasture . . . It was lovely just to sit and watch all these delightful creatures, so quiet and undisturbed that it was evident we were far from the ken of civilisation . . .'

On the other hand he was keen to shoot a lion and noted, 'Few people know how completely nocturnal lions have become in nearly all parts of Africa. It is now possible to live for years in some lion haunted districts and yet never to see a single one in broad daylight. Only a few years ago on the Gwas N'gishu plateau . . . lions could be seen almost any morning returning over the open country to lie up in bush for the day. Nearly all these lions were ridden down and killed and in other parts, especially in forest and bush countries, it is now very rare to see one in broad daylight, except in the very wildest and least frequented places. Lions soon learn it is not safe to be abroad after sun up and make for the dense bush by the rivers, or lie up in dongas, where they are seldom surprised or seen, unless stumbled upon by chance . . .'

Out with Mabruki on another occasion he saw two lionesses about six hundred yards distant and wrote: 'Luckily the lions made for the open park-lands and not towards the river bush which was close at hand, so I set old "Kongoni" on the move at a gentle canter, whilst Mabruki ran alongside me at a good pace with my second gun. My object was to cut off the lions in their advance and bring them to bay, without, if possible, making them too much annoyed, and so get in a quiet shot . . . but as I made a spurt . . . they suddenly threw up their heads and stood looking at me, at the same time uttering two or three angry grunts of disapproval.

'My old horse "Kongoni" though a good enough animal for hunting had no turn of speed and if chased by a lion would certainly have been caught, so I determined to see the rest of the fight out on foot. Wherefore I jumped off and ran forward till within 250 yards of the lions, whose demonstrations now became so alarming that I saw the moment for action had arrived.

'Most unfortunately the ground was covered with longish grass and stunted bush, where I could neither sit, nor lie down, so I was obliged to take my shot from the shoulder, always a bad position for a long shot. Sighting carefully, I saw the bullet strike an ant-heap about two hundred yards beyond the lioness but in a good line, perhaps two or three inches too high. The beast I fired at stood perfectly still . . . I fired again, and this time hit the lioness in the centre of the shoulder. She raised her foreleg, bit it fiercely and then ran about thirty yards, swung round once or twice and fell.

'At this moment I heard the sounds of galloping behind me and knew that Pullar (his companion on the safari) and Judd were coming up at full speed. Glancing towards the second lioness I now saw that she had charged up within 100 yards of me and was lying flat out on the ground, switching her tail from side to side and uttering low growls. I covered her with my sight, but as she was apparently more excited by the advent of the galloping horses and was looking towards them, I thought I would risk her charge and allow Pullar to have the shot, since more than once he had expressed the wish to kill a lion.

'I kept my sight on her chest, however, and must confess that the moment when Pullar to my right jumped off his horse and got into position was a very anxious one. Every moment I thought she would charge, when at last bang went the powerful .416 Rigby and the lioness seemed to be bodily lifted from the ground and placed *hors de combat*, I breathed a sigh of relief, but although done for she still showed fight – the shot was rather low, but had raked her through the stomach. Yet the gallant beast still came on. Pullar's second shot missed and the third laid her out, apparently dead, whilst the fourth caused instantaneous death. In the excitement of the moment both my friend and Judd had a shot at my lioness, which did not seem to require it. I need not describe the joy with which we surveyed our prizes – two full grown lionesses in the prime of life . . . it was splendid that Pullar should have arrived in time to get his first lion . . .'

From his earliest days Millais had been an ardent collector of birds and their eggs and of animal heads and specimens. To him this was entirely natural and he wrote unself-consciously revealing the motives which inspired the trophy hunter: 'I . . . went south in the hope of getting a good head or two of some of the Antelopes. We all wish to get good specimens and this looking for exceptional ones where game is abundant has in itself a great charm, for as numbers are passed in review, it is wonderful how soon one can appreciate the additional inch or two of horn that constitutes the desirable trophy. Record heads are generally obtained by flukes, often without any special skill on the part of the hunter and occur even to the most experienced just once or twice in a lifetime, but when animals are really as abundant as they are here, it is necessary to be selective and not shoot at any beast that just for the moment seems to carry good horns. There are hundreds of most of the common kinds, and as we look them over with the glass and at last see that one individual with an exceptional trophy, it is our object to kill him, even if it takes all day to do so . . .'

This was his last visit to Africa before the outbreak of the First World War. Millais appears to have spent much of the war as consul in Norway, being at forty-nine too old for active service. His work, however, seems to have been connected with Counter-Intelligence and he rated the rank of Commander in the Navy. The Germans had a lot of spies and sympathisers in Scandinavia and his post was clearly of some importance since on several occasions the Germans attempted to capture him. A U-boat once stopped and searched a ship on which he was thought to be travelling, but he had given them the slip by deliberately feeding false information on his movements to a German spy.

As a writer, Millais is probably best remembered for his book *A Breath from the Veldt*, published in 1899, describing his early experiences in Africa and providing a splendidly evocative picture of this period in text and illustrations. In 1919 he published his rather charming book of wide-ranging reminiscences entitled *Wanderings and Memories*. Finally, in 1924 he published *Far Away and Up the Nile*, an account of a journey up the Nile with his son, Raoul, which again has many of his illustrations and is a very good descriptive account of a big game hunting safari. As an artist, observer and naturalist, as well as big game hunter, Millais was amongst the foremost of his generation. After the war he lived mainly in peaceful retirement in the country and died in 1931 at the age of sixty-six.

Notes on two contemporaries:
Abel Chapman and Harold Frank Wallace

Millais' friend and contemporary, Abel Chapman, was another observer naturalist, keen ornithologist and artist, who also hunted big game. He was, however, a wealthy man and *bon vivant*, owning a sizeable estate in Northumberland. A friend of Selous, he made several ornithological expeditions with him to North America. Although quite prepared to rough it with the best, his idea of iron rations was more inclined towards a half bottle of champagne than Selous's rather more basic desire for a cup of strong tea. He wrote a book

Abel Chapman in Kenya, 1906.

on shooting in the Sudan published in 1921, entitled *Savage Sudan*, the first on the subject since Samuel White Baker. His other book on big game hunting in British East Africa was written earlier in 1908, entitled *On Safari*. One extract from this will suffice to indicate the changes which took place in the decades which followed. He had reached Nairobi ill with malaria, and was staying at 'Nairobi's single wood-built hotel' when he wrote: 'Meanwhile, within an hour's walk of the town, my brother Walter had found abundant game — hartebeests and zebra, gazelles, ostrich, cranes and bustard and had already opened our score. But, so soon as the crisis of the fever had passed, he left me and went on alone with the "Safari" — as a mobilised hunting expedition is called; for it was obviously inadvisable to keep a crowd of between forty and fifty "boys" idle among the many temptations of Nairobi.

'In Equatoria, it should be explained, there is none of that monotonous "trekking-in" by ox-waggon that characterised South African hunting . . . Here the terror of the tsetse-fly has eliminated all that, and transport, away from the railway, is entirely effected upon the heads of native porters. Thence springs the genesis of the "Safari".'

With an eye for nature and bird life Abel Chapman, like Millais, never shot to excess, but contented himself with reasonable specimens of each type of game. Today, however, the name of Abel Chapman is probably much more widely associated with wildfowling, not only because of his well illustrated book *The Art of Wildfowling*, but also because he was one of the foremost exponents of his day, being amongst the moving forces behind the formation of the Wildfowlers Association of Great Britain and Ireland, better known today by its modern title of the British Association for Conservation and Shooting. A prolific contributor and letter writer to sporting journals, he thrived on controversy, but was in general extremely well liked by all who knew him. He was truly one of the old class of Edwardian dilettante landowning sportsmen artists and authors, a breed no longer to be found.

Another of the same kind was Harold Frank Wallace, born in 1881. He was better known perhaps in his day as one of the foremost exponents of the art of deer stalking. His book, written in conjunction with Lionel Edwards, *The Pursuit of Red, Fallow and Roe Deer in England and Scotland*, published in 1927, remains a classic of Edwardian proportions. His delightful reminiscences of highland stalking published in 1932 and entitled *A Highland Gathering*, is a charming book. He also wrote *The Big Game of Central and Western China*, published in 1913, which is perhaps less well known. This is, however, a very readable record of an expedition in 1911–12 through China, well illustrated by the author, who restricted himself to shooting specimens of various game and at no time shot more than was required. Examples of restraint such as these were unfortunately not followed as often as they might have been by less experienced would-be big game hunters. Harold Frank Wallace, typical of the artist/author hunters of the Edwardian period, died in 1964 aged 83.

Harold Frank Wallace, 1928, from a painting by Lionel Edwards.

Theodore Roosevelt 1858–1919

Africa 1909

President, Author, Big Game Hunter, Conservationist

*For three-quarters of a century there have been capital books
written on big game hunting in Africa – one of the best being the
earliest, that by Captain Cornwallis Harris . . .*

Theodore ('Teddy') Roosevelt was born in 1858, eldest son of a wealthy New York family, originally of Dutch origin. He was educated at Harvard, where he was a noted boxer, and graduated with honours in 1880. Subsequently he entered politics, but when war with Spain broke out in 1897 he joined a volunteer regiment of cavalry nicknamed the 'Rough Riders' because many of them were ex-cowboys. He was latterly promoted Colonel and led his men personally in a successful dismounted action to capture an enemy position at the battle of San Juan Hill.

In 1900 he was nominated as Vice President under President McKinley and when the latter was assassinated in 1901 succeeded him at the unprecedentedly youthful age of forty-three. He was enormously popular as President, although inevitably also not short of detractors. Nevertheless none could deny that he was outstanding in many ways. A prodigious memory and amazingly wide breadth of reading enabled him to discourse fluently on a surprising diversity of subjects, but amongst his greatest interests was a devotion to hunting in all its forms, particularly big game hunting. It may be argued that the greatest achievement of his Presidency was the building of the Panama Canal and in material terms this might at first appear to be so. In the long term, however, his work as a conservationist was undoubtedly where his greatest legacy to the American people lay.

During his lifetime the American buffalo, or bison, nearly became extinct and might well have shared the fate of the once vastly numerous Passenger Pigeon, the last of which was seen in 1917. Events such as these must have had their effect on him and it is clear that the imminent disappearance of the bison was something that caused him to think deeply about the way the USA was dealing with its natural resources. The fact that his bent was primarily towards hunting did not blind him to the loss of natural timbers, woodlands, or the pollution of rivers and lakes, which was also taking place at a tremendous pace owing to the increasing industrialisation of the country.

The first book Roosevelt wrote on sport, *The Wilderness Hunter*, subtitled 'An Account of the Big Game of the United States and Its Chase with Horse, Hound and Rifle', was published in 1893. It covered the hunting of everything from deer, goat, caribou and elk, to buffalo, grizzly bear, cougar, peccaries and wolves. Regarding the buffalo he admitted that by the end of the Civil War they had been steadily hunted to near extinction.

With his wide breadth of reading, as well as his interest in the subject, it is virtually certain that he had read three very different accounts of shooting bison in the United States all written by Englishmen. But it is still interesting to compare these in view of the different dates of their visits. The earliest of these was that rather strange character, notorious in his own time, the Honourable Grantley Berkeley, sixth son of the fifth Earl of Berkeley, who spent the greater part of his life in various sporting activities. In 1859 he was commissioned by the Editor of *The Field* to go to the USA and shoot bison, sending back an account of his experiences. In September of that year, accompanied by Lt. Bayard of the US Army, he had his first experience of buffalo hunting. They came up to a small herd and he wrote: 'Bayard and myself . . . set off towards them gently . . . when we came within about half a mile off they set in that peculiar up-and-down canter in which they invariably commence their retreat . . . we set off in a gallop [and] Taymouth [his horse] . . . soon overtook them; but . . . slackened his pace a little . . . and . . . I knew . . . he was very much scared . . . A slight touch of the spur, however, and that clasp of the knees which horses well understand, put all direct refusal out of his head, and we came up at three parts speed alongside the bulls, though he swerved from them infinitely further than I desired . . . Oh! What an exciting sight it was, thus close up with them, to see thirty black rusty monsters flying two or three abreast . . . the last old bull (generally the king of the herd) leering out from side to side beneath either horn . . . As Bayard seemed to be holding back for me, I called out for him to go at the bull, when Bayard, on his steady, nice horse, ran alongside, and with his heavy revolver, slightly struck the bull, but not in a spot to stop him. The bull then became mischievous and prone to charge anything that came in his way . . . and . . . went away sulkily by himself. I shot at him without effect . . .

'We now came to a creek . . . Bayard fired his revolver, at a long distance for that weapon, and I got my second shot, and saw that it took effect in a slanting direction in the back of the bison. We then rode over the creek and my third shot, at some distance, broke the shoulder of the huge beast . . . and brought him at once to bay. We drew up at a respectful distance . . . and hit the buffalo close behind and a little above the elbow, when he . . . fell dead.'

Roosevelt indicated that until the American Civil War (1861–1865) the buffalo herds had been one great mass covering the central prairies. The completion of the Union Pacific Railway in 1870 finally split the herds in two groups, the northern and southern. From 1870–1875 the annual destruction of the

Theodore Roosevelt and his son, Kermit, in East Africa; Millais, though a friend of Roosevelt, was critical of the number of photographs taken of him with game he had shot.

American buffalo was estimated to be around the almost unbelievable figure of 2,500,000 a year and this went on for a decade or more. In 1880 the completion of the Northern Pacific Railway led to the northern herd being attacked, and the last of the Dakota herds were destroyed by the Indians in 1883. Thereafter, something less than 1,000 were left. Theodore's brother Elliott shot them as a boy of seventeen in 1877 and Theodore himself shot them in 1883, but writing in 1893 he reckoned there were fewer than 500 remaining. In *The Wilderness Hunter* he wrote: 'No herd of a hundred individuals has been in existence since 1884 . . . in 1877 my brother Elliot then aged 17 . . . hunted buffalo in Northern Texas when herds still darkened the prairies as far as the eye could reach.'

Writing under his familiar pseudonym, 'The Old Shekarry', H. A. Leveson was frankly horrified in 1877 to find that buffalo cows were being slaughtered throughout the year. He wrote feelingly, if vainly, in his book, *Sport in Many Lands*, 'It is to be hoped that Congress will take early action to prevent the extinction of the buffalo . . . Of the various modes of hunting buffalo in the States no true sportsman would hesitate to pronounce in favour of the only legitimate way which is by running them down and killing them at close quarters with a rifle or revolver shot. This is capital fun, for the animal besides being swift enough to give a good horse enough to do to close with him often wheels about with such quickness as to baffle both horse and rider for several turns before there is any certainty of bringing him down . . .'

He was impressed by the cowboys' ability to shoot bison from horseback with a long-barrelled .45 revolver. He remarked on this feat being performed on two occasions by different cowboys. Regarding the grizzly bear he wrote respectfully, 'I should give "Old Ephraim" a wide berth if I was not armed with a thoroughly serviceable breech-loading rifle throwing a heavy bullet. . .'

In 1881 Samuel White Baker visited the USA and stayed on a ranch in the Rocky Mountains where he found there were still plenty of buffalo, although they had vanished from the plains. He was content to stalk them once to secure a good specimen. Thereafter he simply stalked them for the pleasure of observing them, taking aim with his rifle at half cock and touching the trigger without firing a shot, because he saw no point in wasting the meat or killing a rare beast simply for the sake of slaughter. His hunter, however, commented sourly, 'If you came all the way from the Old Country to shoot and you won't shoot when you've got the chance, you'd have done better to stay at home.'

Sam saw his point and could not blame him, but still declined to kill needlessly. Like Leveson, however, he was impressed by the American cowboys' prowess with the long-barrelled .45. When one of them killed a bear from horseback he regarded it 'as an unprecedented triumph in *shikar*.'

These three accounts of American buffalo, or bison shooting indicate the sort of sport available before and after the days of deliberate commercial and political slaughter. In part, the decision to encourage the slaughter of the bison was a political one, aimed at controlling the Plains Indians, whose survival depended on the bison for both meat and hides. Once the buffalo had gone the Plains Indians ability to survive was also gone and since they were seen as an obstacle to 'progress' the political decision to encourage the slaughter of the bison was taken. This is one of the few instances of deliberate near-extinction of an animal being taken by Man and somewhat naturally Theodore Roosevelt was not likely to print such a disgraceful story. On the other hand it is plain that he must have been aware of it and his decision to encourage the conservation of the American natural heritage was very probably in part brought about by it. In his second book, *Outdoor Pastimes of an American Hunter*, published in 1906, he expressed his views very clearly.

'It is entirely in our power as a nation to preserve large stretches of wilderness which are valueless for agricultural purposes and unfit for settlement as playgrounds for rich and poor alike and to preserve the game so that it shall continue to exist for the benefit of all lovers of nature and to give reasonable opportunities for the excrcise of the skill of the hunter whether he is or is not a man of means. But this end can only be achieved by wise laws and a resolute enforcement of the laws. Lack of such legislation and administration will result in harm to all of us . . .'

This was straight talking by a man who had the foresight to see that his country's natural heritage was being wasted at an alarming rate. It was in great part due to his energy and enthusiasm both during and after his Presidency that many conservation plans were got under way in the period up to his death in 1919. Many of the benefits which the American nation is reaping today and will continue to reap for many years to come stem initially from his actions.

On standing down from office in 1909 he took a prolonged safari in Africa, which had been earlier planned for him by his big game hunting friend Frederick Selous. Amongst those who accompanied him at intervals were R. J. Cuninghame, W. N. McMillan and William Judd, who was managing the safari. Roosevelt himself wrote with considerable percipience that 'Many parts of East Africa can and I believe will, be made into a white man's country; and the process will be helped not hindered by treating the black man well . . .'

He was accompanied by his son Kermit and it is plain that it gave him considerable pleasure to chronicle his son's successes, such as one occasion shooting a leopard: '. . . the leopard did not wait to be driven. Without any warning out he came and charged straight at Kermit, who stopped him when he was but six yards off with a bullet in the fore part of the body; the leopard turned and as he galloped off Kermit hit him again crippling him in both hips. The wounds were fatal and they would have knocked the fight out of any animal less plucky and savage than the leopard, but not even in Africa is there a beast of more unflinching courage than this spotted cat . . .[It still required two shots from W. N. McMillan and even then the wounded leopard mauled a beater severely] . . . then – out it came straight at Kermit and this time dropped dead to Kermit's bullet . . .'

In all, the Presidential party killed 9 lions, 5 hyenas, 8 elephants, 13 rhinoceros, 7 hippopotamus, and 6 buffalos. Roosevelt noted: '296 head self: Kermit 216 head: we did not kill a hundredth part of all we could have done . . .'. They did, however, kill 9 white rhinos which was well over the permitted limit and by any standards excessive, particularly as even then they were very scarce. In any event at no time were they considered difficult to shoot, even in the time of Cornwallis Harris when shooting with muzzle-loaders.

Sclous in a letter about the safari to his friend Dennis D. Lyell wrote: '. . . Fortunately for Mr Roosevelt no rain to speak of fell in the country in which he was hunting during the first three months of his trip, so there was no long grass, or heavy dew to trouble him . . .'

Selous also wrote about a narrow escape that William Judd had when out with him after lions: '. . . I saw two lionesses and galloped them, but . . . the grass was rather long and they crouched and disappeared suddenly . . . and as the spoor afterwards showed I galloped past within seven yards of where one of them was lying. Judd (who was managing the caravan) was following me and about 80 yards behind, and when he got near one of the lionesses she charged at him at close quarters.

'Judd's horse reared up and swung round and Judd fell off, but as he did so he pulled off his rifle, holding it across his thighs. By a marvellous piece of luck the bullet went right into the lioness's eye, killing it instantly, and Judd lay on the ground alongside the dead lioness . . .'

In 1910 Roosevelt's account of the safari was published as a book entitled *African Game Trails*; 'An Account of the African Wanderings of an American Hunter-Naturalist'. Inevitably there were many who had criticisms to make of it, not least of the photographs that so offended Millais.

Selous wrote rather bitterly to Lyell: 'I am afraid you cannot hope to make much money by a book on sport and natural history in any part of Africa . . . No doubt Mr Roosevelt's book will sell well and it is a good and interesting book in itself, but that is not the reason it will sell, which is because it was written by a great and well known personality . . . I really think one could make more money by writing articles for . . . magazines than by writing books.'

Kermit Roosevelt shoots a leopard in East Africa, 1910. A drawing by Philip R. Goodwin.

In practice Roosevelt's book, although possibly very successful in the USA, does not seem to have sold more than one edition in England, but this was perhaps not surprising in view of Selous's comments. The market simply seems to have been flooded with books on big game shooting in Africa at this time. Roosevelt, as he would have liked, was regarded as very little different from his friends Selous and Millais. This did not stop him writing a foreword to C. H. Stigand's book, *Hunting the Elephant in Africa*, published in 1913, from which the quotation at the head of this short biography is taken. Throughout the First World War Colonel Theodore Roosevelt was a fervent proponent of US participation, dying the year after the end of hostilities in 1919. Despite his fondness for big game hunting there is no doubt that he was a sincere conservationist who saw that the future for big game lay in natural reserves, or parks, which were already being set up in Africa and it was through his initiatives that similar reserves and national parks were started in the USA.

Perhaps one of the best thumbnail sketches of Theodore Roosevelt was by Millais who knew him well and wrote of him: 'I remember the first time I met him . . . in 1908 . . . he came up to me and said, "I seem to know your face. Who are you?" "Millais is my name," I replied. "What, *Breath from the Veldt* Millais?" he said enthusiastically. "You've just got to sit down right here and have a chat. I don't know when I've been so pleased to meet anyone" . . . and if we did not have a chat I listened at anyrate for some twenty minutes with absorbed interest to his views of Nature and the Zoology of South Africa, of which he displayed, contrary to my expectations, a very considerable knowledge . . . On occasion, Roosevelt was inclined to be dogmatic . . . after he returned from his African trip and his excellent book *African Game Trails* had been published he gave me a lecture of about twenty minutes on the superiority of pictures done on the spot by a zoological artist over all forms of instantaneous photography. At last, when I managed to get a word in, it was impossible to refrain from saying, "If those are your opinions why did you not take an artist with you instead of a photographer?" "Well, you have got me there" he admitted, laughing . . . then we should have been spared that dreadful series of bad portraits of the author standing in fatuous attitudes over mangled corpses of deceased hartebeests, lions and zebras. Roosevelt probably knew this himself but his book was written for the man in the street . . . Theodore Roosevelt was certainly one of the most remarkable men of this or any other time. In person he was the embodiment of physical fitness being an expert rider and shot and skilled in most games. Mentally he was a giant whose broad vision ranged over a vast variety of subjects. At one sitting I have heard him discuss big game hunting, bimetallism, zoology, geography, national policy, European history, botany, palaeontology, archaeology and ancient forms of religion, bringing to each and all a thoroughness, accuracy, wealth of detail and breadth of criticism that was astonishing did we not know the extent of his reading and power of his memory . . .'

141

7

THE LAST EDWARDIANS
IN AFRICA

Chauncey Hugh Stigand 1875–1919

James Sutherland 1876–1930

Chauncey Hugh Stigand, and (below)
pages from his unpublished diary kept on
safari in Uganda in 1912.

with bowler hat & coat.

KK was very enthusiastic about his dance. He said that it was his own & that Bari's couldn't do it. The great feature was hitting a bit of ebony with another stick which sounded rather well when done by about 50 men in time as it gives out a metallic sound.

Trip to Uganda.

Left KK. about 26-2-12. in evening. Slept Ruaha in pen air. Read. mails about midnight.

Crossed over at Shokoli; went to Kagu Uma & then eastwards up Uma.

Saw a group of about 10 males all too small to shoot.

Another day met big herd of females & young, about 50 to hundred. There seemed one possible male but impose. to get anywhere near him. Followed up a valley gradually narrowing.

Came to a place with a big rock in middle of valley. Sent a native to climb the valley one side & circle round in front of them & shout. If he had done this they were almost bound to come back down the valley & whichever side

of the rock they passed I would have got a good view & been able to pick.

Of course he bungled it by going only a few hundred yards & then shouting behind them & driving them up the valley.

I was returning to Shokali on 3rd having got nothing when we saw a group of phant far off on the hills. Sending porters on I went after them. About 25 bulls & some nice tusks amongst them.

Of course the biggest were in the middle & I waited for about an hour & then some natives fired the grass & began shouting, not knowing I was there. The elephant were moving on & something had to be done quickly so I hurried after them over a rise, gave my mind to part of the herd who had stopped just over the rise & as the rest began to go off picked the biggest I could get a shot at.

I estimated the tusks at 60 lbs. but hear from Rumile where I sent them with abdi that they are 69 & 64 so good as I expected in a flying visit.

Chauncey Hugh Stigand 1875–1919

Africa 1900–1919

Accident Prone Hero

. . . the lion sprang . . . and . . . landed on me . . . I scrambled round
with my left arm still in his mouth . . . and started pummelling him
with my right fist . . . He gave me a final shake and then . . .
disappeared into the grass . . .

Chauncey Hugh Stigand was born in 1875 and went to school at Radley, where
he apparently did well at games but did not distinguish himself scholastically.
He then went on to a well known army crammer, after which he entered Sandhurst and was duly commissioned into the Royal West Kents. He served in
Burma and Aden before joining a Special Service Unit in Somaliland in 1900.
He subsequently served in the King's African Rifles in Nyasaland, British East
Africa and Zanzibar from 1902–1907. Rejoining his regiment on the outbreak
of the First World War he was promoted Major in 1916, appointed Governor
of the Upper Nile in the same year and for his services in that post was awarded
the OBE. In 1918 he married an American lady, Nancy Neff of Washington
DC, but the marriage lasted only two years, for he was killed in action in 1919,
ambushed by rebellious natives. Throughout his life in Africa he was a keen
hunter and writer on the subject of big game.

It may be inferred that from an early age Chauncey Hugh Stigand suffered
much from his somewhat unusual Christian names. Small boys fasten on anything of this nature in a cruel manner, which can scar even the most insensitive
youngster. It is significant that Stigand was always known, even by his closest
friends, as Stigand, without reference to either of his Christian names. Dennis
D. Lyell, who was one of his closest friends from his days in the King's African
Rifles, where they met in 1903, always referred to him simply as Stigand. He
recorded admiringly that Stigand was over six feet in height and that when
he was being coached for the army Sandow told him he could train him into
one of the strongest men in the world. This perhaps, tells us quite a lot about
Lyell and Stigand and for that matter, Sandow himself.

Chauncey Hugh Stigand was fairly clearly at first sight a somewhat dogmatic
man of forthright temperament without fear, if also without much imagination.
For it seems that in his youth at least, as is often the way, he simply could
not imagine anything happening to him. In many ways he seems to have been

something of an overgrown schoolboy when Lyell first met him, for he mentions for instance a wrestling match in the billiard room of the King's African
Rifles between this large and powerful Captain and his brother officer, Captain
James Brander Dunbar, who though tough and muscular was only some five
foot three inches tall. Despite the disparity in their sizes both were the same
age, approaching thirty, and both at that time were probably of the same overgrown schoolboy type. According to Lyell they ended up rolling under the
billiard table while a game was in progress and dislodged it so that a spirit
level had to be found to restore the *status quo*, effectively ending the wrestling
match – and doubtless discomforting those playing billiards.

Stigand and Lyell co-operated on a remarkable book, *Central African Game
& Its Spoor*, which was published in 1906. It was a rather strange attempt
to portray the tracks and tracking of African big game on paper. Scarcely surprising there was only one edition, but the experience of producing it
obviously infected both Stigand and Lyell with the writing bug. Stigand himself wrote several more books on big game and related subjects. The first of
these was entitled *Scouting and Reconnaissance in Savage Countries*. This small
145-page manual gave advice on almost all aspects of scouting, tracking and
reconnaissance amongst hostile tribes in Africa. It was somewhat ironic therefore that Stigand himself should be killed in an ambush by hostile Dinka
tribesmen in 1919, when leading a scouting party. But, as he himself had indicated, such an ambush was almost impossible to avoid in thick grass or bush.

His third attempt at authorship, published in 1909, *The Game of British East
Africa*, was a success, and it included many of his own early photographs.
His fourth book, *To Abyssinia: Through an Unknown Land*, published in 1910,
gave an account of a journey from Gilgil in Kenya to Addis Ababa, often accompanied by mutinous porters. It was another book of considerable interest, with
again some surprisingly good photographs. His fifth book, *Hunting the Elephant
in Africa*, published in 1910, was yet another wide-ranging book covering
much more than the titled subject matter, again full of his own decided views
on various subjects. His sixth book, published posthumously and written in
conjunction with his wife, who was obviously a partner entirely suited to him,
was entitled *Cooking for Settler & Trekker*, a small but fairly comprehensive
little book.

Millais wrote fairly strongly on the subject of Stigand to Dennis D. Lyell,
his old friend, in 1918, the year before Stigand's untimely death, saying that
he knew him 'fairly well' and continuing '. . . he showed me his heads the
other day in Eastbourne and had one grand Koodoo, but I do not like his writings, or his patronising remarks on other sportsmen. There are many other
hunters who shoot on the plains (which he despises) who are quite as good
hunters as he, and they look upon game in its proper perspective. Because
a man's views do not agree with yours that is no reason his ideas are wrong.
He perhaps has a different standpoint and interest, and to say that bush shoot-

ing is the only one worth doing is all bunkum. I know for a fact from a man who has lived for the last four years (in close intimacy with Stigand) that the natives found all the game for him as they do for all white hunters – Selous or anyone else included (though many species of course one kills without their aid): so he talked nonsense in adopting his very superior tone. Not that I do not mean to suggest Stigand is not an excellent hunter, he probably is, but I don't like his tone with regard to others, or even beginners who must shoot on the plains to commence with, if only to learn their rifle. After all he was a novice himself once.'

Fairly obviously Millais had little rapport with Stigand and particularly disliked his at times seemingly dogmatic attitudes, which were perhaps particularly obvious in his book *The Game of East Africa*, and possibly something abrasive had occurred in their recent encounter in Eastbourne. In practice it was probably just that they were very differing types. Millais, of course, had been in the Seaforth Highlanders and the Navy whereas Stigand had been in the West Kents and the King's African Rifles, giving them somewhat different backgrounds for a start. It is most likely that Stigand simply seemed to Millais the hearty type of man that he found rather tiresome.

Stigand in fact, like so many people, probably gave a misleading impression of himself. He was obviously a late developer. The boy who was sensitive about his Christian names; the youth who had to be coached for Sandhurst; the man who went out to the King's African Rifles; the soldier in search of action; the big game hunter; the writer; all made up the man. His chief failing, in his younger days at least, seems to have been a lack of imagination. He would follow a wounded lion into a cavern, or an elephant into the bush, or face a charging rhino, thinking in his early days that accidents could never happen to him. Later he learned by bitter experience, that they could. That he then still went on and did the same things, although in some instances admitting to having 'cold feet', shows that he really did possess a high degree of courage and was indeed 'heroic' material.

His description in *Hunting the Elephant in East Africa* of a near fatal encounter with a rhino is typical of the man and Millais could scarcely have objected to it. Indeed one is inclined to think that Millais may have been so put off by reading the earlier dogmatic views expressed in Stigand's book, *Game in East Africa*, that he had never read it. Stigand wrote: 'The lot of an elephant hunter is now a hard one. Girt about on all sides with exorbitant and restrictive licenses and with most of the elephant now driven into unhealthy and impenetrable country, he must needs be an enthusiast who would become a devotee of this sport . . . In 1905 I was looking for elephant in the vicinity of Fort Manning. I had no thought of rhino . . . I met a fresh spoor . . . and . . . bent down . . . to see the tracks . . . I heard the engine-like puffs of a pair of rhinos close at hand . . . they had been lying up close to the spot . . . The next moment a great behorned head burst out of the grass a yard or two from me. I had no time to think, but just shoved my Mannlicher in his face and pulled the trigger. He swerved, but . . . at the same moment I became aware of the second one bearing down on me from my left. There was no time to reload, so I tried to jump out of his path with the usual result in thick stuff that one tripped up.

'He kicked me in passing, then . . . whipped round, and the next moment I felt myself soaring up skywards. I must have gone some height as my men on the elephant track said they saw me over the grass which was ten or twelve feet high . . . I fell heavily on my shoulder blades . . . I looked round for my rifle and . . . picked it up . . . While doing this I suddenly found that a finger nail had been torn off and was bleeding. Directly I discovered it, it became very painful.

'Whilst examining this injury some of my men appeared and uttered cries of horror. I could not make out why they were so concerned till I glanced at my chest and saw that my shirt had been ripped open and was covered with blood whilst there was a tremendous gash in the left side of my chest, just over the . . . heart . . . Small bits of mincemeat were also lying about my chest and shirt . . .

'. . . I felt nothing at all except a rather numb sensation. It struck me that it must have pierced my lungs: I would soon know if this was the case, as I would be spitting blood. I waited a short time and nothing of the sort occurred, so I concluded that the lungs were all right . . .

'I was about thirty miles from Fort Manning, and . . . I started back to the nearest village. After walking [my horse] some time I felt faint [but] I . . . per-formed the rest of the journey on foot.

'Having arrive at the village . . . I dressed the wound as best I could and lay down. . . I had a sleepless night until about two in the morning . . .'

A friend then fortuitously appeared with an Indian doctor, who 'stitched the wound up most skilfully . . . three weeks later I was well enough, though still in bandages, to start on a 240 mile march which I completed in ten days.'

Chauncey Hugh Stigand had at times a somewhat staccato style of writing, especially when trying to impart information. When read by a more natural writer such as Millais, the style could well have been misinterpreted as arrogant, supercilious, or dogmatic. On the other hand he could also write surprisingly well and descriptively at times, if always directly, but with a touch of possibly unconscious humour which was engaging. His description of how he was mauled by a lion is a case in point. He wrote: 'It was at Simba that I was mauled by a lion. In the dry weather they used to come and drink from a small pool . . . under the water tank . . . I stationed myself here one night, sitting astride a girder. After a while a lioness came strolling down . . . It was difficult to shoot as she was directly underneath me . . . she must have heard me as she gave one bound of about four yards to one side . . . I then fired and she raced about two hundred yards up the [railway] line and fell dead across the track.

'I was just thinking of descending . . . when two lions came out on to the track, just opposite the dead body . . . then they began slowly to approach to the water-tank.

'The leading one came on . . . When he got close I fired at him. I found out afterwards that the shot just caught the corner of his jaw, breaking part of the bone of the lower one, and then glanced off into the shoulder. He collapsed into the water trough just below the tank. The second one stopped on hearing the shot, and then advanced again . . . I gave him a shot and he waltzed round and then rushed into the grass where he was found dead next morning . . . By this time the one in the water trough had picked himself out and I just had time to give him another shot as he left the track, after which I heard him collapse in the grass close to the line.

'As the moon had now gone in it was difficult to see. I went up to the station and got my orderly to bring a lamp . . . I then returned and could just make out something lying in the grass . . .

'In the dark, the body, which was just discernible, appeared a long way below the line . . . I approached the edge and immediately the inert mass assumed life and with a roar sprang on me with one bound . . . As the lion sprang I fired into his chest and he landed on me, his right paw over my left shoulder and he seized my left arm in his teeth . . . The weight of his spring knocked me down . . . I scrambled round with my left arm still in his mouth until I was kneeling alongside him and started pummelling him with my right fist on the back of the neck. He gave me a final shake and then . . . disappeared into the grass . . . I reloaded and covered him but could not see clearly enough to fire. I then passed the spot at which he was lying, keeping my rifle pointed towards him. I could not see him in the grass and thinking him well left alone continued towards the station . . . Afterwards . . . I found I had not the use of my wrist, owing to a nerve being practically severed . . . I found that I was drenched with blood and my coat and breeches torn with teeth and claws. I retired to the waiting room, where I got the station-master to syringe out my wounds with strong potassium permanganate. There were eight holes in my arm and I afterwards discovered, three claw marks on my back . . . I sat up in the waiting room for about six hours, when the Nairobi train came in . . . I reached a carriage all right, but just as I got to the steps my legs gave way, as I was very weak from loss of blood . . . After a few days my arm swelled . . . but it was just saved. It was seven months, however, before I could use my wrist, and about two years before I could feel really steady with it when shooting, although I shot my next lion after this event some nine months later . . . as I was afraid I might have lost my nerve; but I seemed to be all right and have bagged seven since . . .'

Stigand was also tossed by an elephant, but lived to tell the tale of that too. It was ironic that in *Shooting and Reconnaissance in Savage Countries* he wrote: 'The usual African punitive expedition is a poor enough show. It usually

*Two contemporaries of Stigand: Frederick Roderick Noble Finley with a
buffalo in Mozambique, 1903, and (below) Colonel R. Meinertzhagen,
CBE, DSO, 1904; explorer, soldier and big game hunter.*

starts by some European being attacked, or murdered, or constant raids being made by some tribe not in an administered area on some tribe which is under the government. In both cases the tribe to be attacked has, as a rule, not the slightest conception of the powers or resources of the government . . . In ninety-nine cases out of a hundred directly an expedition reaches their country, the natives fly in every direction, scattering all over the country and hiding their stock in small herds. It then only remains to break up and catch what stock can be found and shoot down a few men running away until the ''cease fire'' is sounded . . . Possibly one or two soldiers, who have wandered far away by themselves . . . are killed or wounded, but otherwise no casualties occur.

'On the hundredth occasion all starts as before, but either the strength or the courage of the enemy has been underrated, or a small column becomes detached. Nothing is seen of the assailants except a few flying men. Suddenly there is a rush in thick grass or bush and the little column gets massacred . . .'

And that, by a strange quirk of fate, was in the end a fairly exact description of what happened to Major Chauncey Hugh Stigand, KAR, OBE, along with a brother officer and a sergeant leading a column against the Dinkas in 1919. It was later found that before succumbing to the spears of the attackers he had fired about a dozen shots in a final stand. True to his own code, Stigand remained the accident-prone hero to the bitter end, at the age of forty-four.

James Sutherland 1876–1930

Claustrophobic Physical Fitness Enthusiast

The morning coat and silk hat I wore on my last brief visit to
England, I flung into the sea in sheer exuberance of spirits, when
I left Marseilles, glad to be rid of such costly insanity . . .

James Sutherland was brought up in England, although his father had had an adventurous youth gold-digging in New Zealand and Australia. It is not clear whether he was successful and returned home with a fortune, or whether he simply inherited money; whatever the source, his funds ensured that James had a fairly normal middle-class upbringing in England, including a public school education, where it seems he was taught to box and from an early age took a keen interest in physical training. These were both interests which he continued throughout later life. Although comparatively small, no more than five foot six inches, he was well built and physically active. His agility and physical strength were to stand him in good stead throughout his subsequent life in Africa.

He first went out to Africa in 1896 when around twenty years of age. He moved from Cape Town to Johannesburg, where he noted laconically in the preface to his book, *The Adventures of an Elephant Hunter*, he 'spent some time in hospital suffering from the effects of a bullet wound.' It may be inferred that he had joined one of the Irregular Forces during the Boer War and was wounded in action, although he does not say so. After wandering around Matabeleland, Mashonaland, British Central Africa, Tanganyika and the Congo, followed by Portuguese East Africa, he had a spell as a storekeeper in Nyasaland and finally arrived at his favourite hunting grounds in German East Africa. From this stage onwards he remained a hunter, primarily interested in elephants.

In 1905–1906 he was in German East Africa at the outbreak of the Maji-Maji rebellion and for the services he rendered the Germans during this period, fighting as a volunteer with their forces, he not only received the Iron Cross but, much more important from his viewpoint, was given the right to shoot elephants as and where he wished. It was during this period that he shot 447 bull elephants in ten years. He did not count cows, but claimed a world record at the time. His claims in this respect seem to have been regarded as questionable by several experienced hunters such as Selous, on the grounds that he

152

appears to have allowed his native trackers to shoot elephants and claimed any beasts they killed as his own. Whether this was in fact the case is, of course, hard to prove either way, but he certainly laid himself open to the accusation in his book, although this detracts little from his undeniable hunting feats.

On the outbreak of the First World War in 1914 he was still deep in southern German territory and was fortunate in escaping arrest and returning to British territory. He then joined the Nyasaland Forces and by 1916 was acting as an Intelligence Agent patrolling the borders of Portuguese East Africa and German East Africa, probably the only instance of a recipient of the Iron Cross fighting against Germany! His profound knowledge of the natives and their languages, as well as the trust they had in him, made him invaluable to General Sir Edward Northey who made him his Chief Intelligence Officer. He was wounded in action, mentioned in despatches and awarded the Legion of Honour.

He was known as a kind and gentle man, who disliked the trappings of civilisation and was undoubtedly at his best in the outback amongst his native followers and friends, as is clear from his writings. In his book he gives an indication of how he started: 'I left the Old Country for Cape Town in the early part of 1896 with the object of carving out a career for myself. I had no precise knowledge of what that career was to be . . . I have done many things to earn a living . . . contracting for the Beira railway: I have been agent for various African trading companies: I have kept native stores: and I have even been a prize-fighter. None of these occupations . . . seemed . . . to suit my nature, and I was still uncertain as to what I should undertake as a means of earning a livelihood when I reached Portuguese East Africa. It was there I decided to become an elephant hunter and practically speaking I have been on the spoor of elephant ever since . . . my intense love of sport was more a cogent factor in assisting me to come to such a decision than any love of lucre . . . I have never regretted the life I have led. It has been a life of weary days and restless nights, of fever, thirst, hunger, toil and strife: but a life of wild exhilarating excitement, of sunlight and air, vast spaces and solitude . . . far removed from the restricting influences of a complex civilisation . . .'

His description of the hunter's life in the forest (pori) gives a very clear picture of the man himself as well as being very evocative. 'Before dawn I am awakened by the joyful singing of the birds in the forest and, as I lie, I may occasionally hear the loud snort of a buffalo, the screeching, gossiping chatter of monkeys, or the loud booming woof-woof of the lion, which, like an evil dream, seems to lose some of its sinister impressiveness at the approach of day. I am probably about to doze off once more when my boy brings me a steaming cup of delicious cocoa – not the brick-dust and water concoction so often met with – but a beverage made with boiled milk and flavoured with a suspicion of vanilla. Immediately afterwards I spring from my camp-bed, fill my lungs with air, and picking up my dumb-bells, go through a systematic course of exercise, which keeps every muscle of my body supple and gives me complete mental control over the functions of each. It is to this constant care of my physical being that I ascribe my fitness today, after all the vicissitudes of a most strenuous and exacting life under a tropical sun, and to it I also assign a great part of my success as a hunter, for, apart from the temperament suitable for such a calling, the muscular system must be so tuned that it will instantaneously respond to every message of the brain. Upon this co-operation a hunter's life again and again depends. After exercise a cold tub and a brisk rub down! What a splendid tonic and what an absolute necessity in the tropics! Next, my boy brings me a lightly brewed cup of tea and some biscuits, and this frugal meal constitutes breakfast.

'Our camp is now all astir. My men consisting of trackers, carriers, cook and private servants – about ten in number – are ready to start, so off we go into the forest with long, easy, springing strides, the blood tingling in our veins with the joy of life. To all intents and purposes, we are absolutely free: there is no vexatious etiquette to be observed: I can burst into a hearty laugh without shocking the ridiculous propriety of a crowded street: I do not require to wear this kind of waistcoat or that kind of tie. The morning coat and silk hat I wore on my last brief visit to England, I flung into the sea in sheer exuberance of spirits, when I left Marseilles, glad to be quit of such costly insanity – even a bowler hat is a ludicrous menace to my sense of natural comfort . . .'

Describing the tracking of game he wrote: '. . . we have discovered fresh spoor . . . I push ahead with my two trackers . . . [who] can read the bush as plainly as a civilised man reads his newspaper, and yet, after a lifetime spent in hunting, I can state that they are usually inferior to an adaptable and thoroughly trained white man. Even here finer brains count . . . (Approaching our quarry) . . . It now behoves us to advance with the utmost wariness, and I follow my tracker so closely, that he can if necessary touch me with his hand. My rifle is held in my grasp ready to slip to my shoulder in an instant, while my other tracker follows me with my second rifle, so that when I have emptied my first, I have simply to make a half turn and snatch the other from his hands. This action has become almost instinctive with me through years of constant practice, and essentially so, for often one-tenth of a second is in hunting, as in boxing, of vital importance; you may not have the opportunity of saying afterwards: "If only I had been a shade quicker!"'

On wounded elephants he wrote succinctly: '. . . if I merely wound an elephant and he bolts I make every effort to follow him up and finish him, and I am glad to say that in the majority of cases I accomplish this end. I adopt this procedure apart from the question of obtaining ivory, for in my hunting I have always endeavoured to bear in mind the question of pain. Swift death is comparatively little to any living thing – long drawn out pain is terrible, and when the question of hunting is concerned the professional is usually

James Sutherland, East Africa, 1907.

too experienced a shot to entail any unnecessary suffering on the animal he hunts, a compliment which, I fear, cannot always be paid to the amateur, or those who scurry through the country with the object of writing a book . . .

'Sometimes, if elephants are plentiful, I am from ten days to three weeks or more away from my main camp; and after such a period of absence I am generally glad to return, for unless a man wishes to give way under the strain, he must rest and recuperate at intervals . . .

'As we approach camp we see the smoke of our fires . . . My men's wives and children come out to meet them . . . while I am greeted by my little terrier who comes jumping up to me, licking my hands and tugging at my trousers in a frenzy of excitement and joy. At last we are home and I immediately bathe and change my clothes, and all my men, who are wonderfully clean, do the same. A nicely cooked meal is the next luxury, and after that I indulge in a peg or two of whisky and the solace of tobacco. My men make a hilarious night of it . . . I lie and listen to the ebb of the noisy jovialities: a soft wind flaps in at my tent, and . . . my senses are soon steeped in sound and refreshing sleep . . . If anyone has a desire to live, where living is great full-blooded living, let him go and spend some of his time among wild animal life – far away from the insidious comforts and the petty restraints of life in a civilised community . . .'

His description of some of his experiences with elephants are illuminating,

155

as for instance this account of a day when after a lengthy hunt he had shot three elephants and heard a fourth in the bush and had sent his loader and tracker, Simba, to climb a tree to see if he could see it. He continued: '. . . to my horror I heard a terrific scream and next moment saw Simba dashing back towards me . . . with the elephant in hot pursuit. Shouting to him to turn to the left that I might have an unobstructed view of the infuriated animal, who was now only about thirty yards behind his intended victim, I took hasty aim and fired, the bullet striking the brute in the side of the head. For an instant he staggered and then came charging on again! At the same moment, Simba, catching his foot in a creeper, plunged heavily forward on his face and for one awful second I thought it was all up with my faithful old tracker. In a flash, to my intense relief, he was on his feet again, but . . . dashed straight on towards me, completely obstructing my view of the animal. Rushing past and slightly the right of my man I gave the elephant the contents of my second barrel in the forehead, the terrific impact of the bullet hurling him back on his haunches. The shot, however, struck him too high up to prove fatal and, speedily recovering, he made tracks for the long grass . . . I hastily grabbed my light rifle from Simba and gave chase. Ere he had gone far I managed to place a bullet in the vicinity of his heart, whereupon he instantly turned, and uttering a succession of short, shrill screams bore down upon me. When he was within forty yards of me, I fired in his face – the light was too uncertain for taking careful aim – but the small bullet proved absolutely ineffectual . . . I drove another through his forehead hoping to reach his brain and drop him. Still he came on . . . and was within fifteen yards of me, when I pulled back the bolt of my rifle . . . only to discover to my horror that the magazine was empty . . . Fully convinced that . . . this was the end . . . I flung my rifle . . . into the elephant's face and sprang to the left. At the same moment I heard a terrific report a few inches behind me and turned to find Simba standing with my heavy rifle in his hands . . . he had slipped a cartridge into the weapon and fired it in the very nick of time . . . Immediately swerving to the right the elephant . . . continued his wild career for another fifty yards before coming to a standstill. Snatching my heavy rifle from Simba, I slipped a couple of cartridges into it, and rushing up to the unsteady old warrior sent a bullet through his heart. He toppled over with a tremendous crash and, after a few gasps, lay still . . . Dragging my weary limbs over to where Simba stood, supporting himself against a convenient tree, I gave his hand a hearty grip – it was by no means the first time we had faced a life and death encounter together

and being utterly exhausted flung myself on the ground. My tracker followed suit and for a long while we lay, too tired to think, or speak or move . . . The severe exertion of this hunt brought on a bad attack of malaria, which incapacitated me for a few days, but thanks to quinine, tea and whisky, I felt sufficiently well to resume hunting shortly afterwards.'

Unfortunately, there was little scope for a man of Sutherland's qualities and background in post-war Africa. Although throughout his life he kept himself amazingly fit physically and was able to throw off attacks of malaria, he was known latterly to be suffering severely from dysentery and because of failing sight in his right eye he had to creep very close to his quarry and shoot from his left shoulder. In the late 1920s he was last known to be hunting in the far interior of the French Sudan. Because of the scarcity of elephants he was only making a bare living, and it was there that he died in 1930, aged only fifty-four.

Notes on a contemporary: Thomas Alexander Barns

Thomas Alexander Barns, who was more generally known as T. Alexander Barns, was one of the last Edwardian hunters in Africa, very much of the same period as Sutherland. Born in 1882 he arrived in Africa around 1902 and by 1905 was farming a cattle ranch in north-eastern Rhodesia. He was described by Dennis D. Lyell, who was a neighbouring farmer at one time, as an excellent walker with considerable powers of endurance which helped to make him a successful elephant hunter. In those days he used a German 7.9 mm Mauser with a hair trigger and, though not a very good shot, he had a cool temperament and always made a point of pumping the whole of his magazine into an elephant to make sure of it.

Like many of the same period he was forced to act as a white hunter, supplementing his income by taking rich clients on safari. He also collected specimens for museums and shot and preserved the specimen of the African bull elephant that now stands in the Natural History Museum, South Kensington. He was not only a good naturalist but also a sound entomologist. In addition he was a very competent photographer. It was natural therefore that he should go on to write a number of illustrated books.

His first was entitled *The Wonderland of the Western Congo*, published by Putnam in 1920. It was rather grandiosely sub-titled, 'The Region of the Snow-Covered Volcanoes, the Pygmies, the Giant Gorillas and the Okapi'. It is probable that this description was the work of some American sub-editor, for the book itself makes rather stuffy reading and the photographs are the best part of it.

His second book, published in 1923, was entitled *Across the Great Craterland to the Congo*. It was again lengthily and grandiosely sub-titled: 'Describing a journey of Exploration and Research to the Land of the Giant Craters in Tanganyika Territory and To the Forests and Lakes and Volcanoes of the South Eastern Congo with Some Account of the African Apes and the Capture and Taming of the African Elephant: with in addition a Chapter on Elephant Shooting.' In this case the sub-title cannot be blamed on an American, for the book was published by Ernest Benn. It was again well illustrated and was somewhat better reading than his previous book. His description of the Belgian attempts to tame the African elephants under the patronage of King Leopold is of considerable interest, as is his chapter on elephant hunting.

His last book was entitled *An African Eldorado*, published by Methuen in 1926. In this he described gorilla and elephant hunting in the Congo, giving a graphic account of the difficulties he encountered in preserving the elephant skin for Rowland Ward to prepare the specimen for the Natural History Museum. As a field naturalist and animal collector he was clearly carving out a special field of his own.

He was married and his wife often accompanied him on his explorations and hunting trips. It was strange that a man of this kind, who had numerous narrow escapes from wild animals in the jungle during the course of his life, should have died as he eventually did. He was killed in Chicago in 1930, stepping into the path of a train when trying to avoid a motor-car.

8

THE SURVIVORS

James Brander Dunbar 1875–1969

Archibald Dunbar Brander 1877–1953

Walter Dalrymple Maitland Bell 1880–1951

(left) *James Brander Dunbar, and* (right) *Archibald Dunbar Brander.*

The Dunbar Brander Brothers

James Brander Dunbar 1875–1969

Africa 1894–1906

The Original of Buchan's John MacNab

I stalked him at first light. Then I cut off the head and the testicles.
Put a label on them and stopped the mail van. Sent them through
the post and he *had to pay the postage . . .*

Archibald Dunbar Brander 1877–1953

India 1896–1926

Conservator of Forests and Worthy Successor to James Forsyth

. . . I descended quietly, but not so quietly as to escape the tiger's
notice, who accompanied me through the jungle . . . growling . . .
the whole time. It was a terrible experience and one I hope never
to renew . . .

To understand the rather odd relationship of the Dunbar Brander brothers it is necessary to know something of their background and the reason why Jim styled himself Brander Dunbar while Archie remained Dunbar Brander. Their maternal great uncle, Lt Colonel James Brander of Pitgaveny and Kinnedar, who died in 1854, was directly responsible. He had no male heir and his property, duly entailed, was left to his sister, Mary, Lady Dunbar, second wife of the late Sir Archibald Dunbar, Bt, and then to her only son, second son of the baronet, a Captain in the Madras Cavalry. The entailed estate passed to them, however, only on the condition that they adopted the surname of Brander. Lady Mary Dunbar thus reverted to the name Lady Mary Dunbar Brander and her son James became Captain James Dunbar Brander. He in turn had two sons, James, born in 1875 and Archibald, born in 1877. Both were duly baptised with the surname Dunbar Brander.

Jim, who ultimately, like his father, attained the rank of Captain, was always of a somewhat mischievous, not to say wild, nature from the earliest age, a trait which remained marked and even accentuated throughout his long life. Archie was much the more settled character, but was always capable of holding his own against his elder brother. Both were men of short stature, inheriting the Dunbar genes in this respect. As boys, dressed naturally in the kilt of the Pitgaveny tartan, on receiving their first .410 shotguns they took it in turns to fire at each other's backsides from an initial distance of forty yards, advancing a yard at a time until they felt the pellets sting through the thick cloth of their kilts. This distance, some fifteen yards, they mutually agreed would be the nearest at which they fired at each other. They then stalked each other through the woods surrounding Pitgaveny and the one who peppered the other first was acknowledged the victor.

It was from those early days that Jim developed the art of bare-foot stalking and at one time in his life the soles of his feet were like leather; as hard as those of any native. It was also then that the brothers developed the strong, if still affectionate, rivalry that persisted throughout their lives. If one was to take a course of action, this was almost certainly enough for the other to do the opposite.

After they had both been educated at Rugby, their father died and Jim, being the eldest, inherited the estate. As soon as he was of age, he broke the entail. Having taken pride in his kinship to the Dunbar baronetcy and possibly hoping there was a chance he might inherit that estate as well, he then reversed his surname, thus becoming James Brander Dunbar. Archie, differing from his brother as ever, saw no point in changing his name and retained the Dunbar Brander surname with pride. Passing into the Forestry Service in India he then left Scotland for Central India, the same area so well depicted by Forsyth some forty years previously.

In those late Victorian days in Scotland, Jim, still only in his early twenties, was frankly bored with life and in 1897 (aged twenty-two), challenged a neighbouring estate owner for a Twenty Pound wager that he could shoot a stag undetected on his ground. His evocative account of this event always ran on similar lines and ended with a triumphant declaration beneath the mounted head: 'I stalked him at first light. Then I cut off the head and the testicles. Put a label on them and stopped the mail van. Sent them through the post and *he* had to pay the postage.'

The head, a rather rubbishy affair, with a framed photograph of the cheque for 'Twenty Pounds to J. B. Dunbar Poacher', held pride of place over the mantelpiece in his study, and it was this feat which John Buchan commemorated in his famous story *John MacNab*.

With the outbreak of the South African War in 1899, Jim naturally volunteered for service and after the war was over, found himself in the King's African Rifles with the rank of Captain. He then served for a period in British

162

Central Africa and for a while was district officer in charge of a large area of Zululand. The sport he obtained in Africa was, of course, extremely varied and by the time he felt impelled to return home he had collected the nucleus of a considerable collection of specimen heads of big game, which eventually was to number over 200, including 60 different varieties.

During the First World War Jim served with the Cameron Highlanders, still as a Captain, using his fine marksmanship and stalking abilities to good effect as a sniper on many occasions. It is perhaps significant, however, that despite his age (for by this time he was in his thirties) and his obvious experience, he was not promoted to higher rank. He was never averse to voicing his opinions and no doubt this affected his promotion.

On demobilisation after the war, he returned to Pitgaveny and, like his father before him, was appointed Deputy Lieutenant of the County and a JP, serving also on the County Council. Adopting his lifelong habit of planting a tree a day, he continued to keep his interest in deer stalking alive by renting a different deer forest in the hills each year. He would drive a horse-drawn gypsy caravan to his chosen ground to use as his base, while no doubt roving over the neighbouring forests as well, for in those days the Highlands were almost deserted after the summer months.

Meanwhile, at the outbreak of the same war, Archie was already well known as an outstanding sportsman in Central India and was a leading member of the Forestry Service. Because of his position in the Service he was not allowed to volunteer for the armed forces during the War and remained in India throughout the hostilities. He spent much of his service life hunting big game, as had Forsyth before him. In 1923, as Conservator of Forests, he published his book *Wild Animals in Central India*, a classic of its kind and a worthy successor to Forsyth's earlier work.

The copy he presented to Jim in 1924 is inscribed 'To Jim, with love from brother, March 1924.' The copy is, as might be expected, copiously annotated throughout with remarks scribbled in pencil. It was one of Jim's weaknesses that he could not prevent himself scribbling in the margins of books and the copy of his brother's book was clearly a heaven-sent opportunity.

Where Archie had written regarding black bears: 'Very rarely instead of being black the animal is brown. I have seen three specimens, one adult and two immature skins . . .', Jim noted, 'Brown hair is – on black animals – *dead* hair. Commonly seen.'

Writing on the tiger's sense of smell, Archie noted: '. . . they hardly possess any . . .'. Jim's marginal note reads; 'No African beast can smell worth a damn . . . More rubbish written about animal's sense of smell than anything else. I almost completely ignore "wind". Lyell and Stigand fell into the wind error.'

This is almost the equivalent of the Pope renouncing his belief in the Holy Trinity and is rather typical of the provocative statements Jim was fond of making. In practice, no confirmed deer stalker with the successes he had achieved could possibly say that 'wind' did not matter when stalking deer, or, for that matter, most game of all sizes. He was probably just prepared to argue this in the case of some types of African big game on some occasions or in certain types of terrain.

Jim knew most of the big game hunters of his day and particularly Lyell and Stigand, whom he met when out with the King's African Rifles in 1903 while the two were serving with them. In those days Jim used a double oval bore loaded with 9 grams of black powder, which left a copious blood spoor. Lyell subsequently recorded an extract from one of Jim's letters which was fairly typical of his style: 'I once had to follow a wounded bull through swampy ground covered with breast high iris-like growth and clumps of half burned tenka tenka every few yards. I was leading on the blood spoor when it became evident that we were close to our quarry. Although the men trusted me absolutely there was considerable hesitation when I suggested, in order to allow me free to look out for squalls, that an unarmed tracker should take the lead. We had hardly changed places when the bull's head appeared through the tenka tenka at right angles to his tracks. At this duelling range he simply sank into the grass with a bullet in his brain.'

He also wrote: 'I have had a pretty wide experience of all the dangerous beasts existing from the North to South Africa . . . I cannot exactly say how many elephants and buffaloes I have killed, but of lions I have killed a few, though I never particularly looked for them as the fewer shots fired when in elephant country the better.'

In the copy of Archie's book the interjections by Jim are often quite fascinating. For instance, the younger brother wrote, 'I cannot recollect a case in which a sportsman has been mauled when getting out of a machan at night', to which Jim inserted the comment, 'I've twice got one of the frights of my life by wearying of waiting at water and returning (alone) to camp – on foot of course.'

Archie continued: 'Personally, I . . . only consider I was in danger on one occasion . . . the tiger . . . spotted me in the machan and went off and bathed in a neighbouring pool . . . not wishing to spend a cold and supperless night, I descended quietly, but not so quietly as to escape the tiger's notice, who accompanied me in the jungle alongside the path up to the clearing, growling and demonstrating the whole time. It was a horrible experience and one I hope never to renew, and I only just retained sufficient control not to break into a fatal run. I shot this tiger shortly afterwards and many moons previously someone had driven a Martini Henry bullet right through him, which may have accounted for his peculiar behaviour.'

Jim noted in the margin: 'To run or turn is always fatal. I ran ten yards from a lioness once owing to my .303 magazine jamming and only escaped because I'd broken her foreleg at the shoulder and she fell twice 'ere she realised it was useless. I should have stood my ground.'

Archie wrote on the subject of a tiger's vitality: 'Many almost incredible instances of their endurance under the most frightful wounds have been published, which I can endorse from personal experience of a similar nature . . . I have known a tiger receive a .577 bullet which removed a portion of his heart, turn round, and then charge the beaters who were 100 yards behind . . . The tiger died after this effort, but the charge was . . . a determined effort with purpose in it.

'Head shots are not always fatal . . . When gaining experience I was once very nearly killed by assuming that a tiger which was bleeding in the face from the spot which I had aimed at was dead. It lay there apparently dead. It had previously been wounded and had already given me two charges and a great deal of trouble. Thankful that this was now all over, I stepped forward without even reloading the empty barrel, when it suddenly sprang up with a roar and rushed at me. I was lucky enough to get it in the nostrils and did kill it this time, but its dead body, in turning over, struck me in the chest and in turn laid me out for some minutes . . .'

Jim wrote in the margin: 'The hind legs of a lioness I killed in much the same circumstances would have hit me in the face if I had not jumped aside . . .'

Writing on the subject of moving tigers from cover Archie wrote: 'When hunted, tigers naturally lie up in cover and avoid the open, but cover is a relative term and consists of . . . any spot which is more "concealing" than the general average of the surrounding country. Such spots, therefore, should be approached with extreme caution, a position should be taken up which gives the hunter an advantage, i.e. beside a stout tree or on an eminence; the cover should then be stoned before advancing – a stone landed near the tiger will produce a growl or he will slink off or he may charge.'

Jim wrote in the margin. 'I've bombarded a wounded lion with thirty men throwing every conceivable missile besides abundant abuse of parents for half an hour and never a grunt. I once burnt one out (not wounded) and he waited until singed.'

Archie continued: 'In . . . following up a tiger . . . The sportsman should quarter the ground slightly in advance of the trackers and his duties are to defend and protect all concerned from unnecessary risks. Strict silence should be enjoyed so as to give one every chance of hearing the tiger.'

Jim wrote in the margin: 'Until my men knew me well they demurred at my *never* going first on the trail of any dangerous wounded animal. I always went second in the file with a first-class tracker on the spoor, I glancing at it but on the *qui vive* for squalls.'

Further on Archie noted that 'A tigress is more likely to demonstrate, but is more easily moved or turned than a tiger; a tiger, if he has once demonstrated is more likely to charge and charge home, than a tigress.' To which Jim responded by writing, 'A lioness both demonstrates more and is more courageous than the lion.'

At one point Archie recorded surprisingly: 'The flesh of tigers when cooked and eaten much resembles veal and retains none of the disgusting odour of the animal before skinning.' Jim's comment on this was an emphatic: 'Lion is not very good to eat.'

On Archie's retirement from the Forestry Service as Conservator, Jim asked him to take over as Factor (i.e. Manager) of the Pitgaveny estate, but the brothers could not work in harness long together. Indeed, Jim was a difficult person to live with as numerous people discovered. A notorious local figure about whom stories were legion, he became a legend in his own lifetime and it is always difficult living with a legend. He, of course, enjoyed adding to them whenever he could.

He had a story attached to almost every head amongst the many which completely layered the walls of his mouldering ancestral pile at Pitgaveny. The finest head of a deer, however, vying for pride of place with his own 'John MacNab' head, was that of a magnificent swamp deer, over one of the lower tines of which was carelessly hung a gold medal suspended on a faded ribbon. This was the head, shot by Archie, which won the Gold Medal for the best head at the Olympic Games in 1937. At the time it was rumoured that Herman Goering himself had fondly hoped to win this medal with his own entry, but was beaten at the last minute by Archie's magnificent specimen. Attached to the medal, which was of 'ersatz gold' and quite valueless except as a curiosity, was a badly typewritten note which read:

> Presented at the 1937 Olympic Games to Archibald
> Dunbar Brander by Field Marshall Herman Goering,
> who afterwards committed suicide at the
> Nuremburg Trials in 1947.

Archie, having retired with relief from the task of managing the estate, died in 1953. Jim outlived all the other big game hunters of his generation. In old age he remained a small sturdy, kilted figure, with his memory and his irrepressible sense of humour intact.

Although a good performer with both shotgun and rifle (he continued to shoot geese on nearby Loch Spynie and roedeer on the estate until into his late eighties) it was apparently always a slight matter of chagrin to Jim that his brother Archie, from his earliest days, was generally acknowledged the better shot of the two. He was also undoubtably the finer character. Yet, if only through sheer longevity, Jim remained a remarkable example of period survival. If nothing else, he outlasted all the others. He died aged ninety-four in 1969. He was indeed the very last of his kind.

Notes on a contemporary: Frederick Raban Willians

There were so many minor big game hunters in the latter part of the nineteenth and early twentieth century that it is almost invidious to mention some and not others. Frederick Raban Williams was, however, perhaps typical in many ways of those who helped to open up Africa in the late nineteenth century and first decade of the twentieth, shooting big game as a way of life. Son of a merchant banker, he was born in Luton in 1874, later moving to Guildford, where he was taught by a tutor. He studied initially to become a lawyer but soon found this was not his metier and went instead to farm in Canada. He followed this by prospecting for gold in the far north in the 1891–1893 gold rush, where at least he learned to survey land, even if he found no gold.

On his return to England he joined the West Sussex Yeomanry. In 1897 he went out to Bulawayo and joined the Bulawayo Burgher Force in the last Zulu rebellion. He then tried his hand at farming, prospecting and hunting and it was at this time he met Frederick Selous, while acting as trail blazer and surveyor when the gold and diamond mines were being opened up in Rhodesia. In 1901 he spent an unexplained year in Paris and then went to sea as an engineer, returning to Africa in 1905 to act as surveyor, general advance guard, and trouble shooter for the Benguela railway. He opened up several new projects in the Orange River, Zululand and Northern Rhodesia, going as far as the Belgian Congo and into East Africa.

Raban Williams.

In 1914 he was homeward bound to volunteer for war service when he met the charming young nineteen-year-old daughter of one of Cecil Rhodes's partners who had made a fortune in the diamond fields. She was all set to marry well on her arrival in England, but her fiancé in the UK stood no chance against the attractions of the handsome forty-year-old big game hunter and adventurer and she was swept off her feet.

Soon after the marriage he was commissioned into the 8th South Staffordshires as a Lieutenant and was severely wounded at the Battle of Loos as an acting Company Commander. Mentioned in despatches, he was soon back in action at Ypres in 1917, when he transferred to the Royal Flying Corps. In 1918 he was given a permanent commission in the RAF, but in 1920 was forced to retire from the effects of his earlier wounds.

He then took his wife and young family to British Columbia, starting a strawberry farm as well as surveying in Alaska. From there he moved on to surveying the Blue Nile Dam and later the Assuan Dam. In 1925 he was appointed assistant engineer for the Kenya and Uganda Railway, by which time he had more or less given up shooting big game, although opportunities were still available. Finally, in 1930 he retired and continued with various interests in England until, on the outbreak of the Second World War in 1939, he joined the Home Guard. A very good example in many ways of his kind and of his period, he died aged seventy-one in 1944.

Walter Dalrymple Maitland Bell 1880–1951

Africa 1897–1922

Arguably the Greatest: Certainly the Last

We went thirty days on end without seeing an elephant and in the succeeding four days I killed forty-four bulls. A lioness came within a foot of catching a boy and was shot . . .

The greatest elephant hunter of his day and a big game hunter of renown, Captain Walter Dalrymple Maitland Bell, MC, was born in the Lowlands of Scotland in 1880, the tenth child of a wealthy Scots timber merchant. His mother died at the age of two and his father died when he was six. Thereafter he was brought up in the guardianship of his eldest brother who was over twenty years his senior. Perhaps because of this early loss of his parents he grew up a self-contained child, never interested in team games and very much an individualist. At his prep-school, which he loathed, at the age of eight he laid out the sixteen-year-old hero of the school with a cricket bat.

Perhaps influenced by early reading, his first ambition was to shoot bison, but later his enthusiasm switched to elephants. When he proved troublesome at school, he was packed off to sea on a sailing ship, but left it of his own accord in New Zealand. He then worked his passage round the Horn at the age of fourteen. His exasperated elder brother thereafter consigned him to a tutor in Germany, despite his frequently expressed desire to become a big game hunter. Tutorials did not suit him very long and once more he returned home, where he finally persuaded his guardian to let him go to Africa.

At the age of seventeen he set off for Mombasa. From there he found himself working on the projected Ugandan railway, helping to kill man-eating lions. After agreeing to join an expedition into the interior he was left stranded, suffering from malaria, and had to return home travelling steerage, his tail rather between his legs.

His trustees proved unwilling to finance further expeditions to Africa and he set off instead for the newly-found goldfields in the Klondike. Here, with a partner, he hunted and shot meat, selling the food to prospectors in the goldfields near Dawson. His partner left him in the lurch and made off with the profits, but in the meantime he had learned valuable lessons in subsistence.

At this stage in his life war broke out in South Africa and he volunteered in Canada for a mounted unit, passing first-class both in health and shooting

169

ability. In subsequent desultory action against the Boers his horse was shot and he was taken prisoner, but soon escaped and returned to the British lines. By the end of the war he had learned more valuable lessons in personal survival and now at last found himself in Africa with sufficient cash to finance his own expedition. Already he had made close friends with gunmaker, Daniel Fraser of Edinburgh, and he now acquired two sporting models of the .303 he had come to know and like during the war, using with it a solid-jacketed 215 grain bullet. Thus armed, he went into Southern Uganda and on to Unyoro, where elephant were known to be found.

Having been wrongly advised on the whereabouts of the animal's brain, Bell killed his first elephant with a body shot behind the shoulder. He then sawed open the head between the tusks and thus finally discovered to his own satisfaction exactly where the brain lay. Subsequently, he offered his opinion that no-one should be allowed to shoot elephants until they had examined an elephant's skull in this way. It is notable that in this he was following the example of experienced hunters such as Samuel White Baker.

He then learned his next lesson, discovering that if elephant were killed by a brain shot they did not, in falling, cause their companions to panic – as they did when shot in the body, or when falling against a companion. It was therefore as a specialist in head shots, with a light .275 rifle taken from in front, from the side, or from behind, that Bell was later to amass such huge bags of elephants, shooting considerable numbers at a time without unduly alarming the main herd. It was often said that many would-be emulators of this method ended up dead; certainly without his superlative eyesight, reflexes and co-ordination, it was not a reliable method of killing elephants with impunity.

There is an interesting account of just what a remarkable natural shot he was with a rifle, resulting from his wish to test some suspect ammunition. He was trying some rounds from a doubtful batch of ammunition by firing them at cormorants passing across a lake at a range of over a hundred yards or more from the shore. He had been regularly downing these birds for some time when he was approached by two of the locals who wished to enquire what ammunition he was using in his *shotgun* as they had never before seen birds killed at such a range.

His next significant move was towards the unexplored country round Karamojo, where the law knew no bounds and elephants were to be found in plenty. In 1902 there were still slave traders operating in this lawless area. The Karamojo natives set themselves up as raiders, continuing centuries of tribal warfare, but now armed with modern rifles. The situation there was indeed much as Samuel White Baker had found it in the mid-nineteenth century, with armed traders and natives all at each others throats with no-one trusting anyone else. It was not long, however, before Bell had established his party as completely different from other traders. He made it plain that

Walter Dalrymple Maitland Bell in retirement.

he was only interested in shooting elephants, and that any interference would result in a fight. His aggressive attitude clearly impressed the Karamojo, for eventually he became blood brother to one of their more important chieftains. Thereafter he ceased to have any trouble and soon had as much ivory as he could move. From 1902–1907 he hunted this area almost exclusively without any interference from any other parties.

It was not all easy shooting by any means. On one occasion he recorded: 'We went thirty days on end without seeing an elephant and in the succeeding four days I killed forty-four bulls. A lioness came within a foot of catching a boy and was shot . . .'

Subsequently he moved into the Belgian Congo. His elephant hunting here was again extremely successful, but on at least one occasion he found himself hunted by the Belgian frontier police on the grounds that he was poaching ivory. He admitted to having one armed brush with them, when he was forced to fire in self-defence before getting safely across the frontier.

In 1911 he tried hunting in Liberia, where he found the dwarf elephants had tiny tusks, not worth shooting, although he found some exceptions. He then went on to French Equatorial Africa in 1912. Here he hunted up the Ubangi River with a steam launch. This proved both successful and extremely profitable, and he shot a worthwhile number of elephants.

In Liberia he encountered an interesting individual named Phelizot, whose mother was French but whose father was Irish, and who was himself a US citizen. Although Bell had shown him his own method of shooting elephants, Phelizot's method of hunting was to carry a double .450 and a .318 Mauser. According to Bell, he would find an elephant then rush in close and fire the .450 into the body, thereafter following it and shooting with the .318 until it fell dead. By this method he successfully killed individual bulls with magnificent tusks. He was apparently highly successful in killing individual beasts, but never approached herds. When this somewhat eccentric hunter had obtained £3,000's worth of ivory he returned to Paris, sending £500 to his gunmaker against new equipment and a return ticket, then spending the rest on debauchery. In 1914 he joined the Foreign Legion and was killed in the First World War.

During the war Bell served in the RFC, attained the rank of captain and gained a well-earned MC. After the war he married, but still organised one last trip to Africa to the Ivory Coast. He and his companion, a friend named Wynne, an excellent shot, who was inexperienced in shooting elephants, had a meeting with a native chief which reads in modern terms exactly as if it might have been written by any of the earlier travellers of the previous century. It is apparent that nothing in Africa had changed.

Bell found himself involved with parties dealing in slavery. In fact the self-elected king of the area where he and his friend hunted most successfully after the war was in effect a large-scale slaver, raiding and enslaving the neighbouring weaker tribes. Bell and his companion prevented the king's followers collecting slaves and were not popular with him as a result.

Bell found that hunting elephants by using canoes allowed him to cover much greater areas than if he had tried to hunt merely on foot. In places he even encountered elephant still apparently totally unaccustomed to the sound of rifle fire and therefore quite fearless of it. He was thus able to pick and choose which beasts he shot with even more than his usual care. Most of the time he and his friend Wynne lived off teal, eating two at a time entire. He also, while hunting on the Niger and the Bar Aouck rivers, encountered some of the Hamran Arab elephant hunters whose exploits had been graphically described by Samuel White Baker in the previous century.

Finally, Bell and his wife retired to an estate in Easter Ross, near Garve. He then found in his retirement that he had a promising artistic talent as well a considerable latent literary ability. He started writing articles illustrated in the main with his own drawings. He also had a yacht, named *Trenchemer*, specially designed and built in Aberdeen, with which in 1937 he came second in that most testing of Ocean Races, the Fastnet.

During the Second World War he served in the Home Guard, but was too old to take any more active part. In 1948 he had a slight heart attack and in 1950 for health reasons had to give up his yacht. He continued, however, to stalk stags in his estate, Corriemoille. In 1951 he suffered a second and fatal heart attack and thus, at the age of seventy-one, the greatest elephant hunter of them all passed on to the final hunting grounds. His score of elephants cannot be fully assessed as he gave up counting after the first thousand.

His amazing ability as a shot was the secret of his success, plus the fact that he was light on his feet and always alert. Good footwork, superlative eyesight and reflexes were his strength. Although it might seem that he killed too many elephants it must be remembered that they are still being culled at the rate of around five thousand a year. This puts his grand total in a lifetime, at a time when they were far more plentiful, in proper perspective. He killed cleanly for a living and his quarry did not suffer. The same cannot be said for the many animals caught in traps, or wounded by poachers, or simply dying painfully of old age or disease.

Notes on a contemporary: Dennis David Lyell

Dennis David Lyell was born in Calcutta in February 1871 of Scottish parents who soon returned home to Dundee, where he spent most of his childhood. He read 'profusely on Africa, India and America' and later wrote that he 'soon got to know the works of Gordon Cumming, Selous, Baker, Forsyth, Kinloch, Roosevelt and many others almost by heart and could have passed an examination early in life on the type of weapons used by the various hunters of big game.'

After leaving school he took a job as assistant in a tea plantation at Cossipore in Assam. In 1897 he made a hunting trip into the north-eastern frontier area, but it was really only when he left India for Africa that his career as a big game hunter developed. In 1899, having been severely debilitated by recurrent fever in Assam, he returned home and, once recovered, set out for Nyasaland. He ended up in Blantyre, where he heard of an appointment as assistant to the Quartermaster of the King's African Rifles, near Zomba. Here he met Captain C. H. Stigand, whose close friend he soon became.

Lyell shot most of his game with a 7.9mm Mauser from Rigby, because the cartridges were readily available. With this he shot everything from elephants downwards. It would appear from his own modest accounts that he was not in the same league as a shot as Bell, but then few people were. However Lyell seems to have killed most game successfully and was certainly a very experienced hunter.

In conjunction with C. H. Stigand he wrote his first book, *Central African Game and Its Spoor*, published in 1906. This was a rather extraordinary Edwardian attempt to produce a 'How to' book on hunting big game and,

Denis D. Lyell, and (below) with the horns of a kudu bull shot in north-eastern Rhodesia.

scarcely surprisingly, it sold only the one edition. The writing bug, however, then seems to have seized both him and Stigand, but of the two Lyell was much more the natural writer, possibly because of his admitted prodigious reading as a boy. His output was much greater than Stigand's, but then, of course, Stigand was killed in 1919 and Lyell was still writing books in the 1930s.

Lyell tried many means of making a living, from farming, or ranching in Rhodesia, to hunting. By 1910 or thereabouts he decided the newly-introduced restrictions on hunting, with hunters restricted by licence to a limited number of elephants, were making it impossible to live by the rifle any longer. He then started writing fairly extensively. His first solo effort, published in 1910, was a small volume entitled *Hunting Trips in N. Rhodesia*, intended simply as a guide for travellers. In 1912 he wrote *Nyasaland for the Hunter and Settler*, basically the same book revised and enlarged.

Wild Life in Central Africa followed in 1913, and this was really extracts from his diaries over ten years of elephant hunting. In 1923 he wrote *Memories of an Elephant Hunter*, which consisted of somewhat rambling but pleasant reminiscences of his life as a hunter, including a chapter on India and also including some useful tips for the novice hunter. The following year, 1924, saw the publication of *The African Elephant and Its Hunters*, which included interesting accounts of the various elephant hunters known personally to him. Finally in 1935 he published his last book entitled *African Adventure*, sub-titled 'Letters from Famous Big Game Hunters'. This consisted almost entirely of annotated correspondence with all the well known big game hunters of his day and was perhaps the nearest anyone had come at this stage to writing a history of hunting in the late Victorian and Edwardian period.

He included thumbnail sketches of now largely forgotten figures whom he had met in his travels when hunting big game in the period before the First World War. Lyell also corresponded with many well known figures most of whom he met at the Shikar Club, the big game hunter's club which met once a year. Amongst these was his fellow Scot from Ayrshire, R. J. Cuninghame, MC, who was with Roosevelt at intervals during his African safari. Clearly a man of humorous outlook, he and numerous other characters are well described by Lyell.

He was an industrious letter writer, enquiring from almost all the well-known hunters of the day such questions as what beasts they considered most dangerous and so on. He received, on the whole, remarkably interesting replies. As the 'Big Game Boswell' of his day he thus deserves acknowledgement for recording much that might otherwise have been lost or forgotten. Apart from his letter-writing activities, he also contributed numerous articles to publications such as *The Field* and *The Lonsdale Library*. Indeed, prior to his death in 1949, aged 78, writing and replying to correspondents appears to have been his full-time occupation.

AFTERMATH AND CONCLUSION

The outbreak of the First World War in 1914, when Man concentrated on killing his fellow Man rather than large or small game animals, marked the end of the old full-time big game hunters; the men who pursued big game hunting for sport, for collections, or for profit. Admittedly, numerous safari hunters continued to offer wealthy clients the opportunity to shoot big game in Africa under licence. Similarly, some big game was also shot under licence in India. This state of affairs continued up to the Second World War of 1939–1945.

By this time the need to preserve the vanishing resources of wild life, first recognised by the creation of the Kruger National Park in South Africa as early as the 1880s and brought to world attention by President Theodore Roosevelt's conservation programmes in the USA, had begun to spread more widely. Efforts to prevent the extinction of the remaining big game were intensified. Yet it was not the old big game hunters who had been to blame for the steady erosion of so many endangered species. Indeed, it was they who had almost always been the first to draw attention to the dangers threatening the big game.

It was the outward spread of civilisation, ever encroaching on the wild spaces, clearing the jungles for timber or for agriculture, ploughing the plains for corn, or enclosing them to farm cattle or sheep, which drove away big game, just as happened in the Mediterranean basin over a thousand years earlier. With the presence of domestic beasts, the lions, tigers, leopards and other predators had to be discouraged, or shot. The elephants damaging the forests and herbage at random, had to be driven back, or shot. In addition, widespread poaching by irresponsible natives armed with modern high-powered weapons firing from moving vehicles, or working with lights by night, simply for meat or skins, or for the tusks of elephants or rhinoceros, inevitably affected the big game numbers drastically. Such mindless butchers shot with their automatic weapons, or snared and trapped without caring whether they were killing immature young or pregnant females, or future breeding stock.

The spread of modern farming methods, the increase of population and the need for meat, or the high prices paid in far eastern markets for the supposed aphrodisiac qualities of the rhinoceros horn, or elephant ivory for carving ornaments, all must weight heavily against the survival of big game. There are places where game cannot hope to survive, but in other places the picture is not quite so bleak. There are even some small signs of hope.

The Indian tiger, at the end of the Second World War and later at the time of Partition, was estimated to number around 40,000. By 1972 it was down to around 2,000 and was certainly amongst the threatened species of the world. The creation of sixteen tiger reserves in India between 1978 and 1979 was a big step forward. From the Corbett National Reserve, named after the famous post-war tiger hunter and naturalist, Colonel Jim Corbett, in the foothills of the Himalayas to the north, to the Sundarabans Reserve in the mangrove swamps of southern Bengal where the Royal Bengal tiger still flourishes, these reserves have proved successful. At one time the tiger numbers in the Sunderabans swamps were estimated to be down as low as 400, but they are now estimated to be up to 2,000, with 4,000 as the overall figure and improving. Man-eaters, of course, must sometimes be killed, or else captured and caged, but others can still be tolerated and even encouraged, where they do little harm.

Unfortunately, elephants in India are still hunted by illegal poachers for their ivory, and are also rapidly approaching danger point. The herds in the reserves are persecuted by poachers and the rangers have insufficient powers to deal with them. It is the old story of man's greed threatening to destroy his natural heritage. It is the history of commercial killing for profit without thought for the future; it is the story of the American bison once again being repeated in another part of the world. Yet instances have been successful, where governments have joined forces to combat the problem. It is, of course, a major concern in many parts of Africa. It has been reliably estimated that the elephant population has been reduced from around one and a half million to around five hundred thousand in the last fifteen years, chiefly because of the demands for illegal ivory and the expanding population armed with automatic weapons. The rhinoceros population has all but vanished. Of course when confronted with the choice of starvation because of famine on the one hand, or shooting a protected species on the other, it is understandable why the inhabitants feel justified in killing. This is the fault of governments, not individuals, and it is up to governments to find the answer. The World Wildlife Organisation exists to help them do just that.

Anyone with an interest in wildlife today and especially in the preservation of the remaining big game should support the efforts of the World Wildlife Organisation. The paradox is that in areas where game has to be culled and where tourism is encouraged, there are still those who may wish to shoot a grizzly bear, an elephant, a tiger, or a leopard. Strictly controlled hunting parties can still provide a useful tourist return. If there is such a demand then paradoxically enough this will mean the preservation of the species specifically to fulfil that demand.

This is certainly not advocating a return to wholesale shooting of big game, but merely pointing out that where game must be culled to prevent numbers increasing beyond reasonable bounds, it is as well to make a virtue of necessity and offer the opportunity to those so minded to cull a limited number under strict supervision. There is evidence that where this is taking place in limited areas today the big game is surviving, since it is seen as a source of government income rather than as a threat to farming interests. That the old big game hunters would have regarded such hunting as a travesty is undeniable, but of little concern. Their way of life has gone for ever and it is necessary for the sake of preserving what wild life remains to adapt to present-day needs and circumstances.

To a man, the early big game hunters would have been appalled by the picture presented today, although many of the later hunters had foreseen much of what has happened and warned against it. The World Wildlife Organisation on a global scale is doing its best to preserve the steadily vanishing species by monitoring their numbers and keeping abreast of the world situation, as well as by encouraging governments to take action wherever necessary. They face an uphill struggle, but no-one can help but wish them well. It is only by the education of government first and individuals thereafter; by monitoring the numbers of endangered species; by lobbying the leading world powers; by getting concerted action on a world scale, that action is likely to be forthcoming. It is ultimately only by providing National Reserves, wherever a species is threatened; by preventing the unauthorised carrying of arms; and in some cases by enforcing draconian methods, that the big game can be helped to survive.

The Reservations, the National Parks, Safari Parks, or similar centres, call them what you will, where animals may survive in an approximation of their wild habitat, are perhaps the only final answer. Man has been persecuting big game for long enough and now the pressures have increased to the stage where the big game will otherwise simply become extinct. There have been examples enough already to show that this is not improbable. It is up to Man to provide a refuge of some sort. Such refuges may not be ideal, but they are surely better than nothing. Let us look to the future and try to preserve the big game that remains for future generations. That is what the old big game hunters themselves, above all, would have wished.

RIFLES USED BY THE
BIG GAME HUNTERS

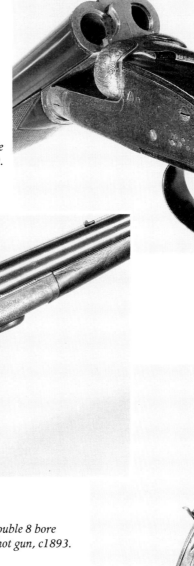

(right) *Holland & Holland
double ejector hammerless rifle
in .577 Express 3" case, c1900.*

(above) *Holland & Holland double 8 bore
hammer 'Paradox' ball and shot gun, c1893.*

(right) *Double .400/.350 Nitro Express by
Alexander Henry, Edinburgh, 1885.*

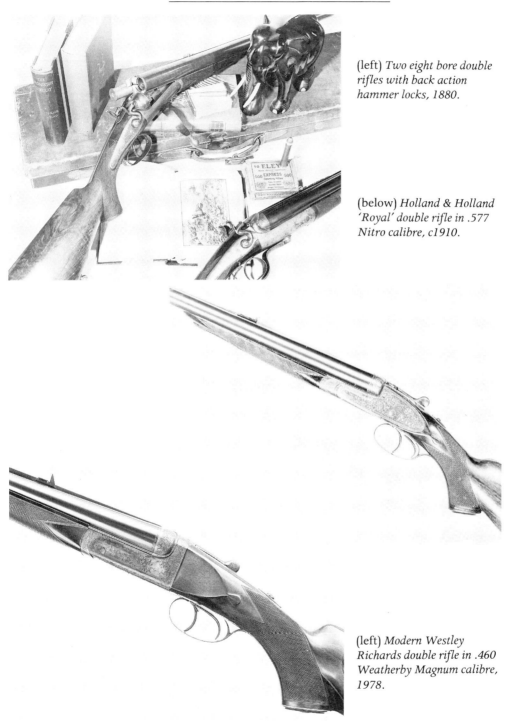

(left) *Two eight bore double rifles with back action hammer locks, 1880.*

(below) *Holland & Holland 'Royal' double rifle in .577 Nitro calibre, c1910.*

(left) *Modern Westley Richards double rifle in .460 Weatherby Magnum calibre, 1978.*

181

CRITICAL BIBLIOGRAPHY

Aflalo, F. G., joint editor with the Earl of Suffolk and Hedley Peek, *The Encyclopedia of Sport*, Lawrence & Bullen, 1897.

Aardvark to Zebra: contributions on Big Game: Africa by H. A. Bryden: India by J. D. Inverarity: N. America by J. Turner: other contributors Theodore Roosevelt, R. Lydekker, etc.

Akroyd, R. A., contributor, *see* Lonsdale Library.

Allen, Hugh, *The Lonely Tiger* , Faber & Faber, 1960.

An interesting commentary on big game shooting in post-partition India: night poaching and the wounding of game. Good reading.

Anderson, Kenneth, *Nine Man-Eaters & One Rogue*, Allen & Unwin, 1954.

Very readable account of the lives and ends of varied big cats that had taken to man-eating in the 1930s.

Man Eaters and Jungle Killers, Allen & Unwin, 1957.

A good the deal of the 'still smoking muzzle' cliché but still some good material of the 'Wide World' variety.

The Black Panther of Sivanipalli, Allen & Unwin, 1959.

'And other adventures of the Indian Jungle:' by a writer whose admitted aim is 'to keep his readers interested'.

The Call of the Man Eater, Allen & Unwin, 1961.

More of the 'adventure' genre by this expatriate turning towards naturalist/folklore.

This Is The Jungle, Allen & Unwin, 1964.

More of the 'adventure in the jungle' kind and still some good material amongst the rest.

The Tiger Roars, Allen & Unwin, 1967.

Amongst the best of these, showing a critical appreciation of the game poaching and developments in modern India.

An Old Shekarree, *The Spear & The Rifle or Recollections of Sport in India*, Ward & Lock, no date, c.1830–40.

Hog hunting, elephant catching and tiger shooting with a little treasure hunting for good measure. Author unknown.

Aramilev, Ivan, *Beyond the Ural Mountains*, 'The Adventurers of a Siberian Hunter', translated from the German, Allen & Unwin, 1961.

Mainly about small game shooting but includes wolf shooting and killing a bear with a knife. Unusual glimpses of Russian life.

Arbuthnot, Col. A. G., CMG, DSO, RA, *See* Burrard, Major G. Contributor of chapters on Ibex, Markhor, Oorial and Kashmir Stag.

Armstrong, Major Nevill A. D., OBE, FRGS, *Yukon Yesterdays: or Thirty Years of Adventure in the Klondike*, 'Personal memories of the famous Klondike Gold Rush, first-hand accounts of lucky strikes, stories of Dawson in the wild Nineties, together with adventures in mining exploration and big game hunting in the unknown sub-Arctic', 54 illustrations and map, John Long, 1936.

Very little on big game hunting but one or two mentions of encounters with grizzly bears.

After Big Game in the Upper Yukon, John Long, 1937.

With records of four hunting trips after caribou, grizzly bear and moose, with evocative pictures and text.

Badminton Library of Sport & Pastimes, *Big Game Hunting*, 2 Vols, Longmans Green, 1894.

Vol I: Ed. by Clive Phillips-Wolley. Contributions by Sir Samuel White Baker; W. C. Oswell; F. J. Jackson; Warburton Pike; F. C. Selous; Vol II: Ed. by Clive Phillips-Wolley. Contributions by Lt. Col. R. Heber Percy; Major Algernon C. Heber Percy; W. A. Baillie-Grohman; Sir Henry Pottinger, Bart; the Earl of Kilmorey; Abel Chapman; Walter J. Buck; St George Littledale.

Baillie-Grohman, W. A., contributor, *see* Badminton Library of Sport & Pastimes.

Baillie-Grohman, W. A., *Camps in the Rockies*, 'Being a narrative of life in the Frontier and Sport in the Rocky Mountains with an account of the Cattle Ranches of the West', Sampson Low, 1882.

Disappointingly prolix account of various sporting expeditions on horseback through the Rocky Mountains.

Fifteen Years Sport & Life in the Hunting Grounds of Western America and British Columbia, Horace Cox, 1900.

A trophy hunter's sport in the '70s and '80s: tedious, but interesting photographs. A chapter on Western servants by Mrs Baillie-Grohman.

Baillie, Mrs. W. W., *Days & Nights of Shikar*, Bodley

Head, 1921.
Not uninteresting in places regarding the larger cats, but reveals throughout the power of the Mem Sahib in India of the 1920s.

Baker, Edward R., *Sport in Bengal*, Ledger Smith, 1886.
Rather muddled sporting records by retired Director of Police, but some good first-hand accounts with attitudes indicative of period.

Baker, Sir Samuel White, contributor, *see* Badminton Library of Sport & Pastimes.

Baker, Sir Samuel White, *Eight Years in Ceylon*, Longmans, 1853.
Autobiographical account of the settlement formed by the Baker brothers in the highlands of Ceylon with details of elephant shooting.

With Rifle & Hound in Ceylon, Longmans, 1855.
Riveting account of Baker's method of hunting *par force* with hounds in pursuit of wild boar, and of elephant-shooting exploits.

The Albert N'yanza, Great Basin of the Nile, Macmillan, 2 Vols, 1866.
Details of exploration including numerous accounts of big game hunting, from elephants and hippopotami to lions and antelope.

The Nile Tributaries of Abyssinia, Macmillan, 1867.
Account of varied big game hunting expedition including elephant hunting with swords in Sudan. Very graphic and readable material.

Ismailia, Macmillan, 2 Vols, 1874.
Mainly on putting down the slave trade in Sudan interior, but some good accounts of big game hunting included. Very readable.

Wild Beasts & Their Ways, Macmillan, 1890.
Very good material on almost all big game with personal accounts of hunting in Far East, Africa and N. America.

Baldwin, Captain J. H., FZS, *The Large & Small Game of Bengal & The North Western Provinces of India*, King, 1877.
One of the early How-To books on big game shooting. Good and detailed with many first-hand accounts of shooting.

Baldwin, William Charles, *African Hunting from the Natal to the Zambesi*, New York, Harper, 1863.
From 1852 to 1860, includes Kalahari. Readable and likeable account of sport and commercial hunting in the early pioneering days.

Ball, V., *Jungle Life in India*, De la Rue, 1880.
The journals of a geologist in India, Burma, Malaya. Not a great deal on big game, but pro-vides a picture of the period.

Barns, T. Alexander, FRGS, *The Wonderland of the Western Congo*, 'The Region of the Snow-covered Volcanoes, the Pygmies, the Giant Gorilla and the Okapi', Putman, 1920.
Well illustrated but rather ponderous reading; not up to expectations aroused by the sub-title.

Across the Great Craterland to the Congo, 'Describing a Journey of Exploration & Research to the Land of the Giant Craters in Tanganyika Territory & To the Forests & Lakes & Volcanoes of the South Eastern Congo with Some Account of the African Apes & the Capture & Taming of the African Elephant: with in addition a chapter on Elephant Shooting', Ernest Benn, 1923.
Again well illustrated and rather better reading than the earlier companion volume, but still heavy going.

An African Eldorado, Methuen, 1926.
Gorilla and elephant hunting in the Congo by field naturalist preparing elephants for Rowland Ward.

Baze, William, *Just Elephants*, translated from the French by H. M. Burton, Elek Books, 1955.
Recollections of a hunter in pre-1945 Viet Nam (Indo-China) who spent many years capturing and taming wild elephants. Some good material.

Tiger! Tiger! translated from the French by H. M. Burton, Elek Books, 1957.
Tigers in Indo-China (Viet Nam) written from notes by experienced sportsman/planter shooting from elephants and machans 1916–1940.

Beard, Peter Hill, *The End of Game*, Hamlyn, 1965.
A good, evocative picture of the passing of the big game and their hunters in Kenya and Tanganyika. Well illustrated.

Bell, Captain W. D. M., *The Wanderings of an Elephant Hunter*, Macmillan, 1923, reprinted Spearman, 1960, 1976.
One of the most enduring classics of African big-game hunting. A first-hand view of 25 years hunting by a first-rate shot and artist.

Bell, Captain W. D. M., *Bell of Africa*, Neville Spearman, 1960.
Posthumous autobiography of Captain Walter Dalrymple Maitland Bell, arguably one of the greatest African elephant hunters of all time.

Bergman, Sten, *Sport & Exploration in the Far East*, translated by Frederic Whyte, Methuen, 1933.
Impressions of visit to Kurile Islands off Japan 1929–30. Little sport, but mention of bears.

Berkeley, The Hon. Grantley F., *The English Sportsman in the Western Prairies*, Hurst & Blackett, 1861.

Racy account of a visit by a well-known British sportsman to U.S. Western Prairies to hunt bison before their virtual extinction.

Best, Capt. J. J., *Excursions in Albania*, 'Comprising a Description of the Wild Boar, Deer & Woodcock Shooting in that Country & a Journey from Thence to Thessalonica & Constantinople & up the Danube to Pest', W. H. Allen, 1942.

Result of notes taken over two tours and six years. Hardly sport, but evocative of place and period.

Best, The Hon. James W., *Indian Shikar Notes*, Pioneer Press, 1921.

Excellent general introduction to all forms of sport in India and requirements. Dated but sensible.

Tiger Days, John Murray, 1931.

Some good accounts of various sporting episodes mainly after tiger, using a bobbery mixed pack for hunting tigers.

Blaine, Capt. G., MC, contributor, *see* Lonsdale Library.

Bland-Sutton, J., *Man & Beast in Eastern Ethiopia*, Macmillan, 1911.

Covers a wide field, but includes comments on all the important big game species and provides a good period picture.

Blaney-Percival, A., *A Game Ranger's Notebook*, ed. E. D. Cuming, Nisbet, 1924.

Observations over 30 years in Africa of which 22 as Game Ranger in Kenya. Hunting lions with hounds: change of habits of elephants, etc.

A Game Ranger on Safari, ed. E. D. Cuming, Nisbet, 1928.

Kenyan Game Ranger's very readable reminiscences of safaris, animals, natives and incidents encountered. Well illustrated.

Blunt, Cdr. David Enderby, *Elephant*, East Africa, 1933.

Retired RN Commander turned Elephant Control Officer in Tanganyika for six years. Interesting conclusions sometimes open to question.

Boyes, John, FRGS, FZS, *The Company of Adventurers*, East Africa, 1928.

Rambling but very interesting reminiscences of one of the earliest pioneers of Kenya, known as 'King of the Kikuyu'.

Braddon, Sir Edward, KCMG, *Thirty Years of Shikar*, Blackwood, 1895.

Meandering memories of distinguished administrator/sportsman from pre-Mutiny with good period material on big game.

Brander, A. A. Dunbar, *Wild Animals in Central India*, Arnold, 1926.

Engrossing result of years of hunting and observing tiger, leopards, panthers, deer, bison, buffalo, antelopes, pig and wild dog.

Brander, Michael, *Hunting & Shooting*, Weidenfeld, 1971.

A history 'from the earliest times to the present day'. Includes India, Africa and N. America. Very well illustrated.

The Perfect Victorian Hero, Mainstream, 1982.

A biography of Sir Samuel White Baker, concentrating particularly on the big game hunting aspects of his career.

Brander, Michael, with Ed. Zern, joint editors, *An International Encyclopedia of Shooting*, Rainbird/Pelham, 1972, Peerage Books, 1982.

Well illustrated world directory of big and small game shooting, with contribution by Earl of Enniskillen on African big game shooting.

Browne, Major E. D., OBE, contributor, *see* Lonsdale Library.

Bryden, H. A., *Kloof & Karoo*, 'Sport, Legend & Natural History in Cape Colony with a Notice of the Game Birds & of the Present Distribution of the Antelopes & Larger Game', Longmans Green, 1889.

Some good period material but tediously written. Notes how commercial over-shooting caused elephant to leave the area.

Bryden, H. A., contributor on African big game shooting, *The Encyclopedia of Sport*, *see* Aflalo. Also editor, *The Big Game of Asia & N. America*, Contributors: Millais, J. G.; Wallace, H. Frank; Barclay, Ford G.; Kennion, Lt. Col. R.C.; Carruthers, D.; Van der Byl, P.B., London Counties Press Association, 1915.

A massive 400-page Edwardian production, well illustrated, showing most big game including New Zealand and N. America.

Buck, Walter J., contributor, *see* Badminton Library of Sport & Pastimes.

Buck, Walter J., *Wild Spain*, *see* Chapman, Abel.

Burrard, Major G., DSO, contributor, *see* Lonsdale Library.

Burrard, Major G., DSO, *Big Game Hunting in the Himalayas and Tibet*, Herbert Jenkins, 1925.

An instructional guide with sections by Arbuthnot, Col. A. G.; Cotton, W. B.; Evans, Col. G. A.; Lowis, F. C.; Wheeler-Cuffe, Sir Otway, Bt.

Burton, Lt. General E. F., *Reminiscences of Sport in India*, W. H. Allen, 1885.
Straightforward and mainly sporting reminiscences from 1840 to 1880 showing changes taking place.

An Indian Olio, Spencer Blackett, 1888.
An overall picture of India, including the Mutiny and Burma, with some chapters on sport with tigers and elephants.

Burton, Brig. General R. G., *Sport & Wildlife in the Deccan*, Seeley, Service, 1928.
Son of General E. F. Burton in India 1839–1883. His first book on big game hunting, from c.1890. Sometimes confusing coverage of periods.

A Book of Man-Eaters, Hutchinson, 1931.
Some good material on tigers and leopards, with some unnecessary extraneous material on werewolves, cannibalism, etc.

The Book of the Tiger, Hutchinson, 1933.
Some very good material on tigers, repeated from above. Shooting on foot, including man-eaters. Also chapter on lions in India.

The Tiger Hunters, Hutchinson, 1935.
Wide-ranging reminiscences of retired Indian Brigadier in his old age and not entirely reliable, but still some good material.

Butler, A. L., contributor, *see* Lonsdale Library.

Caldwell, Harry R., *Blue Tiger*, Duckworth, 1925.
Sporting American missionary tiger, wild boar and wapiti hunting in China amongst bandits. Unusual reminiscences and photographs.

Campbell, Colonel Walter, *The Old Forest Ranger* or *Wild Sports In India*, Hall, 1853.
A fictionalised biography of early sport in India, substantiated by notes from diaries. Rewarding, even if sometimes tedious reading.

My Indian Journal, Edmonstone & Douglas, 1864.
The original diaries of his experiences in India, 30 years previously, on which his first book was based. Excellent reading.

Cane, Col. Claude, *Summer & Fall in Alaska*, 'The Record of a Trip to Cook's Inlet after Big Game', Horace Cox, 1903.
Tedious account of 1902 expedition to Alaska moose- and bear-hunting with C. Little, English colonist.

Chapman, Abel, contributor, *see* Badminton Library of Sports & Pastimes.

Chapman, Abel, with Buck, Walter J., CMZS, *Wild Spain*, Gurney & Jackson, 1893.
Bear, boar, ibex and lynx amongst other animals mentioned in very wide-ranging sporting reminiscences of many years spent in Spain.

Chapman, Abel, *On Safari*, 'Big Game Hunting in British East Africa', Edward Arnold, 1908.
Shooting lion, elephant, etc; with brother. Sporting safari by experienced sportsman with eye for country, nature and bird life.

Savage Sudan, Gurney & Jackson, 1921.
First book on sport in Sudan since Sir S. W. Baker. Personally conducted tour up White Nile, through Sudd to Blue Nile and beyond.

Retrospect, 'The Reminiscences and Impressions of a hunter naturalist in Three Continents 1851–1928', Gurney & Jackson, 1928.
Includes memories of big game, elephant and lions in British East Africa and N. E. Transvaal.

Churchill, Winston S., *See* Leslie, Lionel, A. D.

Cooch Behar, Maharajah of, *Thirty Seven Years of Big Game Shooting* (In Cooch Behar, the Duars & Assam), Rowland Ward, 1908.
Subtitled 'A Rough Diary' and very much 'leaves from a game book' record of sport over 37 years with some good photographs.

Cooper, Major A. C., DSO, contributor, *see* Lonsdale Library.

Corbett, Jim, *Man-Eaters of Kumaon*, Oxford University Press, 1946.
Seven accounts of shooting man-eaters in the '20s–'30s: also a chapter on his dog and fishing. Very good material, excellently written.

The Temple Tiger, Oxford University Press, 1954.
Five accounts of tiger hunts on foot from 1920s to '40s by this Anglo-Indian Colonel and master-hunter/writer.

Cotton, W. B., *See* Burrard, Major G., contributor of chapter on the Leopard.

Cranworth, Lord, MC, *see* Gurdon.

Cuming, E. D., Editor, *see* Blaney-Percival.

Cumming, Sir A. D. Gordon, Bt., contributor *see* Lonsdale Library.

Cumming, Roualeyn Gordon, *Five Years of a Hunter's Life in the Far Interior of Southern Africa*, John Murray, 2 Vols, 1850.
Bloody account of commercial hunting in Africa, shooting everything from elephants to springbok with twelve-bore and solid shot.

Cumming, Lt. Col. William Gordon, *Wild Men & Wild Beasts*, Edmonston, 1872.

Good accounts of sport before and after Mutiny, by kinsman of 'Old Forest Ranger'. Political officer with Bheels.

Deasy, Captain H. H. P., *In Tibet & Chinese Turkestan*, 'Being The Record of Three Years Exploration', Fisher & Unwin, 1901.

Mainly exploration and very little sport; but relates how the record Ovis Ammon skull was picked up by accident.

Drake-Brockman, Lt. Col. R. E., DSO, MD, contributor, *see* Lonsdale Library.

Dunbar Brunton, James, *The Sportsman's Guide to N. E. Rhodesia*, Scientific Press, 1909.

Simple and straightforward 32-page little handbook for any sportsman visiting the area for the first time.

Big Game Hunting in Central Africa, Andrew Melrose, 1912.

Recollections of a sporting doctor in N. E. Rhodesia, shooting all big game from elephant and lion to bush buck and duiker.

De Watteville, Vivienne, *Out in The Blue*, Methuen, 1927.

Account of safari by half-English daughter, aged 24, accompanying Swiss hunter mauled and killed by lion. White rhino and lions shot.

Speak to the Earth, Methuen, 1935.

Attempt at photographic safari written in the irritating determinedly casual chatty style popular in 1930s.

Digby Davies, the subject of *Tiger Slayer by Order*, *see* Gouldsbury, C. E.

Dixon, J. Willmott, writing as 'Thormanby', *see* 'Thormanby'.

Drayson, Capt. A. W., *Tales of the Outspan*, 'Adventures in the Wild Regions of S. Africa', Saunders, Otley & Co, 1862.

Some good period descriptions of outspanning, attacks by natives, elephant hunting, etc.

Eardley-Wilmot, Sainthill, CIE, *Forest Life & Sport in India*, Edward Arnold, 1910.

Sometimes rather rambling reminiscences of big game shooting in India and Burma, but some good material and evocative pictures by wife.

Elliott, General J. G., *Field Sports in India 1800–1947*, Gentry Books, 1973.

Good general history of field sports in India over the period: everything from pig-sticking to tiger shooting.

Elliott, Hon. William, *Carolina Sports by Land and Water*, Richard Bentley, 1867.

Post-American Civil War memories by an exiled Southerner of sport earlier in the century, written in very tedious flowery fictional style.

Ellison, Bernard C., FRGS, Ed. Sir H. Percy Robinson, *H.R.H The Prince of Wales's Sport in India*, Heinemann, 1925.

Somewhat nauseating account of Prince of Wales's Indian Tour, slaughtering big game. It has points of interest and is well illustrated.

Enniskillen, Earl of, contributor on African big game shooting, *An International Encyclopedia of Shooting*, See Brander, M., Zern, Ed., Joint Editors.

Faulkner, Henry, *Elephant Haunts*, Hurst & Blackett, 1868.

Six-months hunting expedition disguised as abortive search for Dr Livingstone. Demonstrates effect of breech-loading rifle on game.

Fayrer, J, MD, FZS, *The Royal Tiger of Bengal*, Churchill, 1875.

Early attempt at detailing natural history, habits and habitat of the tiger with some interesting period concepts and attitudes.

Fife-Cookson, Lt. Col. J. C., *Tiger Shooting in the Doon & Ulwar*, Chapman & Hall, 1887.

Tedious prose but some enthusiastic descriptions of tiger shooting alone or with one friend from elephants, from machans and trees.

Foran, Major W. Robert, *Kill or Be Killed*, 'The Rambling Reminiscences of an Amateur Hunter', Hutchinson, 1933.

Written 34 years after leaving Africa in early pioneering Kenya days. Some good photographs and stories.

A Hunter's Saga, Hale, 1961.

Wide-ranging reminiscences of India, the Rockies and Mexico as well as Africa. No illustrations but good material by competent writer.

Forsyth, Captain J., *The Highlands of Central India*, 'Notes on Their Forests and Wild Tribes, Natural History and Sports', Chapman & Hall, 1871, 1919.

The author died aged only 33 on publication, but his book gives a very good account of sport in Central India, starting in 1857. An early classic.

Fraser, Lt. Col. Thomas Gamble, *Records of Sport & Military Life in Western India*, W. H. Allen, 1881.

Somewhat difficult reading, but some good accounts of early sport, especially tiger shooting, from 1823–1856.

Gerard, Jules, *Lion Hunting & Sporting Life in Algeria*, Addey & Co, 1856.

Perhaps badly translated. Lions, panthers, deer and boar hunting, and native methods by a Spahi Lieutenant, a slayer of 30 lions from 1844–56.

Gerard, Lt. General Sir Montague Gilbert, KCB, KCSI, *Leaves from the Diaries of a Soldier & Sportsman During Twenty Years Service in India, Afghanistan, Egypt and Other Countries: 1865–1885*, John Murray, 1903.
Good accounts of tiger and leopard shooting on foot and from elephants; with good sketches by sporting soldier/author.

Glasfurd, Captain A. I. R., *Rifle & Romance in the Indian Jungle*, Bodley Head, 1905.
Written after 13 years in the Indian Army. Aspirations to literary style make it almost unreadable, but there are some points of interest.

Gouldsbury, C. E., ed., *Tiger Slayer By Order*, Chapman & Hall, 1915.
Edited autobiography of Digby Davies, starting in 1880s to early 1900s, shooting much big game in India and Africa. A good period piece.

Grew, J. C., *Sport and Travel in the Far East*, Constable, 1910.
Wealthy American's account of 3-month Far East Sporting Safari in 1902. Tiger in China; markhor, ibex and bear in Kashmir.

Gurdon, Captain Bertram E., Baron Cranworth, *A Colony in the Making Profit and Sport in British East Africa*, Macmillan, 1912.
A review of Kenya's post-1918 War prospects and sporting possibilities. Very much in period. Game safaris already proliferating.

Hamilton, Lord F., *Here, There & Everywhere*, Hodder & Stoughton, 1921.
Reminiscences including big-game shooting with Maharajah of Cooch Behar in 1891. Also mention of sport in S. Africa and S. America.

Hamilton, Col. J. P., *Reminiscences of an Old Sportsman*, Longman, 2 Vols, 1860.
Nothing larger than boar in Europe and Sardinia, but some interesting, if rambling, material on shooting and dogs.

Handley, Major Leonard M. H., MC, *Hunter's Moon*, Macmillan, 1938.
Good accounts of tiger hunting from machans and on foot. Elephants and poachers also hunted in India and Burma in tough conditions.

Harcourt, Edward Vernon, *Sporting in Algeria*, Hastings, no date.
Written in the form of letters and covers hunting lion, gazelle, boar, ostrich, bustard and hare. Not much sport involved.

Harris, Captain William Corwallis, *The Wild Sports of Southern Africa*, John Murray, 1838.
The first account of sport in Africa, foreshadowing most of the problems encountered by others: hostile natives, climate, disease, etc.

Haughton, Captain H. L., *Sport & Folklore in the Himalayas*, Edward Arnold, 1913.
More folklore than sport, with some indifferent photographs: mostly on bear, urial and ibex, fishing and small game shooting.

Heber Percy, Major Algernon C., contributor, see Badminton Library of Sports & Pastimes.

Heber Percy, Lt. Col. R., contributor, see Badminton Library of Sports & Pastimes.

Hemans, H. N., *The Log of a Native Commissioner*, 'A Record of work and sport in S. Rhodesia', Witherby, 1935.
Includes some good if rather disorganised material on varied big game shooting.

Hook, Col. Hilary, *Home from the Hill*, Sportsman's Press, 1987.
Colourful autobiography of sport in India, Sudan and Kenya by soldier turned safari hunter.

Inglis, Hon. James, *Sport & Work on the Nepaul Frontier*, Macmillan, 1878.
Twelve years sporting reminiscences of an indigo planter: some good material on shooting tigers from machans and elephants.

Inglis, Hon. James, *Tent Life in Tigerland*, Sampson Low, 1888.
Mainly on shooting tigers from elephants. Numerous stories of hairbreadth escapes with illustrations in period.

Inverarity, J. D., contributor on big game shooting in India, *The Encyclopedia of Sport*, see Aflalo.

Jackson, F. J., contributor, see Badminton Library of Sports & Pastimes.

Johnson, Daniel, *Sketches of Indian Field Sports*, Jennings, 2nd Edn, 1827.
Contemporary of Williamson, 1800–09. Poorly illustrated, but corrects Williamson on some points. Good on Indian methods of hunting.

Kemp, Kenneth, ed., *Tales of the Big Game Hunters*, Sportsman's Press, 1986.
Anthology covering over a hundred years of big game hunters, from Pester in 1804 to Radclyffe in 1904. Excellent material well presented.

Kennion, Major R. L., *Sport & Life in the Further Himalaya*, Blackwood, 1910.
Edited notes during 8 years service in N. West

India, including driving game with hounds and falconry. A regular *Blackwood's Magazine* contributor.

By Mountain, Lake and Plain, Blackwood, 1911.
Sporting consul's account of game shooting in Persia, from ibex and wildfowl to Maral stag and Hyrcan tiger. Pleasant writer.

Kilmorey, The Earl of, contributor, *see* Badminton Library of Sports & Pastimes.

Kinloch, Brig.-General Alexander A. A., CMZS, *Large Game Shooting in Thibet & The North West*, Harrison, 1869.
Very sound account of the game likely to be encountered in Tibet with suggestions as to kit required, etc. Illustrated with mounted heads.

Large Game Shooting in Thibet and the North West, Harrison, 1876.
Expanded 2nd edn with chapters on tigers and elephants. Damns those who let Shekarries shoot game, or females in young.

Large Game Shooting in Thibet, The Himalayas, North West and Central India, Thacker Spink & Co, 1892.
The expanded 3rd edn. Organised by species, including rhinoceros. The final definitive volume and well worth reading.

Kinloch, Bruce, *The Shamba Raiders*, 'Memories of a Game Warden', Collins, 1972.
Very good picture of attempts to save wildlife in modern post-Colonial Africa.

The Shamba Raiders, revised edition, Ashford Press, 1988.
Updated reprint of this classic, giving all-too clear picture of large scale commercial poaching of elephants and rhino amid civil unrest.

Kirby, Frederick Vaughan, FZS, *In Haunts of Wild Game*, Blackwood, 1896.
Mainly on antelope, lions and leopards hunted principally on horseback with dogs. Illustrated by Whymper and contains some good material.

(Maqaqamba), *Sport in East Central Africa*, 'Being an Account of Hunting Trips in Portugeuse and Other Districts of East Africa', Rowland Ward, 1899.
Based on diaries written at the time and mainly about elephant, rhinoceros and lion shooting. A prolix *Boys' Own* style of writing.

Lang, Conyers, *Buffalo*, 'The Lone Trail of a big Game Hunter', Ivor Nicholson, 1934.
Account of intended Cape to Cairo big game shooting journey, ended after a year with author gored by wounded buffalo near Nairobi.

Leslie, Lionel A. D., *Wilderness Trails in Three Continents*, brief foreword by Winston S. Churchill, Heath Cranton, 1931.
Somewhat dated amateur big game hunter and 'explorer' giving his accounts of varied sport in Africa, India, Burma and Labrador.

Leveson, H. A. (The Old Shekarry), *The Hunting Grounds of the Old World*, First Series, Asia, 3rd Edn, Longmans Green, 1865.
The Deccan, Southern India, the Mountain Ranges, the Himalayas and Circassia. Somewhat tedious reading today.

Wrinkles, 'Hints to Sportsmen and Travellers on Dress, Equipment and Camp Kit', Chatto & Windus, 1874.
Comprehensively covers the subject with numerous illustrations of the period which are of interest in themselves.

The Forest & The Field, Chatto & Windus, 1874.
Travel and sport through India and Africa; action in the Crimea with the Turkish forces.

Sport in Many Lands, 2 Vols, Chapman & Hall, 1877.
Includes sport in the Rocky Mountains and buffalo on the prairie. Also India, Asia, S. Africa, Abyssinia, Far West and N. America.

Littledale, St George, contributor, *see* Badminton Library of Sports & Pastimes.

Locke, Lt. Col. A., *The Tigers of Trengganu*, Museum Press, 1954.
Interesting account by district officer shooting tigers in Malaya by torchlight within areas controlled by terrorists 1949–53.

Lonsdale Library, *Big Game Shooting in Africa*, Ed: Major H. C. Maydon, Seeley Service, 1932.
Contributors: H.R.H. Duke of Gloucester; R. A. Akroyd; Captain G. Blaine, MC; Lt. Col. R. E. Drake-Brockman, DSO, MD; Major E. D. Browne, OBE; Major G. Burrard, DSO; A. L. Butler; Major A. C. Cooper, DSO; Major P. H. G. Powell-Cotton; Sir A. P. Gordon-Cumming, Bt; Dennis D. Lyell; Captain A. T. A. Ritchie; Captain M. W. Hilton Simpson; N. B. Smith; Col. H. G. C. Swayne; Col. J. L. F. Tweedie, DSO; H. F. Varian; R. C. Wood.

Luard, Nicholas, Lt. Col., *The Last Wilderness*, Elmtree Books, 1981.
A record of a journey across the Kalahari Desert with graphic description of the decline of big game and shooting.

Lydekker, R., *The Game Animals of India, Burma, Malaya & Tibet*, Rowland Ward, 1907.

A nearly successful attempt to classify, with pictures, all the larger game animals of the areas.

The Game Animals of Africa, Rowland Ward, 1908.
Over 489 species, but the number of unknowns admitted made this a gallant, if impossible, effort.

Lyell, Dennis D., contributor, *see* Lonsdale Library.

Lyell, Dennis D., FZS, *Hunting Trips in N. Rhodesia*, Horace Cox, 1910.
Intended basically as handy 'Instructions to Travellers', including approximate costs of hunting tours and detailed requirements.

Nyasaland For the Hunter & Settler, Horace Cox, 1912.
Larger version of the 1910 handbook. 'Nowadays one can hardly live by the rifle as the game regulations limit the number . . . killed'.

'Wild Life in Central Africa', *The Field*, 1913.
Extracts from diaries of ten years' elephant hunting in Nyasaland, Central Africa and N.E. Rhodesia by good hunter and writer.

The African Elephant and Its Hunters, Heath Cranton, 1924.
Interesting coverage of the various elephant hunters known to the author, who was himself a very able and experienced African hunter.

Memories of an African Hunter, Fisher Unwin, 1923.
With a chapter on Eastern India. Somewhat rambling but interesting account of the author's adventurous life as a hunter.

African Adventure, 'Letters from Famous Big Game Hunters', John Murray, 1935.
Annotated correspondence with Selous, Stigand, Millais, Chapman, Brander Dunbar, Bell, and others. Some good material.

also see Stigand, Capt. C. H.

Lytton, The Earl of, *Pundits & Elephants*, 'The Experiences of Five Years as Governor of an Indian Province', Peter Davies, 1942.
Only one chapter on sport, shooting tiger and rhinoceros from elephants, but interesting material.

Maydon, Major M. C., editor, *see* Lonsdale Library.

Meinertzhagen, Col. R., OBE, DSO, *Kenya Diary: 1902–06*, Oliver & Boyd, 1957.
Diaries of the period kept by ardent soldier sportsman and good observer of the period. Compulsive reading.

Army Diary: 1899–1926, Oliver & Boyd, 1960.
Straightforward diary of an army officer with some sporting experiences in India and Africa.

Very interesting picture.

Diary of a Black Sheep, Oliver & Boyd, 1964.
Early diaries and background of noted observer sportsman and big game hunter, showing upbringing and sporting background in U.K.

Melland, Frank, *Elephants in Africa*, Country Life/Scribners, 1938.
Observations of ex-colonial administrator and keen hunter, with 26 years experience in Africa. Well illustrated by Stuart Tresilian.

Millais, J. G., FZS, *A Breath from the Veld*, Sotheran, 1899.
Delightfully illustrated and well written account of the author/artist's travels in Africa with Boer hunter guide.

Wanderings & Memories, Longmans, 1919.
Wide-ranging reminiscences illustrated by gifted author/artist, including much on big game and hunter friends, notably Neumann.

Life of Frederick Courteney Selous, DSO, Longmans Green 1919.
Excellent biography of this outstanding African hunter's life, extremely well illustrated by his close friend and famous artist/hunter.

Far Away Up the Nile, Longmans Green, 1924.
Description of a journey through the Sudan with superb illustrations.

Neumann, Arthur H., *Elephant Hunting in East Equatorial Africa*, Rowland Ward, 1898.
Well illustrated straightforward account from diaries of elephant hunting in the then still largely unknown interior of Kenya.

Newall, Captain J. T., *The Eastern Hunters*, Tinsley Bros, 1866.
Fictionalised account of sport in India around 1850–60s. Somewhat ponderous reading and illustrations uninspired.

Onslow, The Earl of, *see* Melland, Frank.

Oswell, W. Cotton, contributor, *see* Badminton Library of Sport.

Oswell, W. Edward, *William Cotton Oswell: Hunter & Explorer*, William Heinemann, 2 Vols, 1900.
Depicts his father's life mainly through correspondence covering both Indian and African hunting and exploring with Livingstone.

Patterson, Lt. Col., DSO, *The Man-Eaters of Tsavo*, Macmillan, 1907.
Unvarnished account of killing eight man-eating lions while constructing the Ugandan Railway in 1898, meriting bar to DSO.

Pease, Sir Alfred E. Bt., *Travel & Sport in Africa*, 3

Vols, Arthur L. Humphreys, 1902.
Monumental piece of Edwardian book production on sumptuous scale following ten years of travel by very wealthy sportsman:
Vol I Algeria and the Sahara 1892–95: 359 pages extremely well and lavishly illustrated.
Vol II Somaliland 1896–99. Everything from lions and elephants to butterflies and moths: 314 pages lavishly illustrated.
Vol III Southern Abyssinia and Somaliland 1900–01. Lion, elephant and rhino. Details of armoury, including 25 .303s for escort, not particularly readable but quite amazing three volumes.
The Book of the Lion, John Murray, 1913.
299 pages of recollections by vastly experienced African sportsman, with good observations on disturbance of game by settlers.
Pester, Lt. John, *War and Sport in India*, Heath, 1913.
The edited diaries of an East India Company officer 1802–06. Superb accounts of early tiger shooting and sport. Excellent period picture.
Phillips-Wolley, Clive, *see* Badminton Library of Sports & Pastimes.
Pigot, Brig.-General Sir Robert, Bt., DSO, MC, *Twenty-Five Years of Big Game Hunting*, Chatto & Windus, 1928.
Norway; Sardinia; Suikim; India; Burma; Mongolia; Siam; Siberia; Newfoundland; China; Pamirs; New Zealand. Well written.
Pike, Warburton, contributor, *see* Badminton Library of Sports & Pastimes.
Pollok, Col. F. T., *Sport in British Burmah, Assam & the Cassyah & Jyntiah Hills*, 'Indicating the best localities in these countries for sport with natural history notes, illustrations of the people, scenery, and game together with maps to guide the traveller & sportsman & hints on weapons, fishing tackle, etc., best suited for killing game met with in these provinces', 2 Vols, Chapman & Hall, 1879.
Attempts to be too all-embracing and is somewhat heavy in the hand as a result.
Incidents of Foreign Sport & Travel, Chapman & Hall, 1894.
Some good and genuine records of sport with some rather more unusual accounts of exceptional events in Burma and India.
Pollok, Col. F. T., and Thom, W. S., *Wild Sports of Burma & Assam*, Hurst & Blackett, 1900.
First book on sport in Upper Burma (recently

annexed). Records from diaries include some good graphic descriptions. Good photographs.
Pottinger, Sir Henry, Bt., contributor, *see* Badminton Library of Sports & Pastimes.
Powell, Col. A. N. W., *Call of the Tiger*, Hale, 1957.
Notes that cost of beaters are now beyond reach of most sportsmen. Ends with good answers to stock questions on tigers. No illustrations.
Powell-Cotton, Major R. H. G., contributor, *see* Lonsdale Library.
Powell-Cotton, Major R. H. G., FRGS, FZS, *A Sporting Trip Through Abyssina*, 'A Narrative of a Nine Months' Journey from the Plains of the Hawash to the Snows of the Simien with a Description of the Game from Elephant to Ibex & Notes on the Manners and Customs of the Natives', with illustrations and maps. Rowland Ward, 1902.
Interesting journey and some good illustrations evocative of place, period and game shooting. On the whole, good.
In Unknown Africa, 'A Narrative of Twenty Months' Travel and Sport in Unknown Lands & Among New Tribes', Hurst & Blackett, 1904.
Some interesting experiences in the early pioneering days shooting big game in Kenya and neighbouring Uganda.
Radclyffe, Major C. R. E., *Big Game Shooting in Alaska*, Rowland Ward, 1904.
Indifferently written account of sporting expedition shooting bear, sheep and moose in 1903, the year after Cane, (See Cane).
Round the Smoking Room Fire, John Murray, 1933.
Ex-ADC to Redvers Buller with some stories no doubt frequently repeated in his club. Not much on sport or big game.
Rice, Major-General William, *Tiger Shooting in India: (Rajpootana) From 1850–1854*, Smith Elder, 1857.
Early accounts of tiger and big game shooting on foot. Very readable *Boys' Own* style. The follow up of wounded tigers in wedge-shaped phalanx.
Indian Game (From Quail to Tiger), W. H. Allen, 1884.
Covers everything from quail to lions and tigers, but more importantly notes the effects of change from muzzle to breech-loaders.
Ritchie, Captain A. T. A., contributor, *see* Lonsdale Library.
Robinson, Sir H. Perry, ed., *H.R.H. The Prince of Wales's Tour of India*, *see* Ellison, Bernard C.

Roosevelt, Theodore, Introduction to *African Nature Notes & Reminiscences, see* Selous, Frederick Courteney; *see also* Stevenson-Hamilton, Major James; *see also* Stigand, Captain C. H.

Roosevelt, Theodore, *African Game Trails*, John Murray, 1910.
Account of safari in Africa with Selous and others, shooting 296 head to his own gun. Profusely illustrated.

The Wilderness Hunter, Putman, 1893.
Everything from deer, caribou, goat, elk, buffalo and grizzly bear, also cougar, peccary and wolf.

Outdoor Pastimes of An American Hunter, Longmans, 1906.
With cougar hounds, wolf coursing, bear and pronghorn hunting, covering all U.S. outdoor sport.

Ronaldshay, The Earl of, *Sport & Politics under an Eastern Sky*, Blackwood, 1902.
400 pages of 3 years' travel and sport. Another book with very little sport and some fairly boring travel.

Sanderson, G. P., *Thirteen Years Among the Wild Beasts of India*, W. H. Allen, 4th Edn, 1890.
Developed the kheddah method of catching elephants. Much also on shooting, elephants, tigers, panthers, bears, bison, etc., in 1864–77.

Selous, *Life of Frederick Courteney Selous, DSO, see* Millias, J. G.

Selous, F. C., contributor, *see* Badminton Library of Sports & Pastimes.

Selous, F. C., *A Hunter's Wanderings in Africa*, Macmillan, 1881.
Absorbing account of nine years in Africa learning to hunt all the game available. Good observation by fine hunter and sportsman.

African Nature Notes & Reminiscences, Introduction by President Theodore Roosevelt, Macmillan, 1908.
Wide-ranging but very absorbing reminiscences and nature notes by keen observer/hunter after more than thirty-five years experience.

Shakespear, Major Henry, *The Wild Sports of India*, Smith Elder, 1860.
The first edition of this early classic. Written with great zest, it provides a period picture and is still good reading.

The Wild Sports of India, Smith Elder, 2nd Edn, 1862.
One of the early classics on sport in India, covering 25 years from 1838. O. C. Irregular Cavalry

writes with vigour and enthusiasm.

Sheldon, Charles, *The Wilderness of Denali*, 'Explorations of a hunter/naturalist in Northern Alaska', Scribner, 1930.
Well illustrated, readable record by a millionaire hunter/naturalist from 1906–08 in Alaska. Shooting sheep, grizzly bear and caribou.

Simpson, Captain M. W. Hilton, contributor, *see* Lonsdale Library.

Smith, N. B., contributor, *see* Lonsdale Library.

Stebbing, E. P., *Jungle Byways in India*, 'Leaves from the Note-book of a Sportsman & Naturalist', John Lane, 1910.
Ex-Forest Officer's well-written and illustrated accounts of his sporting activities and observations. A good period piece.

Sterndale, R. A., *Seonee or a Tale of Indian Adventure*, Sampson Low, 1877.
Fictionalised account of big-game hunting in India. Good artist/bad author. Makes rather tedious reading of good basic game book.

Stevenson-Hamilton, Lt. Col. J., *The Barotseland Journal of J. Stevenson-Hamilton*, ed. Wallis, J. P. R., Chatto & Windus, 1953.
Journals in 1898–99 in virtually uncharted N. Rhodesia. Breathes sporting spirit of the day.

Stevenson-Hamilton, James, *Animal Life in Africa*, foreword by Theodore Roosevelt, Heinemann, 1912.
Warden of the Transvaal Game Reserves from 1902. One of the earliest game warden/author's views on the animals of Africa.

The Low-Veld & Its People, foreword by Lt. General the Rt. Hon. J. C. Smuts, PC, KC, *Cassell*, 1929.
A good evocative picture of the Transvaal Low Veld country and its inhabitants, human and animal, as well as insects.

South African Eden, Cassell, 1937.
Account of 35 years as Chief Ranger of the Sabi National Game Reserve from 1900 almost up to the Second World War.

Stigand, Capt. C. H., FRGS, FZS, with Lyell D. D., *Central African Game & Its Spoor*, Horace Cox, 1906.
A remarkable Edwardian attempt to produce a 'How To' book for big game hunters. Illustrates tracks and dung; includes some sound advice.

Stigand, Capt. C. H., FRGS, FZS, *Scouting & Reconnaissance In Savage Countries*, Hugh Rees, 1907.
A remarkable small, 145-page, manual on all aspects of scouting, tracking and reconnaissance

amongst hostile tribes of Africa.

The Game of British East Africa, Horace Cox, 1909.

A very wide-ranging book with many extremely interesting observations by a vastly experienced African hunter and early photographer.

To Abyssina Through an Unknown Land, Seeley & Co, 1910.

An account of a journey from Gilgil in Kenya to Addis Ababa with often mutinous porters. Surprisingly good photographs.

Hunting the Elephant in Africa, foreword by President Theodore Roosevelt, Macmillan, 1913.

Undoubtedly one of his best books with numerous anecdotes and interesting reminiscences by accident-prone naturalist/hunter hero.

Stigand, Captain and Mrs C. H., *Cooking for Settler & Trekker*, The Field Press, 1920.

124-page, ambitious guide to cooking in the wild with some fairly odd mixtures proposed. A mating not only of minds, but stomachs.

Stockley, Lt. Col. C. H., DSO, OBE, MC, FRGS, FZS, *Big Game Shooting in the Indian Empire*, Constable, 1928.

Very much a practical 'How-To' book with some good reminiscences covering the post-1918 War period, including Burma and Tibet.

Strachan, Arthur W., *Mauled by a Tiger*, The Moray Press, 1933.

Tea planter author followed wounded tigers on foot once too often. Some good observations. Covers snakes, elephants, etc., to tigers.

Sutherland, James, *The Adventures of an Elephant Hunter*, Macmillan, 1912.

A stirring classic of African big game hunting by a professional ivory hunter/diarist: a realistic first-hand account of a passing era.

Swayne, Col. H. G. C., contributor, *see* Lonsdale Library.

Thesiger, Wilfred, *The Life of My Choice*, Collins, 1987.

Autobiography of explorer who shot 70 lions, elephant, etc., when in Sudan Political with Danakil tribe in the late 1930s. A graphic writer.

'Thormanby' (Dixon, J. Willmott), *Kings of the Rod, Rifle & Gun*, Hutchinson, 2 Vols, 1901.

Racily written sporting biographies. Including Gordon Cumming, Sir Samuel White Baker, Grantley Berkeley, William Cotton Oswell.

Treatt, Major C. Court, FGS, *Out of the Beaten Track*, Hutchinson, 1930.

Writes interestingly on wild animal photography in Africa. Good material on elephants and other animals such as the honey badger.

Turner, J., contributor on big game shooting in North America, *The Encyclopedia of Sport*, See Aflalo.

Tweedie, Col. J. L. F., DSO, contributor, *see* Lonsdale Library.

Tyacke, Mrs R. H., *How I Shot My Bears*, 'Two Years Tent Life in Kullu & Lahoul', Sampson Low, 1893.

Somewhat tediously written and poorly illustrated, but this late Victorian wife was clearly not bound by convention.

Varian, H. F., contributor, *see* Lonsdale Library.

Von Blicken-Finecke, Bror, *African Hunter*, translated by F. H. Lyon, Cassell, 1937.

Reminiscences of a sporting Swedish farmer settled in Kenya from 1913. Guide to Prince of Wales and Hemingway. Notable lion hunter.

Wallace, Harold Frank, FRGS, FZS, *The Big Game of Central & Western China*, with frontispiece and 10 full page and 12 half-page illustrations by the author and 35 photographs, John Murray, 1913.

Account of sporting safari from 1911–12 in China. Some good observations and illustrations by able artist/author/big game hunter.

Wardrop, Major-General A. E., with chapters by Morris, C. W. G., *Days & Nights With Indian Big Game*, Macmillan, 1924.

Mainly post-1918 War, chiefly shooting from machans with some good experiences well portrayed by both authors. Good photographs.

Williamson, Captain Thomas, *Oriental Field Sports*, Edward Orme, 1807.

First definitive work on sport in India. Sumptuously produced but text owes much to the 40 superb drawings by Samuel Howitt.

Wood, R. C., contributor, *see* Lonsdale Library.

Zern, Ed., with Michael Brander, joint editors, *An International Encyclopedia of Shooting*, See Brander, Michael.